#A Book Of

BUSINESS STATISTICS

For B.B.A. & B.B.M. Semester – II
As Per Revised Syllabus Effective from June 2013

Prof. P. G. DIXIT
M.Sc., M.Phil. (Stats.)
Head of Statistics Department,
Modern College, Pune - 5.

Prof. A. V. RAYARIKAR
M.Sc. (Maths.), M.Sc. (Stats.), M.Phil. (Maths.)
Former, Head of Mathematics Department,
Modern College, Pune - 5.

NIRALI PRAKASHAN
Advancement of knowledge

N2915

B.B.A. & B.B.M. BUSINESS STATISTICS (SEMESTER – II)   ISBN 978-93-83750-08-5

Second Edition : November 2015

© : **Authors**

The text of this publication, or any part thereof, should not be reproduced or transmitted in any form or stored in any computer storage system or device for distribution including photocopy, recording, taping or information retrieval system or reproduced on any disc, tape, perforated media or other information storage device etc., without the written permission of Authors with whom the rights are reserved. Breach of this condition is liable for legal action.

Every effort has been made to avoid errors or omissions in this publication. In spite of this, errors may have crept in. Any mistake, error or discrepancy so noted and shall be brought to our notice shall be taken care of in the next edition. It is notified that neither the publisher nor the authors or seller shall be responsible for any damage or loss of action to any one, of any kind, in any manner, therefrom.

Published By :
NIRALI PRAKASHAN
Abhyudaya Pragati, 1312, Shivaji Nagar,
Off J.M. Road, PUNE – 411005
Tel - (020) 25512336/37/39, Fax - (020) 25511379
Email : niralipune@pragationline.com

Printed By :
Repro Knowledgecast Limited,
Thane

DISTRIBUTION CENTRES
PUNE

Nirali Prakashan
119, Budhwar Peth, Jogeshwari Mandir Lane
Pune 411002, Maharashtra
Tel : (020) 2445 2044, 66022708, Fax : (020) 2445 1538
Email : bookorder@pragationline.com

Nirali Prakashan
S. No. 28/27, Dhyari,
Near Pari Company, Pune 411041
Tel : (022) 24690371
Email : dhyari@pragationline.com
bookorder@pragationline.com

MUMBAI
Nirali Prakashan
385, S.V.P. Road, Rasdhara Co-op. Hsg. Society Ltd.,
Girgaum, Mumbai 400004, Maharashtra
Tel : (022) 2385 6339 / 2386 9976, Fax : (022) 2386 9976
Email : niralimumbai@pragationline.com

DISTRIBUTION BRANCHES

NAGPUR
Pratibha Book Distributors
Above Maratha Mandir, Shop No. 3, First Floor,
Rani Jhanshi Square, Sitabuldi, Nagpur 440012,
Maharashtra, Tel : (0712) 254 7129

JALGAON
Nirali Prakashan
34, V. V. Golani Market, Navi Peth, Jalgaon 425001,
Maharashtra, Tel : (0257) 222 0395
Mob : 94234 91860

BENGALURU
Pragati Book House
House No. 1, Sanjeevappa Lane, Avenue Road Cross,
Opp. Rice Church, Bengaluru – 560002.
Tel : (080) 64513344, 64513355,
Mob : 9880582331, 9845021552
Email:bharatsavla@yahoo.com

KOLHAPUR
Nirali Prakashan
New Mahadvar Road,
Kedar Plaza, 1st Floor Opp. IDBI Bank
Kolhapur 416 012, Maharashtra. Mob : 9850046155

CHENNAI
Pragati Books
9/1, Montieth Road, Behind Taas Mahal, Egmore,
Chennai 600008 Tamil Nadu, Tel : (044) 6518 3535,
Mob : 94440 01782 / 98450 21552 / 98805 82331, Email : bharatsavla@yahoo.com

RETAIL OUTLETS
PUNE

Pragati Book Centre
157, Budhwar Peth, Opp. Ratan Talkies,
Pune 411002, Maharashtra
Tel : (020) 2445 8887 / 6602 2707, Fax : (020) 2445 8887

Pragati Book Centre
676/B, Budhwar Peth, Opp. Jogeshwari Mandir,
Pune 411002, Maharashtra
Tel : (020) 6601 7784 / 6602 0855

Pragati Book Centre
Amber Chamber, 28/A, Budhwar Peth,
Appa Balwant Chowk, Pune : 411002, Maharashtra,
Tel : (020) 20240335 / 66281669
Email : pbcpune@pragationline.com

PBC Book Sellers & Stationers
152, Budhwar Peth, Pune 411002, Maharashtra
Tel : (020) 2445 2254 / 6609 2463

MUMBAI
Pragati Book Corner
Indira Niwas, 111 - A, Bhavani Shankar Road, Dadar (W), Mumbai 400028, Maharashtra
Tel : (022) 2422 3526 / 6662 5254, Email : pbcmumbai@pragationline.com

www.pragationline.com   info@pragationline.com

Dedicated to
    My Son
        Mr. Kalpak Dixit
            in his loving memory

Statistical Thinking will one day be necessary for effective citizenship as the ability to read and write

H.G. Wells

Preface ...

We are indeed very happy to place this book is in the hands of **first year 'B.B.A. and B.B.M.'** students. This book is written according to new prescribed syllabus by Pune University which comes into force from the academic year 2013.

The main purpose of the book is to provide foundation as well a comprehensive background of 'Descriptive measures of statistics' to beginners in simple and intersecting manner. In order to make the contents of the book easier to comprehend, we have included a requisite number of illustrations, remarks, figures, diagrams etc. To elucidate statistical concepts, Applications of Statistics in real life situations is emphasized through illustrative examples. We have included the additional features MS-EXCEL commands in to obtain summary statistics. It will give an exposure to statistical computing package. Ample number of graded problems, are provided at the end of each chapter along with hints and answers. A specimen paper is set for student's self assessment.

While writing the book we have borne in mind that many students have not offered mathematics at XIth and XIIth std.

This book will also serve the purpose of reference book for M.B.A., C.A., B.C.A., I.C.W.A., M.P.M., classes.

We are thankful to Mr. D. K. Furia and the staff of Nirali Prakashan for bringing out this book in short time. Mrs. Anagha Medhekar, Mr. Santosh Bare and Mr. Pandya deserve special thanks for the co-operation they have extended to us. Finally, our families deserve special thanks for their support, encouragement and tolerance.

We requires our colleagues, teaching Statistics to offer their criticisms and suggestions, for further improvement of the book.

Deepawali

1st Nov. 2013-11-09   **Authors**

Syllabus ...

FOR B.B.A.

1. **Population and Sample** (8)
   1.1 Definition of statistics, scope of statistics in economics, management sciences and industry. Concept of population and sample with illustration.
   1.2 Methods of sampling – SRSWR, SRSWOR, stratified, systematic. (Description of sampling procedures only). Data condensation and graphical methods : Raw data, attributes and variables, classification, frequency distribution, cumulative frequency distributions.
   1.3 Graphs – Histogram, frequency polygon. Diagrams – Multiple bar, Pie, Subdividied bar.

2. **Measures of Central Tendency and Dispersion** (11)
   2.1 Criteria for good measures of central tendency.
   2.2 Arithmetic mean, median and mode for grouped and ungrouped data, combined mean.
   2.3 Concept of dispersion, absolute and relative measures of dispersion, range, variance, standard deviation, coefficient of variation, quartile deviation, coefficient of quartile deviation.

3. **Correlation and Regression (for ungrouped data)** (10)
   3.1 Concept of correlation, positive and negative correlation.
   3.2 Scatter diagram, Karl Pearson's coefficient of correlation.
   3.3 Meaning of regression, two regression equations, regression coefficients and properties (statements only)

4. **Time Series** (14)
   4.1 Definitions and utility of time series analysis, components of time series, trend, seasonal variation and cyclic variation, irregular or erratic variations.
   4.2 Measurement of trend : Freehand or graphical method, method of semi-averages, moving average method, method of least squares.
   4.3 Measurement of seasonal variations : Method of seasonal averages, ratio-to-trend method, moving average method, link relative method. (Only application, no proof required).

5. **Index Numbers** (5)
   5.1 Important definitions of index numbers.
   5.2 Characteristics of index numbers, uses of index numbers, types of index numbers : Price index, quantity index, value index, numerical problems.
   5.3 Problems in the construction of index numbers : Methods of constructing index numbers. (Only application, No proof required).

FOR B.B.M.

1. **Population and Sample** (15)

    Definition of statistics, scope of statistics in economics, management, sciences and industry.

    Concept of population and sample with illustration. Methods of sampling – SRSWR, SRSWOR, stratified, systematic. (Description of sampling procedures only).

    Data condensation and graphical methods : Raw data, attributes and variables, classification, frequency distribution cumulative frequency distributions.

    Graphs – Histogram, frequency polygon.

    Diagrams – Multiple bear, pie *chart, subdivided bar.

    Using excel draw all graphs and diagrams.

2. **Measures of Central Tendency and Dispersion** (18)

    Criteria for good measures of central tendency, arithmetic mean, median and mode for grouped and ungrouped data, combined mean concept of dispersion, absolute and relative measure of dispersion, range, variance, standard deviation, coefficient of variation, quartile deviation, coefficient of quartile deviation. Using excel calculate measures of central tendency and dispersion.

3. **Correlation and Regression (For Ungrouped Data)** (08)

    Concept of correlation, positive and negative correlation, Karl Pearson's, coefficient of correlation, meaning of regression, two regression equations, regression coefficients and properties.

4. **Linear Programming Problems** (07)

    Meaning of LPP, formulation of LPP, solution by graphical methods, problems relating to two variables only.

•••

Contents ...

1.	Population and Sample	1.1 – 1.14
2.	Frequency Distribution	2.1 – 2.40
3.	Measures of Central Tendency	3.1 – 3.32
4.	Measures of Dispersion	4.1 – 4.30
5.	Correlation and Regression	5.1 – 5.40
6.	Time Series (For B.B.A. Only)	6.1 – 6.44
7.	Index Numbers (For B.B.A. Only)	7.1 – 7.24
8.	Linear Programming Problems (For Two Variables Only) (For B.B.M. Only)	8.1 – 8.16
	University Question Paper	P.1 – P.4

Chapter 1...
Population and Sample

Contents ...

1.1 Introduction
1.2 Definition
1.3 Importance of statistics
1.4 Scope and Applications of Statistics
1.5 Population and Sample
1.6 Types of Sampling

Key Words :

Uses of statistics, Scope of Statistics, Limitations of Statistics, Sample, Population, SRSWOR, SRSWR, Stratified Sampling, Random Sampling.

Objectives :

In this chapter the various aspects of statistics, uses, scope and applications in various fields are discussed. The concept of statistical population and sample is also introduced. Random sample and methods of drawing sample are introduced.

1.1 Introduction

It is believed that Statistics is in use from the time when man began to count and measure. In ancient days kings used to maintain records of land, agricultural yield, wealth, taxes, live stock, soldiers, weapons, deaths and births etc. There are references that Hebrews conducted population census. In ancient days Maurya kings, King Ashoka, Gupta kings had collected Statistics. Kautilya's Arthashastra mentions that the statistics of population, land etc. were collected from time to time. Emperor Akbar gave details of population, land, agriculture etc. in his publication Ain-i-Akbari.

It is considered that the word Statistics seems to be derived from the Italian word 'statista' or the Greek word 'statistika'. Both the words have the same meaning 'political states'.

The word statistics carries several meanings. Many times statistics is considered as statistical data, which contains numerical information of a characteristic under study. *For example :* Statistics of a batsman, population statistics etc.

Statistics or statistical methods is treated as a branch of science which deals with **(i) collection, (ii) presentation, (iii) analysis and (iv) interpretation of data.**

Wherever data are generated, the use of statistics becomes inevitable. Statistics performs number of functions such as (i) presentation of facts and figures. This enables to get an overall idea about the phenomenon. (ii) forecasting, (iii) planning, (iv) controlling, (v) exploring etc.

Statistics plays a role in every walk of life, right from simple situation such as finding average marks in examination to a very complex phenomenon such as rainfall prediction or measuring changes in prices.

Statistics helps in decision-making whenever phenomenon contains uncertainities. LIC, banks, defence department, government agencies, industries, business, trade etc. make use of statistics in planning, forecasting, controlling, decision-making. Index numbers are widely used in almost all fields such as economics industry business, import, export etc. Now-a-days ISO 9000 makes use of statistical tools for standardising the quality of industrial production.

1.2 Definition (Oct. 2014)

Statistics can be defined as the science of collection, presentation, analysis and interpretation of data.

Number of statisticians had made an attempt to define statistics. They used statistics for different purpose, with a different view-point. Accordingly they defined statistics emphasizing their view point. Two definitions are given below.

(a) Webster's Definition : Webster defines statistics as "the classified facts representing the conditions of people in the state, especially those facts which can be stated in a table or tables of numbers or in any tabular or classified arrangement."

The above definition gives importance to presentation of facts and figures. Remaining aspects of statistics are not considered in this definition.

(b) Horace Secrist's Definition : Secrist defines statistics as follows : 'By statistics we mean aggregates of facts affected to a marked extent by multiplicity of causes numerically expressed, enumerated or estimated according to resonable standards of accuracy, collected in a systematic manner for a predetermined purpose and placed in relation to each other.

The above definition takes into account almost all functions and aspects of statistics. It covers the fair important aspects viz. (i) collection, (ii) presentation, (iii) analysis and (iv) interpretation of data.

1.3 Importance of Statistics

We know that many phenomena in nature and activities, experiments are subject to measurements, moreover variation in different types of characteristics is inevitable. For example, income of a family, height of a person, sales of a company, electricity consumption of a city etc. This produces voluminous data. It becomes difficult to comprehend. This forces the use of statistical methods. Thus statistics is important from the following view points.

(i) Statistical methods enable to condense the data. It facilitates several functions apart from summerisation.

(ii) Statistical methods give tools of comparison.

(iii) Estimation, prediction is also possible using statistical tools.

(iv) We can get idea about the shape, spread, symmetry of the data.

(v) Inter-relation between two or more variables can be measured using statistical techniques.

(iv) Statistical methods help in planning, controlling, decision-making etc.

(vii) The use of statistical methods is important because considerable amount of time, money, manpower can be saved.

(viii) Uncertainties can be reduced to get reliable results.

(ix) Statistical methods give systematic methods of data collection and investigation.

Thus statistics reveals several aspects of phenomena.

H. G. Wells expresses the importance and need of statistics in the following words.

"Statistical thinking will one day be necessary for effective citizenship as the ability to read and write".

1.4 Scope and Applications of Statistics

The tools and techniques given by statistical methods are used in almost all fields at several phases. Because of diversified applications of statistics, an exhaustive list of fields is difficult to prepare. However, some of them are stated below. We find use of statistics indispensable in the agriculture, business, commerce, demography, economics, education, government agencies, industries, social sciences, biological sciences, medical sciences, management sciences etc. We discuss briefly the scope of statistics in some of the above stated fields.

(a) **Statistics in industry :** Industry makes use of statistics at several places such as administration, planning, production, growth and development. In many industries 'Statistical Quality Control' division is separately operating. Mainly, whether manufactured goods possess a desirable standard or not is examined using various control charts. These inspections are done at the time of production. On-line process capability study is conducted to set-up the machines to give desired standards. Moreover purchased goods or semifinished goods are inspected using acceptance sampling plans of various types. Now-a-days, ISO 9000 makes use of Statistics to a large extent. Apart from this in some industries the technique known as designs of experiment is also used. Newly installed machinery is tested for its performance using statistical methods. Sampling is required to be used because of its several advantages. Multiple regression planes are used for forecasting, when several factors are interlinked. Efficiency measurement, index number of production, work sampling etc. are very much useful for administration and planning department.

(b) **Statistics and Economics :** In the field of economics, huge amount of data are needed to be processed and interpreted. Statistics is very much helpful in this field. In order to collect data, various statistical methods of investigations are used. Many a times questionnaires are drafted. A proper representative of a group is selected using sampling methods. Statistical methods are used in this activity to get reliable results. Estimation of national income, per capita income, poverty line, industrial production etc. is done using statistical techniques. Probability distribution of income can be useful in various economic activities. A tool known as index number developed in Statistics is used every now and then in economics. It performs number of functions. It measures average increase in prices, production, income, volume of import, export etc. Index numbers are called as economic barometers. Index numbers are used in determining real income, deflation, cost of living index numbers. To measure the changes in prices of shares in stock market index number provides the best tool. Several interlinked activities in economics can be studied. For example, (i) the relation between prices and supply (ii) the relation between demand and prices (iii) the relation between sales and profit.

Demand analysis, time series analysis techniques are mainly developed to study economics. Those are the gifts given by statistics.

Richard Lipsey says " The role of statistical analysis is two fold. First, we wish to use observations from the real world to test our theories. Second, we wish to use such observations to give us measures of the quantitative relations between economic variables.

(c) Statistics and Management Sciences (April 2015 B.B.A., B.B.M. B.B.A. Oct. 2014): Most of the managerial functions make use of statistics. For efficient working of various sections of management such as sales, production, marketing statistical method are used. Different statistical tools such as forecasting, tests of significance, index numbers, time series analysis, statistical quality control, estimation play vital role in management activities. Apart from this, various optimisation techniques known as linear programming, transportation techniques, job assignment problems, sequencing, CPM and PERT, replacement problems, inventory control are also useful.

Portfolio management makes use of regression analysis. The regression coefficient called beta index in portfolio is used in decision-making. Risk measurement is done using standard deviations, covariance. Various statistical techniques are used in decision-making.

(d) Statistics and Social Sciences : Bowley says "Statistics is the science of measurement of social organism, regarded as a whole in all its manifestation". Research in social sciences need questionnaire. Further analysis is required to be done using statistical tools. In social sciences we need to test association between two variables such as (i) education and criminality (ii) education and marriage adjustment score (iii) sex and education (iv) richness and criminality etc.

1.5 Population and Sample

In order to study a group of large number of items we require to draw sample. We use technique of sampling several times in every day life. *For example,* while purchasing food grains we inspect only handful of grains and draw conclusion about the whole sack. Similarly while examining blood of an individual, few drops are enough for diagnosis. Quality of milk is tested with the help of a small quantity of milk taken out of can, instead of entire milk in the can. Sampling is a well accepted means of collecting information. Moreover it is believed to be scientific and objective procedure of selecting items. Sampling plays very important role in statistical inference.

Population : In the technical language of statistics the word population is used in somewhat a wider sense. It does not mean only a human population. For example, (i) In the study of industrial development, all the industries under consideration is the population. (ii) In the study of socio-economic conditions of a particular village, all families or houses in the village will be a population. (iii) In the study of agricultural yield, all the cultivated farms together will be a population. (iv) In titration experiment solution in beaker is a population. Thus population may be a group of employees, collection of books, total industrial production, a group of persons suffering from a particular disease, collection of explosives, group of students etc.

We give a specific definition below :

Definition : An aggregate of objects or individuals under study is called *population or universe.*

Population may contain finite or infinite elements. Accordingly, it is called as *finite* or *infinite* population.

Statistical Population : We have defined population as an aggregate of objects or individuals; however, many a times we record some quantitative or qualitative characteristic of each member in the population. These observations (or data) are collectively called as *statistical population.* Thus in the further study we will be interested in 'statistical population'.

In order to study the population, one of the ways is to collect information about each and every element in the population. This method is called as *census* or *complete enumeration.*

After every ten years 'population census' of India is conducted. In this census, information regarding every individual is collected.

Limitations of census method : (1) Census method provides reliable results; but due to voluminous work, it is expensive and time consuming. It requires a large amount of manpower.

(2) There are some situations where census is possible but impracticable. For example, testing blood of an individual. In this case, entire blood cannot be tested. Thus census cannot be used here. Similarly in testing explosives, testing of average life of bulb produced in a lot, testing strength of construction material, census method cannot be used.

(3) If the population is infinite, census cannot be used.

Sampling (Oct. 2014) : In order to overcome the limitations of census, sampling is used. In this case, some representative items are selected from the population, so that all important characteristics of population are covered in the items of this group. Such a group is called a sample and the method of selecting such a group is called as sampling method.

Definition : Any part of population under study is called a *sample*.

Illustrations : (i) While purchasing food grains, we inspect only a handful of grains and draw conclusions about the quality of the whole lot. In this case, handful of grains is a sample and the whole lot is a population.

(ii) While examining blood of an individual, a few drops are taken out of human body for diagnosis. These drops form a sample whereas entire blood in the body is a population. In this case, conclusions based on sample are accepted for population without any doubt as far as the method is concerned. In this case, census is impracticable. Sampling method is appealing in such situations.

(iii) For testing quality of milk, a small quantity of milk is tested instead of entire bulk.

(iv) A housewife confirms whether the food is properly cooked or not with the help of few particles taken out of the container. Clearly, the food in the container is a population, whereas food taken out of container for inspection is a sample.

Note that (a) Sampling is a well accepted means of collecting information. (b) It is believed to be scientific and objective procedure of selecting items. Thus, sampling plays important role in further statistical analysis.

As the sampling methods are used to study population, the samples should be chosen carefully. A natural requirement would be that the sample should be representative of concerned population. There are several methods of sampling in practice. We shall deal with some of these in later sections.

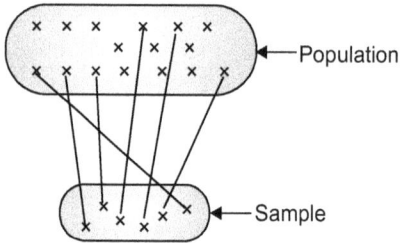

Fig. 1.1 : Nature of Sample

Advantages of Sampling Over Census : (B.B.A. April 2015)

1. **Reduced Time :** As compared to census, sample consists of a less number of elements. Hence there is a considerable reduction in processing time. The results can be obtained quickly due to time saved in data collection and further analysis.

2. **Reduced Cost :** There is reduction in cost, both in terms of time and manpower. In sampling, only a part of population is under consideration. Therefore expenses incurred in collection of data and its analysis are always less than those in census. Thus sampling is economical.

3. Greater Accuracy : As compared to census, only limited number of elements are to be processed. Therefore, sophisticated machinery, well-trained staff can be used and accuracy can be increased. Due to the reduced volume of work, it can be completed efficiently and without fatigue. Moreover, elements will be free from non-sampling errors such as incompleteness of returns, biases due to interviews, inaccurate returns etc.

4. Greater Scope : (a) If population is infinite or too large or cost per unit is too high, census is impracticable. (b) If testing is destructive i.e. element gets destroyed in the analysis, sampling is the only alternative available to us; for example, testing the life of a bulb, testing strength of building construction material, testing fat percentage of milk, testing human blood etc. (c) Suppose a company manufactures a remedial medicine for a certain disease. All the patients suffering from the particular disease may not be ready to try the newly manufactured medicine. In this case sampling has larger scope than census.

Sampling Unit : Members or elements of population are called sampling units. In the sampling process, population is divided into small units which are called the sampling units. For example, in a socio-economic survey, a family is a sampling unit; whereas in a health survey, an individual will be a sampling unit. Sampling units must be distinct and unambiguous in nature. Sampling units together must cover the entire population. In other words, sampling unit is the smallest part of the population which cannot be further subdivided for the said purpose.

Sampling Frame : It is an exhaustive list of all members or elements of population. Sampling frame gives guidelines to cover the entire population. The frame should be up-do-date and suitable for the purpose of survey or enquiry. In a socio-economic survey, frame may be determined from the records at grampanchayat or ration cards. To prepare a good frame is a difficult job. Defective frame does affect the result of the survey.

Samples can be selected in two ways :

(i) Deliberate selection of items or non-random sampling : In this method investigator selects elements in any manner which is suitable to him. For example, he may select elements on first come first served basis.

This method is unscientific. It may produce unreliable results. There is a likelihood of a partial view in this method. The figures collected in this way do not obey statistical laws or laws of probability. Hence, such data will not be useful for further analysis and interpretation. To avoid such problems, another method is used.

(ii) Random Sampling : In this method, the selection of units in sample is done impartially. Personal or any kind of bias in selection is avoided in random sampling.

Further, it each unit has an equal chance of selection, the sample is called as **simple random sampling.**

Discussion regarding need of randomness and how to achieve it is included in later part.

1. Sample is selected with a view to study the concerned population. Therefore, sample should be so selected that it will represent all important characteristics of the population. This may be achieved if elements in sample are selected at random. Thus, sample is a miniature of population.

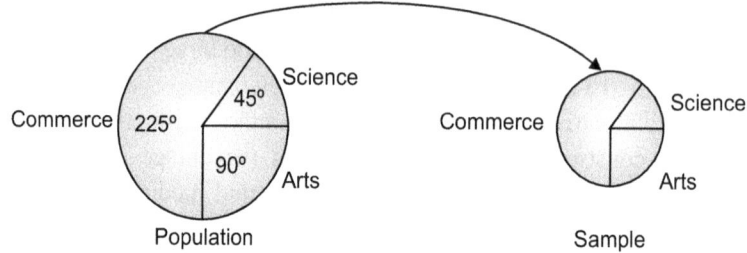

Fig. 1.2

In sample the components of population should be in more or less same proportion.

2. Sampling units should be independent.

3. Sample should be evenly spread over the population. It can be achieved by dividing population in homogeneous sub-groups and selecting a random sample from each sub-group.

Randomness and its need : It is really required to decide the way in which sampling units are selected. In order to draw a sample of suitable size (which is pre-determined) we need to select the elements from the population one by one. Which element should be chosen ? If we select elements according to our convenience or wish, then personal bias is likely to creep in. Some elements may be deliberately selected in sample. This may result in getting unreliable conclusions.

In a random selection, equal chance of selection is given to each sampling unit. This avoids biased selection, or purposive selection. Moreover, random selection is objective.

Methods of Achieving Randomness :

It is noted above that randomness is quite essential while selecting a sample. It can be achieved by the following two ways :

(a) Lottery method : In this method, we serially number the elements from 1 to N. If possible we put all the elements together or put N different slips bearing numbers 1 to N together. Slips are made of the same size and shape. Thus, the slips represent the elements in population. All these elements or slips are kept in a drum with a handle for proper mixing. With the help of the handle, slips are thoroughly mixed and n elements or slips are drawn one by one.

The 'n' elements corresponding to the numbers on the selected slips will form a sample.

(b) Use of 'random numbers' : Instead of lottery method, use of random numbers is made for selecting a sample just for operational convenience. There are several random number tables available for this purpose. Random number tables are so prepared that each of the digits 0, 1, ..., 9, will have same frequency or chance. The digits are arranged in rows and columns. For selecting two digit numbers, two columns are considered together so that we get numbers from 00 to 99. Similarly for 3 digit numbers, 3 columns are read together which give rise to numbers from 000 to 999.

In order to draw a random sample by this method, we select any page of random numbers and choose the numbers serially in row or column selected at random. If the number selected in this manner is between 1 and N, the corresponding element is taken in the sample. Thus n elements are chosen.

(c) **Random Numbers Generated by Computer :** Now-a-days random numbers within a required range can be generated on computers. These numbers satisfy the properties of the random numbers, however, they are generated by using some formula, hence those random numbers are called as pseudo random numbers. In most of the computer languages and software packages there are inbuilt functions which generate pseudo random numbers.

1.6 Types of Sampling

A success of sampling method mainly depends upon proper selection of sampling method. Different sampling methods are used in practice. A sampling method which suits to the purpose is selected. Sampling methods are mainly classified into two classes viz. (i) non-random sampling and (ii) random sampling (or probability sampling). In the earlier discussion we have studied the importance of random sampling. We discuss two popularly used random sampling methods. (1) Simple random sampling (2) Stratified random sampling.

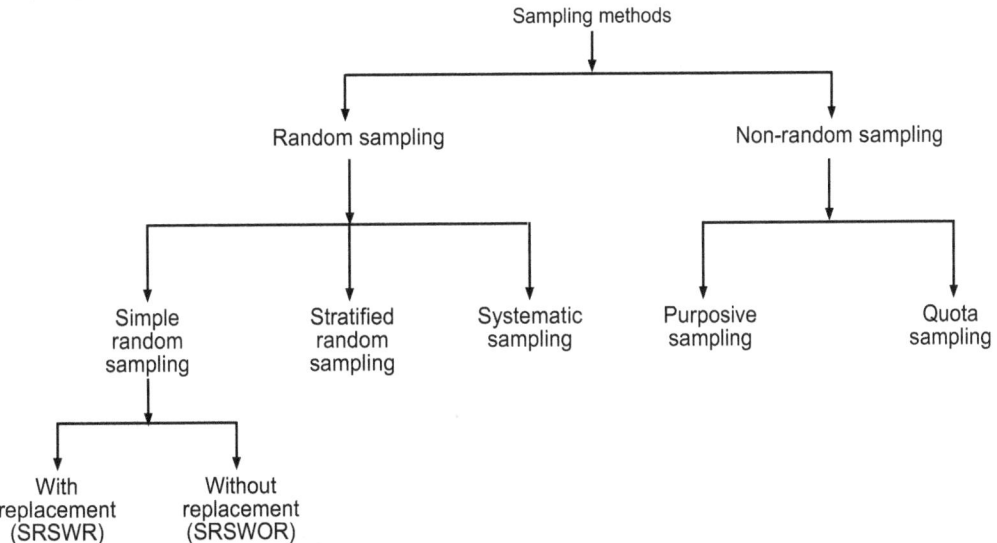

1. Simple Random Sampling (SRS) (B.B.A. Oct. 2014) : It is the easiest and most commonly used method of sampling. In this method each element of population is given same chance of getting selected in the sample. If population consists of N elements then probability of selecting any element at any draw is $\frac{1}{N}$.

Further, there are two types of simple random sampling due to slight difference in procedure of selecting the elements.

(a) Simple Random Sampling with Replacement. (SRSWR) : In this method, first element is selected at random from the population. It is recorded or studied completely and then replaced back in the population. Afterwards second element is selected similarly. This process is continued till a sample of required size is selected. In this method population size remains the same at every draw. This method of sampling is called as *simple random sampling with replacement*.

One of the serious drawbacks of this method is that, the same element may be selected more than once in the sample.

(b) Simple Random Sampling Without Replacement (SRSWOR) : There is another procedure of selecting elements in which, elements are selected at random but those are not replaced back in the population. This method of selecting sample is called as simple random sampling without replacement. In this method population size goes on decreasing at each draw. The drawback of getting the same element selected more than once is overcome in SRSWOR.

Illustrations of Simple Random Sampling :

(i) Suppose a lot of 500 articles is submitted for inspection to determine the proportion of defective articles one can use SRSWOR.

(ii) In order to conduct a socio-economic survey of certain village we can take SRSWOR and find per capita income of a village.

(iii) In order to test average petrol consumption of a lot of scooter manufactured SRSWOR or SRSWR can be used.

(iv) To find diameter of a rod, generally we take reading at few points on a rod and then find the average of readings. These readings form SRSWOR. This is practised for physical measurements of articles.

(v) Testing human blood by taking few drops out an individual's body is a SRSWOR.

(vi) In order to find average life of a bulb we take SRSWOR from a manufactured lot.

Simple random sampling is widely used due to its simplicity and convenience. However, it suffers from some drawbacks such as, it may not be proper representative when population is heterogeneous, widely spread etc. Some part of population may not be represented in simple random sample at all. In order to avoid these problems some other sampling methods are in use.

2. Stratified Random Sampling (B.B.A., B.B.M. April 2015) : If population is not homogeneous, SRS is not very effective. Therefore the entire population is divided into several homogeneous groups called as strata (singular stratum). A simple random sample of a suitable size is selected from each stratum and then combining these sampled observations we can form a sample. The sample thus formed is called as a *stratified random sample*.

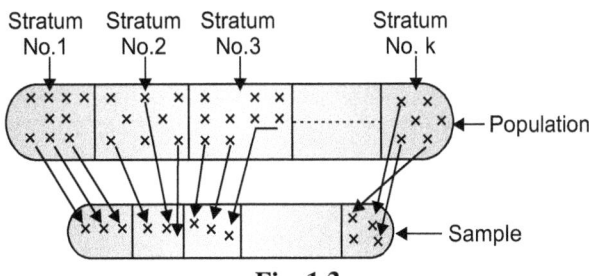

Fig. 1.3

A properly designed stratified random sampling gives better results than simple random sampling. Moreover this method is more suitable from administrative point of view.

Illustrations of Stratified Random Sampling : (B.B.M. April 2015)

(i) To estimate annual income per family we divide the population into homogeneous groups such as families with yearly income below ₹ 20,000; between ₹ 20,000 - ₹ 50,000; between ₹ 50,000 - ₹ 1 lakh and above ₹ 1 lakh. Afterwards we use stratified random sampling taking above groups as strata.

(ii) Suppose the proportion of defective articles is to be estimated in a manufacturing process. Then we can use stratified random sampling by taking strata as production in the different shifts.

(iii) In order to estimate crop yield we can divide the field under cultivation in plots, which are equally fertile considered as strata.

(iv) To conduct health survey in a college we can use stratified random sampling by considering strata as the faculties or classes or sex etc.

In the above discussion we have seen how stratified random sampling is better than simple random sampling. However, in practice an another simple procedure is adopted which we discuss below.

3. Systematic Sampling : To draw a systematic sample of size n, sampling units are numbered 1 to N, where N is the population size. In this method we divide population in n equal parts according to serial numbers. Suppose each of the part includes k units (we assume N = nk).

Note that 1st group will contain units bearing serial numbers 1 to k, 2nd group will contain units bearing serial numbers k + 1 to 2k and so on. Then we select a number at random from 1 to k. Suppose this is j then j^{th} unit in serial order from each group is taken. Thus it will form a sample of size n which is called as *systematic sample*. If j^{th} unit is selected then systematic sample will include j^{th}, $(j + k)^{th}$, $(j + 2k)^{th}$ ....., $j + (n - 1) k^{th}$ observations from original list.

For example : If a sample of size 15 from 150 units is to be drawn, we need to make 15 groups, each of size 10. Thus, here N = 150, k = 10, n = 15. We need to select one unit from first group. Suppose 3rd unit gets selected at random. Then other 14 units will be automatically selected. Those will be bearing serial numbers 13, 23, 33, ..., 143.

Entire sample can be selected by selecting every k^{th} unit after the unit selected from the first group. Thus only one unit drawn at random from first group determines entire sample.

Illustration of Systematic Sampling :

(i) To select houses for a survey we can use house numbers, in this case systematic sample is preferred.

(ii) Suppose a shopkeeper wants to study customers' purchasing habits, he may use bill book. He can choose a systematic sample using the numbers on bill he has.
(iii) Farms can be selected by taking systematic sample using survey numbers.
(iv) Suppose a committee of n = 6 students is to be selected from a class of N = 60 students then we can make 6 groups each of k = 10 students using their roll numbers. We select a student at random from first group. If 7th student is selected, then from each of the next groups we select 7th student. Thus a systematic sample will include students with roll numbers 7, 17, 27, 37, 47, 57.

Population

1	2	3	4	5	6	7	8	9	10
11	12	13	14	15	16	17	18	19	20
21	22	23	24	25	26	27	28	29	30
31	32	33	34	35	36	37	38	39	40
41	42	43	44	45	46	47	48	49	50
51	52	53	54	55	56	57	58	59	60

One of the systematic Sample ↑

Generally, systematic sampling gives better results than that of simple random sampling. It is easier to implement than the stratified sampling. However, there are two drawbacks which are given below :

(i) Systematic sample may not be proper representative if population has hidden periodicities. For example, suppose sales during a year are available. If we take sales of every seventh day in a sample, then sample may contain all Sundays, on which sales might be high.

(ii) If $N \neq nk$, sample, size does not remain fixed.

Case Study

A manager on a highway mall observed that, customers demand for tea and coffee was increasing and it should to be served at the earliest. He was thinking of installing automatic tea and coffee machine. He decided to take customers' opinion. Whether the customer would like the test of tea, coffee prepared on machine. He gathered opinion of customers for a week by using simple random sampling and installed the machine due to favarable opinion about machine made tea and coffee. He also took review for a month by asking the customers at random whether they were satisfied with the tea and coffee. It saved time and gained customers' satisfaction also.

Points to Remember

1. Advantages of sampling are (i) reduction in time, cost, manpower, (iii) increases accuracy, (iii) greater scope.
2. Random sample is preferred to non-random sample because it is proper representative. The result based on random sample are statistically valid. It is unbiased selection procedure.
3. Stratified sampling is used if population is heterogeneous.

Exercise 1.1

A. Theory Questions :
1. Define 'statistics'.
2. Explain the importance of statistics or statistical methods.
3. Describe the scope and utility of statistics in the field of (i) industry, (ii) economics, (iii) management sciences, (iv) social sciences.
4. Mention the application of statistics in the following fields :
   (i) industry, (ii) economics, (iii) management sciences, (iv) social sciences.
5. Explain the terms with illustration : Population, sample, sampling unit, sampling frame.
6. (a) Describe the limitations of sampling over census.
   (b) Describe the advantages of sampling over census.
7. What are the requirements of a good sample ?
8. Explain what is a random sample. Why random sample is preferable ? Explain the various methods of achieving randomness.
9. Explain the procedure of drawing
   (a) SRSWR (b) SRSWOR
   (c) Stratified random sample (d) Systematic sample.
10. State the advantages of simple random sampling and drawbacks of the same. Also explain how these drawbacks can be overcome.
11. (a) State the advantages and limitations of stratified sampling.
    (b) State the limitations of stratified sampling.
12. How does SRSWR differ from SRSWOR ?
13. Make critical comparison between
    (a) Sampling and census.
    (b) Stratified random sampling and sample random sampling.
    (c) SRSWR and SRSWOR
    (d) Random sampling and non-random sampling.
14. Give illustrations of each of the following sampling methods :
    (a) SRSWR (b) SRSWOR (c) Stratified sampling (d) Systematic sampling.
15. Explain the situation where sampling has larger scope as compared to census.

Exercise 1.2

B. Numerical Problems :
16. Explain with illustration the terms (i) finite population (ii) infinite population.
17. In a population of size N = 6, the observations were 3, 4, 7, 9, 11, 14. Draw all possible SRSWOR of size 2.
18. In a population of size N = 8, the observations were 2, 4, 7, 9, 11, 0, 25, 14. Draw all possible SRSWOR of size 5.
19. If a population consists of 50 items then how many :
    (a) SRSWOR each of size 10 can be selected.
    (b) SRSWR each of size 10 can be selected.
20. Suggest appropriate sampling methods, giving reason, in each of the following situations.

(a) To estimate the average price of books in a library a sample of 500 books is to be selected from 10,000 books having accession numbers.
(b) In order to estimate average pocket money spent by the students in a certain college having 3000 students, a sample of 400 students is to be selected.
(c) A market surveyer wants to select a sample of 1000 persons using telephone directory.
(d) To find the daily total requirement of electricity consumption in township containing 3000 houses, 500 offices, 600 shops, 100 factories; a sample of 1000 units is to be selected.
(e) To find the daily total requirement of petrol for two wheelers in a certain city a sample of 5% of two wheelers using RTO registers is to be selected.
(f) In a socio-ecnomic survey a sample of 1000 families is to be selected from a certain village.
(g) To find the average house tax paid by citizens a sample of 500 families is to be selected using municipal corporation records.
(h) To find the average income of employee, in a certain factory employing various categories such as managers, supervisors, clerks, workers.
(i) In an industrial survey a sample of size 50 is to be selected. The area under consideration includes 100 small scale, 200 medium scale and 50 large scale industries.

21. Identify the sampling scheme used in the following situations :
(a) For a exhibition, 5 students are to be selected from each class to work as volunteers.
(b) A teacher distributed hand-outs to the students in the first row only.
(c) An examination question paper contains 10 questions of which any 5 are to be attempted. Ramesh selected questions bearing even serial numbers.
(d) Salesman contacted the first 100 customers visiting the shop for survey.
(e) Suppose there are 10 divisions of F.Y.B.Com. named as A, B, ... J in a certain college. A sample of 10 students from each division is chosen for managing sports activity.

Answers 1.2

17. (3, 4); (3, 7); (3, 9); (3, 11); (3, 14); (4, 7); (4, 9); (4, 11); (4, 14); (7, 9); (7, 11); (7, 14); (9, 11); (9, 14); (11, 14).
18. In all 56 samples are possible.
19. (a) $^{50}C_{10}$ (b) 50^{10}
20. (a) stratified   (b) stratified
    (c) stratified   (d) stratified
    (e) stratified   (e) SRSWOR, stratified
    (g) stratified, SRSWOR (h) stratified
    (i) stratified.
21. (a) stratified (b) non-random (c) stratified
    (d) non-random (e) stratified.

Chapter 2...
Frequency Distribution

Contents ...
2.1 Variables and Attributes
2.2 Classification
2.3 Frequency Distribution
2.4 Methods of Classification
2.5 Cumulative Frequencies
2.6 Relative Frequencies
2.7 Guidelines for the Choice of Classes
2.8 Graphs
2.9 Diagrams (Simple Bar, Multiple Bar, Sub-divided Bar and Pie Diagram)
2.10 Choice of Diagram
2.11 Advantages and Limitations of Graphs
2.12 General rules for Construction of Graphs

Key Words :
Variable, Attributes, Discrete Variable, Continuous Variable, Raw Data, Primary Data, Secondary Data, Classification, Frequency, Inclusive and Exclusive Method of Classification, Class Limits, Class Boundaries, Class Mark, Open End Class, Relative Frequency, Cumulative Frequency, Histogram, Frequency Polygon, Frequency Curve, Ogive Curves.

Objectives :
This chapter explains the first two aspects of statistics viz. collection and presentation of data. Classification is a tool of data condensation. It becomes easier to analyse the data after classification. Graphical representation has several advantages.

2.1 Variables and Attributes   (B.B.M. April 2015)

While studying any phenomenon we come across two types of characteristics : (i) constant and (ii) variable. The characteristic which does not change its value (or nature) is considered as **constant**.

For example : Height of a person after 25 years of age, altitude of a certain place from sea level etc. On the other hand there are many characteristics which are qualitative or quantitative in nature and change their values (or nature). *For example :* Examination result of a candidate can be recorded as pass or fail which is a qualitative variable characteristics, whereas we can express a candidate's performance as percentage of marks which is a quantitative variable.

Statistics involves the study of variable characteristics. Hence, we include the related and necessary definitions.

Attribute (B.B.M. April 2015) : A qualitative characteristic like sex, nationality, religion, grade in examination, blood group, beauty, defectiveness of an article produced by a machine is called as *attribute*.

Variable (B.B.M. April 2015) : A quantitative characteristic (which changes its value) like weight of person, examination marks, population of a country, profit of a salesman, is called as *variable*.

It can be clearly noticed that variables can be measured by numbers.

Further the variables can be divided into two categories : (i) discrete and (ii) continuous.

Discrete variable : A variable taking only particular values or isolated values is called as *discrete variable*.

For example : Number of students in a class, number of articles produced by a machine, population of a country, number of workers in a factory etc. are discrete variables. Most of the discrete variables have integral values.

Continuous variable : A variable taking all possible values in a certain range is called as *continuous variable*.

For example : Weight of a person, length of a screw produced by a machine, temperature at a certain place, agricultural production, electricity consumption of a family, speed of a vehicle are the examples of continuous variable.

It is observed that many continuous variables such as marks, income, weight of a person etc. look like discrete variables after the measurement. This is mainly due to the limitations of the measuring instruments. Using better instruments one can have accurate measurement and overcome this difficulty.

The following diagram summarizes the various types of data :

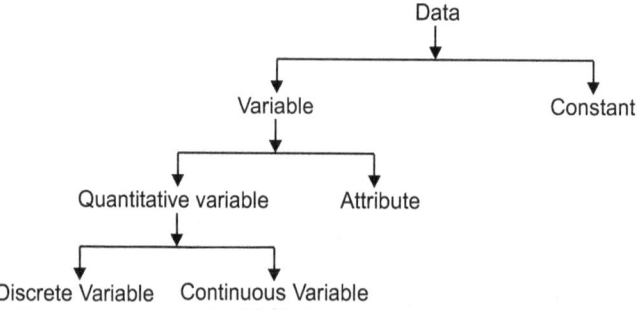

2.2 Classification

In order to study a characteristic or a group of characteristics of any type, the first phase is to collect the data.

Raw data : The unprocessed data in terms of individual observations are called as raw data.

For the sake of further statistical analysis, the data items are arranged in increasing (or decreasing) order. However, if there is a huge amount of observations, merely ordered arrangement is not enough. It does not furnish much useful information nor does it reduce the bulk of data. Data in this form are difficult to comprehend, analyse and interpret.

For example : Income of 5000 individuals is given for analysis.

It becomes quite essential to condense the data in a suitable form. Classification can be used as a tool to condense the data.

Classification : The entire process of making homogeneous and non-overlapping groups of observations according to similarities is called as *classification.*

The groups so formed are called as **class intervals or classes**.

Objectives of Classification : The objectives of classification can be summarised as follows :

1. It condenses the data.
2. It omits unnecessary details.
3. It facilitates the comparison with other data.

For example : In case of classification of income of 5000 individuals, one can find the number of individuals below poverty line or income distribution of two countries can be compared.

4. It reveals prominent features of the data.

For example : We can find the income group in which majority of families lie.

5. It enables further analysis like computation of averages, dispersion etc.

2.3 Frequency Distribution

We proceed to study how the observations are classified and a frequency distribution is formed.

Frequency distribution of continuous variable :

The procedure of classification of continuous variable differs slightly from that of a discrete variable.

Procedure :

1. Find the smallest and the largest observation. Calculate the difference between them. This difference is called as the *range*.
2. Decide the classes, by dividing the range into several intervals. The number of classes be preferably between 7 to 20.
3. Prepare first column of table by entering the class intervals.
4. Classify the observations one-by-one in the appropriate class by putting tally marks in the second column against the corresponding class. Cross the observation from the original data to avoid double counting.
5. Count the tally marks and enter the number in the third column.

Illustration 1 : *The following are the scores in intelligence test conducted for 80 candidates of a certain class.*

112	77	115	91	137	88	89	71
100	93	64	116	95	95	106	92
84	86	97	124	84	117	97	80
103	114	83	77	94	114	63	61
120	126	98	98	116	108	94	105
108	99	87	96	88	95	73	92
91	129	108	81	82	102	86	111
119	90	109	101	107	75	123	104
106	84	75	99	72	128	114	93
83	82	124	114	130	81	101	91

Prepare the frequency distribution of the data by taking suitable class intervals.

Solution : In the given problem we note that the highest and the lowest observations are respectively 137 and 61. Hence, the range is 137 – 61 = 76. In this case it is suitable to make 8 classes each of width 10. Since the lowest observation is 61, it is convenient to choose the first class as 60 to 69, the next as 70 to 79 and so on. The last class will be 130 to 139. According to the procedure described above, we classify the observations and prepare a table of three columns. First column includes classes, seconds includes tally marks and the third includes frequencies. The first observation is 112, it lies between 110-119, therefore, we put a tally mark to include the observation in this class. Likewise all the observations are classified and the process gives the following table 2.1.

Table 2.1 : Frequency Distribution of Scores of 80 Candidates

Class Intervals	Tally Marks	Frequency
60 – 69	III	3
70 – 79	N̄ II	7
80 – 89	N̄ N̄ N̄ I	16
90 – 99	N̄ N̄ N̄ N̄	20
100 – 109	N̄ N̄ IIII	14
110 – 119	N̄ N̄ I	11
120 – 129	N̄ II	7
130 – 139	II	2
Total	–	80

Frequency : The number of observations in a class is called as *frequency* or *class frequency.*

Frequency Distribution : A table containing class intervals along with frequencies is called as *frequency distribution.*

2.4 Methods of Classification

There are two methods of classification : (I) inclusive method (II) exclusive method. We bring out the difference between the two methods.

I. Inclusive Method : In this method the observation equal to upper limit is included in the same class. Therefore, the method is called as *inclusive method*. It can be observed that the upper limit of class is not the same as the lower limit of succeeding class. Therefore, a discontinuity is observed between the classes. *For example,*

Table 2.2

Daily Sales in ₹
2000 – 2999
3000 – 3999
4000 – 4999

II. Exclusive Method : In this method the observation equal to upper limit does not belong to the same class. It is included in the next class. Therefore, the method is called as *exclusive method.* For example, the observation 4000 is included in 4000 – 5000. In other words, the observation equal to upper limit is excluded from the same class.

For example,

Table 2.3

Daily Sales in ₹
2000 – 3000
3000 – 4000
4000 – 5000

In this case upper limit of one class is the lower limit of subsequent class. The classes are observed to be continuous without any gap in between them.

We explain below few more terms related to the frequency distribution.

Class-limits : The two numbers designating the class-interval are called as *class limits.* With reference to table 2.1, the first class interval is 60–69, in this case 60 and 69 are the class limits. The smallest possible observation that can be included in the class is *lower limit* and the largest possible observation that can be included in the class is the *upper limit.* In the above example 60 and 69 are lower and upper limits of the class interval 60–69.

Class boundaries : The class boundaries are the numbers upto which the actual magnitude of observation in the class can extend. The class boundaries are also called as actual limits or extended limits. For the sake of clarity, let us consider the frequency distribution with classes 10–19, 20–29, ... etc. In this case an observation 19.2 will be rounded-off to 19 and placed in 10–19, whereas the observation 19.6 will be rounded-off to 20 and will be placed in 20–29. Therefore, the actual magnitude of the observation in the class 20–29 will be between 19.5–29.5.

Note : If the classes are not continuous then, we need to determine class boundaries. If d is the gap between two classes then

$$\text{lower boundary} = \text{lower limit} - \frac{d}{2}$$

$$\text{upper boundary} = \text{lower limit} + \frac{d}{2}$$

The illustration below will make out the difference between class limits and class boundaries.

Illustration 2 : *Convert the class limits 10-19, 20-29, 30-39 into class boundaries.*

Class limits	Class boundaries
10 – 19	9.5 – 19.5
20 – 29	19.5 – 29.5
30 – 39	29.5 – 39.5

Solution : Note that the gap between the first and second class interval is

$$d = 20 - 19 = 1$$

$$\therefore \quad \text{lower boundary} = \text{lower limit} - \frac{d}{2} = 20 - \frac{1}{2} = 19.5$$

$$\text{upper boundary} = \text{upper limit} + \frac{d}{2} = 29 + \frac{1}{2} = 29.5$$

It can be clearly seen that in case of exclusive method of classification, class limits and class boundaries are same.

Using class-boundaries the classes are made continuous however original frequency associated do not alter.

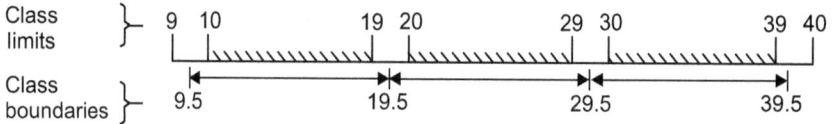

Fig. 2.1

Class-mark or Mid-values : It is the mid-point of class interval and the same can be obtained as follows :

$$\text{Mid-value} = \frac{\text{Upper limit} + \text{Lower limit}}{2}$$

$$= \frac{\text{Upper boundary} + \text{Lower boundary}}{2}$$

Class-width : It is the actual length of the class interval. We can find class width as follows :

Class width = Upper boundary − Lower boundary

= $\begin{pmatrix} \text{Lower limit of the} \\ \text{succeeding class} \end{pmatrix} - \begin{pmatrix} \text{Lower limit of the} \\ \text{class under} \\ \text{consideration} \end{pmatrix}$

= $\begin{pmatrix} \text{Upper limit of the} \\ \text{class under} \\ \text{consideration} \end{pmatrix} - \begin{pmatrix} \text{Upper limit of the} \\ \text{preceding class} \end{pmatrix}$

Open end class : A class in which one of the limits is not specified is called an open end class.

For example, in the following frequency distribution there are two open end classes.

Table 2.4

Daily Sales in ₹
below 2000
2000 – 3000
3000 – 4000
4000 and above

→ Open end classes

The class 'below 2000' has no lower limit and the class '4000 and above' has no upper limit. Therefore, these classes are open end classes. Whenever the extreme observations are widely spread, open end classes are used. In case of income distribution or the classification of sales of a company, open end classes may be required. Open end classes create some problems in further analysis, therefore, as far as possible the open end classes should be avoided.

Ilustration 3 : Find the mid-point and width of each class given the classes below 10, 10-20, 20-40, 40-60, 60-70, above 70.

Solution :

Class	Mid-point	Width
below 10	Not defined for open end class	
10 – 20	$\frac{10 + 20}{2} = 15$	10
20 – 40	30	20
40 – 60	50	20
60 – 70	65	10
above 70	Not defined for open end class	

Illustration 4 : Given the classes 0-9, 10-19, 20-29, 30-39 find the mid-point and width of each class.

Solution :

Class	Mid-point	Width
0 – 9	$\frac{0 + 9}{2} = 4.5$	10
10 – 19	14.5	10
20 – 29	24.5	10
30 – 39	34.5	10

Note : Width = Difference between two successive lower limits.

2.5 Cumulative Frequencies

In many situations it is required to find the number of observations below or above a certain value. *For example* : In case of a frequency distribution of income, the number of persons below poverty line or in case of frequency distribution of examination marks, number of candidates above 60 etc. is required to be found. In this case cumulative frequencies are much useful. There are two types of cumulative frequencies : (i) less than type cumulative frequency (ii) more than type cumulative frequency.

Less than type cumulative frequency of a class is the number of observations less than or equal to the upper limit of the corresponding class. Similarly more than type cumulative frequency is the number of observations more than or equal to the lower limit of the corresponding class.

It is clear from the above explanation that the less than type cumulative frequencies can be obtained by computing cumulative sum of frequencies from the lowest class to highest class. We illustrate the procedure of computing the less than type and more than type cumulative frequencies.

Illustration 5 : *For the following frequency distribution find (i) less than cumulative frequencies (ii) more than cumulative frequencies.*

Marks	0-10	10-20	20-30	30-40	40-50
Frequency	5	12	15	4	4

Solution :

Marks	Frequency	Less than cumulative frequency	More than cumulative frequency
0 – 10	5	5	4 + 4 + 15 + 12 + 5 = 40
10 – 20	12	5 + 12 = 17	4 + 4 + 15 + 12 = 35
20 – 30	15	5 + 12 + 15 = 32	4 + 4 + 15 = 23
30 – 40	4	5 + 12 + 15 + 4 = 36	4 + 4 = 8
40 – 50	4	5 + 12 + 15 + 4 + 4 = 40	4
Total	40	–	–

It can be noted that the less than cumulative frequency is increasing in nature. Less than cumulative frequency of the lowest class is same as the usual frequency and the less than type cumulative frequency of highest class is the total number of observations. In case of more than cumulative frequencies exactly reverse observations will be seen.

A table containing upper limits along with less than type cumulative frequency or lower limits along with more than type cumulative frequency is called as *cumulative frequency distribution*.

2.6 Relative Frequencies

Two different frequency distributions may not have the same total frequency, hence for the purpose of comparison and interpretation, sometimes it is better to express the frequency of a class in terms of proportion (or percentage) of the total number of observations. The proportion of number of observations in a class is the *relative frequency*. Therefore,

$$\text{Relative frequency} = \frac{\text{Class frequency}}{\text{Total frequency}}$$

It can be noted that the relative frequency maintains the same pattern which is observed in class frequencies. The total of relative frequencies is 1.

Relative frequencies are widely used in economics, commerce etc. We illustrate how the relative frequency helps comparison.

Illustration 6 : *The following table gives the frequency distribution of marks in accountancy out of 60. Find the relative frequencies.*

Marks	0-10	10-20	20-30	30-40	40-50	50-60
No. of students	5	25	27	32	6	5

Solution :

Marks	Frequency	Relative Frequency
0–10	5	0.05
10–20	25	0.25
20–30	27	0.27
30–40	32	0.32
40–50	6	0.06
50–60	5	0.05
Total	100	1.00

2.7 Guidelines for the Choice of Classes

Classification of data is a sort of compromise, therefore, it becomes important to choose appropriate number of classes. The classes should be chosen, so that it will condense the data and it will also maintain the patterns in the original data.

(1) The number of classes should not be too large, otherwise it will not serve the purpose of condensation.

(2) The number of classes should not be too small. If the number of classes is too small it will not reveal the pattern in the original data. Moreover, due to the small number of classes, each class will be too wide. For further computations it is assumed that the observations in a class are situated at the centre of the class. The assumption will not remain valid for wider classes.

The number of classes should be between 7 to 20. However, according to the needs and requirements of the situation appropriate number of classes is chosen.

If the number of observations is large, naturally the number of classes will be large.

(3) As far as possible, classes should be of uniform width.

Sturge's Rule : If N is the total number of observations to be classified, then according to sturge's rule, the number of classes is approximately $1 + 3.222 \log N$. By the other approach as a thumb rule, the number of classes is approximately $\sqrt{N}$.

(4) As far as possible, open end classes should be avoided.

(5) The class width should be preferably 5 or multiple of 5.

(6) The lower limit of the starting class be preferably multiple of 5.

For example : The classes may be of the type 0–9, 10–19… or 11-20, 21-30 … etc.

2.8 Graphs

Here we discuss the various graphs associated with frequency distribution. Generally graphs are used to represent mathematical relationship between two variables, otherwise diagrams are used.

(i) Histogram : It is one of the popularly used graphs for the representation of frequency distribution. It is a series of adjacent rectangles erected on X-axis with class interval as base, hence width of rectangle is equal to class width. Height of rectangle is taken as proportional to class frequency. In case of inclusive method of classification, extended class interval is used as base, where extended class interval is an interval designated by class boundaries.

Note :

1. A serious drawback of histogram is that, it cannot be drawn for a frequency distribution with open end class.

2. In case of discrete variable, histogram need not contain adjacent rectangles, those may be separated like bar diagram.

3. Histograms are useful to find mode, which is discussed in the next chapter.

Illustration 7 : *Draw a histogram to represent the following frequency distribution :*

Size of farm in hectares	1–20	21–40	41–60	61–80	81–100	101–120
No. of farms	12	38	16	5	3	1

Solution :

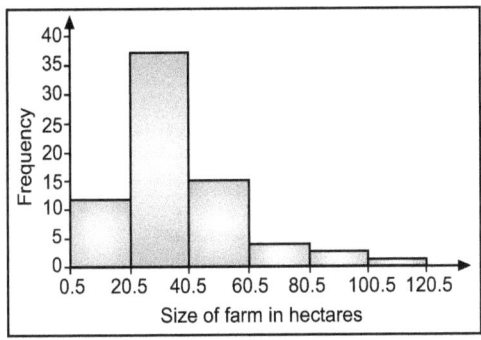

Scale :
X-axis : 1 unit = 20 Hectors
Y-axis : 1 unit = 5 Farms

Fig. 2.2 (a) : Histogram

Histogram using MS-Excel : To draw histogram follow steps given below. Take mid-values on X-axis and frequency on Y-axis. Enter mid values in column A and corresponding frequencies in column B on worksheet. Select the frequencies by clicking the mouse then go to insert command on main menu. Select

Insert – – > chart.

Then following windows will appear on the screen one-by-one.

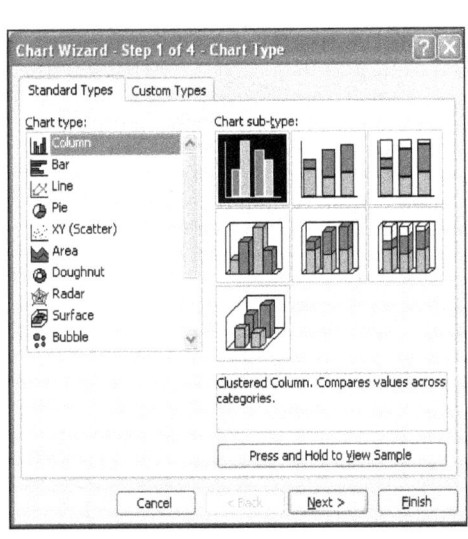 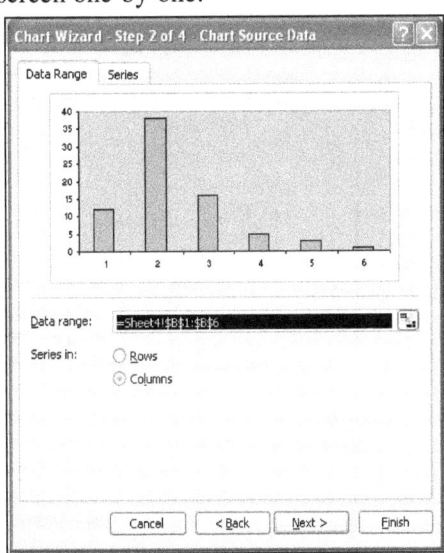

Fig. 2.2 (b)

Select chart type **(column)** and click **next**.

It is at bottom command line.

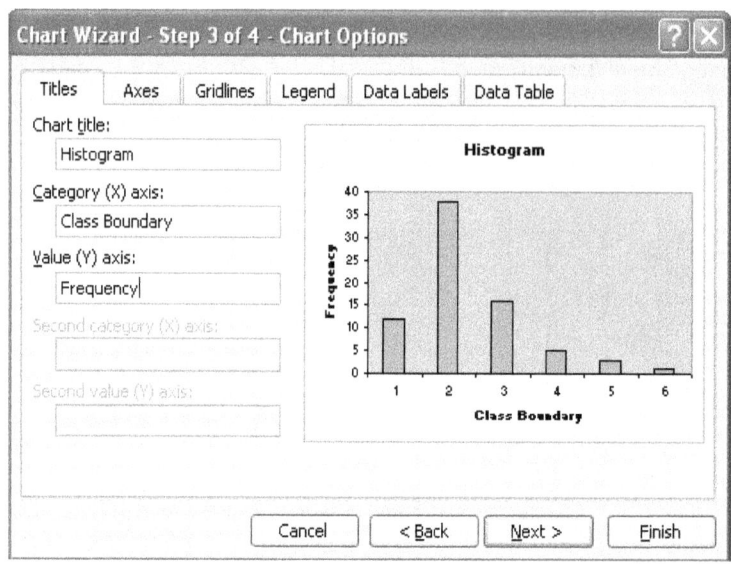

Fig. 2.2 (c)

In the data range, select frequencies and click Next.

Give chart title and x, y axis, click Finish, Right click on one of the bar as shown in Fig. 2.2 (d), select sub-menu Format Data Series to get Fig. 2.2 (b) then select Gap width 0 as shown in Fig. 2.2 (d). Click OK to get histogram as shown in Fig. 2.2 (e).

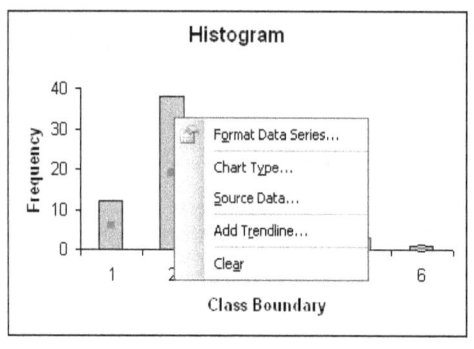

(d)

(e)

Fig. 2.2

After going through all steps of chart wizard, following histogram will appear on the screen.

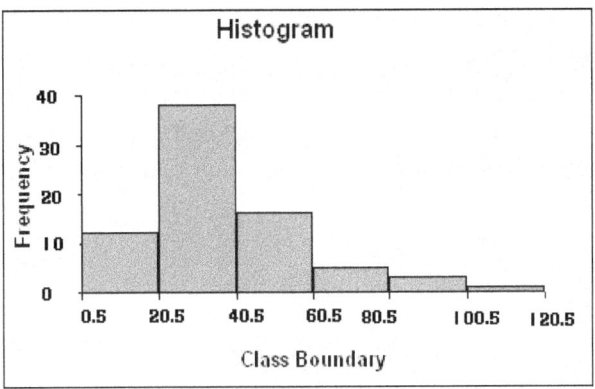

Fig. 2.2 (f)

Histogram and ISO 9000 : Now-a-days manufacturing units and industries have to maintain quality of their product as per norms laid down by Indian Standards (IS) or International Standards Organisation (ISO). To achieve quality standards several statistical tools are used. Such tools are known as Quality Control (QC) or Process Control (PC) tools. Histogram is an important tool. It has three fold purpose (i) It displays the pattern of variation, (ii) It gives idea about process behaviour, (iii) It helps to decide where to focus the efforts for improvement. Some interpretations based on histogram are illustrated below :

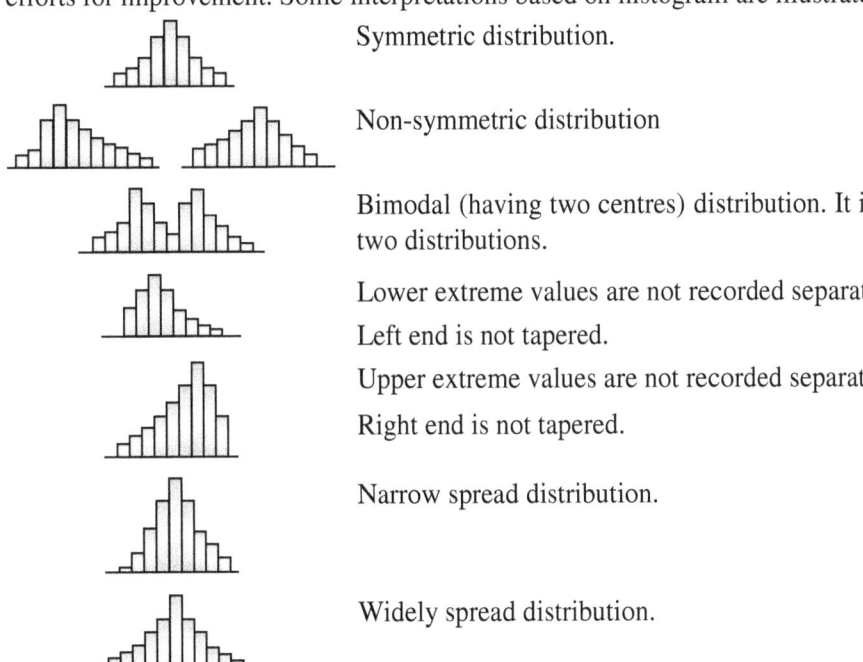

Fig. 2.3

(ii) Frequency Polygon : Generally a graph is expected to be in the form of a smooth curve. Histogram does not fulfil this requirement. Therefore, another important way of presentation of frequency distribution is frequency polygon or frequency curve. This type of graph enables us to understand the pattern in the data more clearly. Mid-values are taken on X-axis and frequencies on Y-axis to draw the graph. Successive points are joined by the line segments. Further, to complete polygon we obtain closed figure by taking two more classes. One preceding to first class and the other succeeding to last class. Frequency of each class is taken to be zero. Mid-points of these classes are used to get closed figure. The figure so obtained is called as frequency polygon.

Note :

1. We can draw frequency polygon using histogram. In this case we join the mid-points of upper sides of all the rectangles by line segments. Further to get closed figure we join the mid-values of preceeding class and succeeding class to the frequency distribution.

2. Histogram gives rough idea about the nature of frequency distribution. The border of histogram represents the frequency distribution. the boarder is zigzag, so we need to make it more smooth. Using frequency polygon and frequency curve it is possible to do so. The following figures will demonstrate how to make the border smooth by reducing the class width.

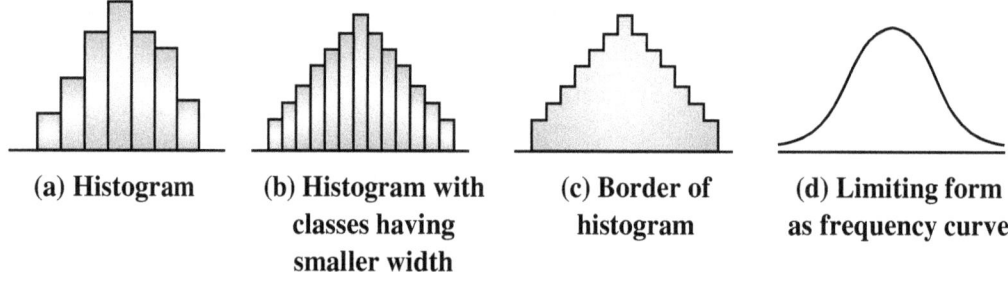

(a) Histogram   (b) Histogram with classes having smaller width   (c) Border of histogram   (d) Limiting form as frequency curve

Fig. 2.4

(iii) Frequency Curve : There is little difference in frequency polygon and frequency curve. If the points (or vertices of frequency polygon) are joined by a smooth curves instead of straight lines we get a closed figure called as *frequency curve*. While drawing frequency curve we should take care that the area under the curve is same as that of frequency polygon.

It can also be noticed that, we can draw frequency curve using histogram by the similar procedure which is used in case of frequency polygon.

Illustration 8 : *Draw a frequency polygon and a frequency curve for the following data :*

Monthly house rent	100-300	300-500	500-700	700-900	900-1100	1100-1300
No. of families	6	16	24	20	10	4

Solution : Mid-values of classes are taken on X-axis and frequency is taken on Y-axis. First point we need to plot is (200, 6), second point will be (400, 16) and so on. The last point will be (1200, 4). To get a closed figure we take two more points (0, 0) and (1400, 0). Joining these points by line segments (or smooth curve) we get frequency polygon (or frequency curve).

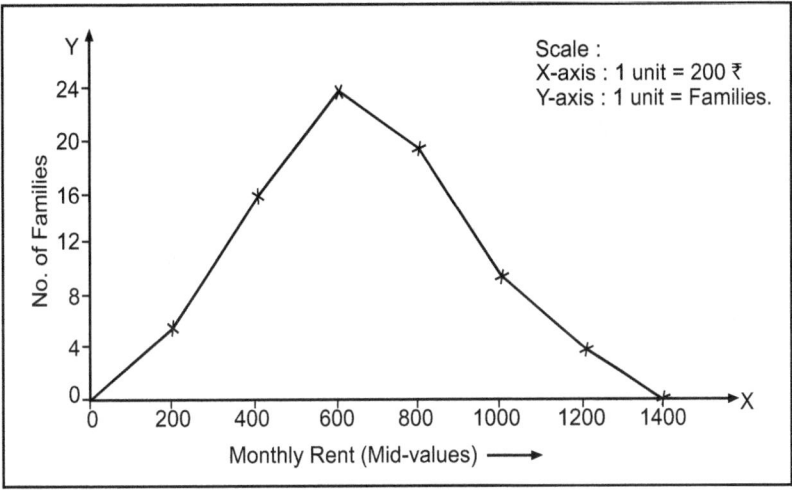

Fig. 2.5 : Frequency Polygon

(iv) Cumulative Frequency Curve or Ogive (B.B.M. April 2015) : Cumulative frequency distribution is represented by cumulative frequency curve (or ogive). There are two types of cumulative frequencies, hence, there are two types of cumulative frequency curves. For less than type cumulative curve upper boundaries of classes are taken on X-axis and less than cumulative frequencies on Y-axis. A preceding class before first class is also taken into consideration for drawing this curve. Cumulative frequency of this class is taken to be zero. Similarly, to draw more than type cumulative frequency curve lower boundaries are taken on X-axis and more than cumulative frequencies on Y-axis. In this case a succeeding class to the last class is taken with cumulative frequency zero. Those points are joined by smooth curve to get the cumulative frequency curve.

This type of curve is useful in finding median which is discussed in the subsequent chapter.

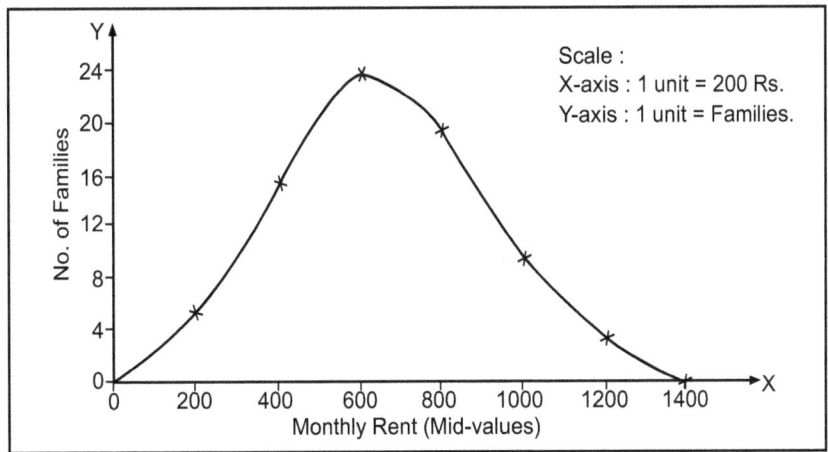

Fig. 2.6 : Frequency Curve

Illustration 9 : *Draw less than cumulative frequency curve and more than cumulative frequency curve for the following frequency distribution :*

Marks	0–10	10–20	20–30	30–40	40–50
No. of students	5	12	43	32	8

Solution : To draw less than type cumulative frequency curve we find out the required cumulative frequencies. In this problem class limits and class boundaries are same.

Upper limits	0	10	20	30	40	50
Cumulative frequencies	0	5	17	60	92	100

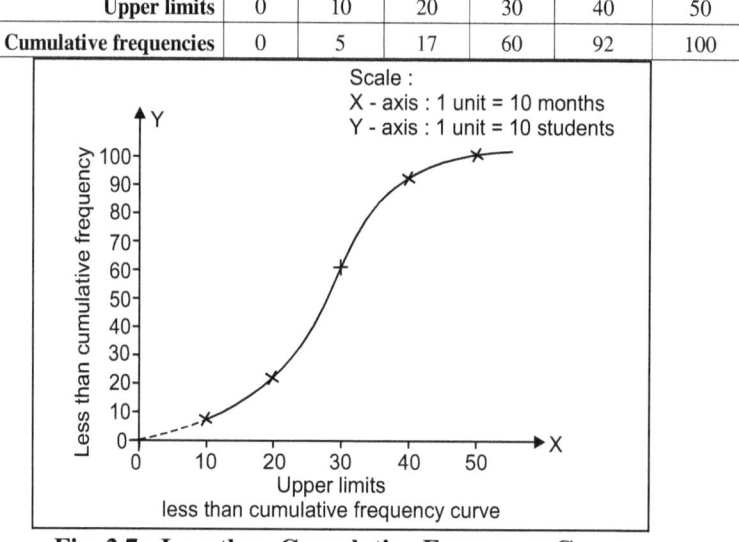

Fig. 2.7 : Less than Cumulative Frequency Curve

In order to draw more than cumulative frequency curve we obtain more than cumulative frequencies.

Lower limits	0	10	20	30	40	50
Cumulative frequencies	100	95	83	40	8	0

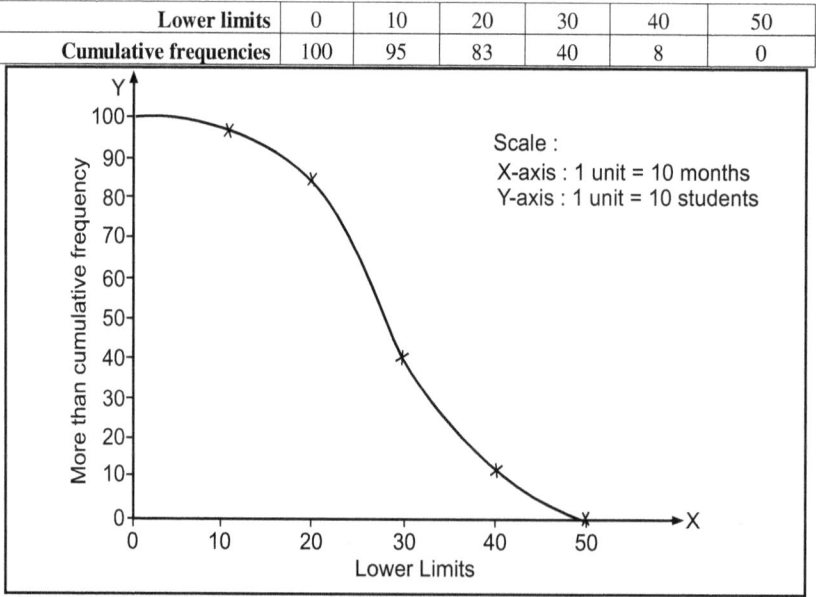

Fig. 2.8 : More than Cumulative Frequency Curve

2.9 Diagrams
(Simple Bar, Multiple Bar, Sub-Divided Bar and Pie Diagram)

In the earlier discussion we have studied the methods of summarising voluminous data. Those methods are adopted to serve the purpose of condensation, comparison and for revealing patterns. However, these methods have their own limitations. Especially when table is large in size, comparison becomes difficult. Perhaps a more effective way to serve the purpose of comparison and revealing the patterns, is graphical or diagrammatic representation. Diagrams and graphs are easy to understand and create an effect which lasts for a longer time. They use voluminous, uninteresting, dry data and present the facts in an attractive and impressive manner. They facilitate comparison and hence, conclusions can be drawn quickly, which is not possible with the help of a table or frequency distribution to the same extent. Moreover, patterns present in the data are more clearly exhibited by graphs and diagrams. Due to such several advantages, graphs and diagrams are believed to be powerful tools to convey information to a layman. Therefore, graphs and diagrams are found to be of immense use in several fields to emphasize the facts. LIC, banks, government agencies, industries use graphs to show their growth, development, extension activities etc.

There are several types of diagrams used in practice to represent the information in statistical table viz. simple bar diagram, multiple bar diagram, subdivided bar diagram, percentage bar diagram and pie diagram. Two of which are discussed below,

(i) Simple bar diagram : In order to represent data related to a single variable, simple bar diagram or bar diagram is used. For example : Yearly sales, monthly production, yearly population, countrywise population, yearly inputs etc. In this type of diagram, year, month, country etc. are taken on X-axis and corresponding values of the variable are taken on Y-axis. In this case rectangles of equal width and height proportional to the value of variable are erected on horizontal axis.

Illustration 10 : Represent the following data using simple bar diagram :

Year	1981	1982	1983	1984	1985
Production in (milion tonnes)	45	40	50	52	47

Solution :

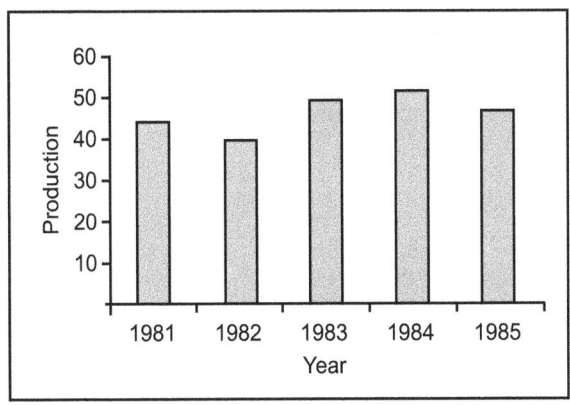

Scale :
X-axis : 1 unit = 1 Year
Y-axis : 1 unit = 10 millian

Fig. 2.9 : Bar diagram

Illustration 11 : Use a bar diagram to represent following data :

Year	1983	1984	1985	1986	1987
Profit of a company (in lakhs ₹)	2.5	2.0	– 1.0	2.8	3.0

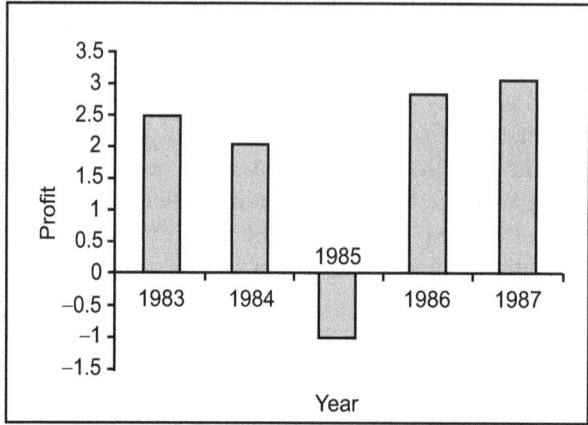

Scale :
X-axis : 1 unit = 1 Year
Y-axis : 2 unit = 1 Lakh ₹

Fig. 2.10 : Bar diagram

Note :

1. Sometimes horizontal bars are used instead of vertical bars.

2. When two or more variables are involved, bar diagram cannot be used. However, in order to overcome this drawback **multiple bar diagram** can be used.

(ii) Multiple bar diagram : In case of two or more variables multiple bar diagram is used. Similarly, whenever there are two or more components associated with a variable, this type of diagram is preferred. *For example :* Yearwise strength of a college can be divided into two components, girls and boys. In this diagram, with respect to each variable or component, separate bar is used. Such bars are drawn adjacent to each other for the same year or month etc. (to which change in data is related). Bars associated with different variables or components are displayed in different shades or colours. As usual the bars are of same width and height is maintained proportional to the value.

Illustration 12 : Draw a multiple bar diagram to represent the following data :

Profit of company (₹ in lakhs)	Year				
	2003	2004	2005	2006	2007
Company A	200	250	400	600	570
Company B	250	260	350	610	590
Company C	300	315	415	390	400

Solution :

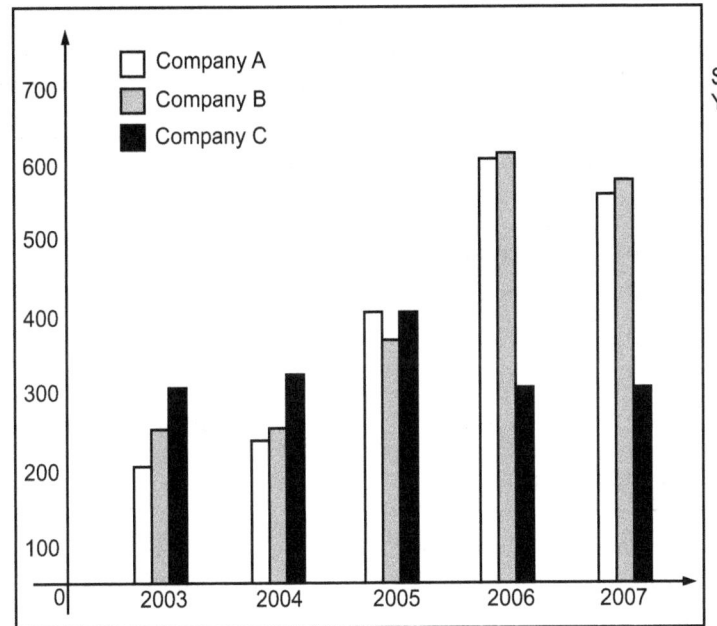

Fig. 2.11

Illustration 13 : Yearwise and sexwise strength of certain college is given below.

Year	2003	2004	2005	2006	2007
Boys	1250	1500	1600	1900	2000
Girls	1000	1300	1600	1800	1900

Represent the data by multiple bar diagram.

Solution :

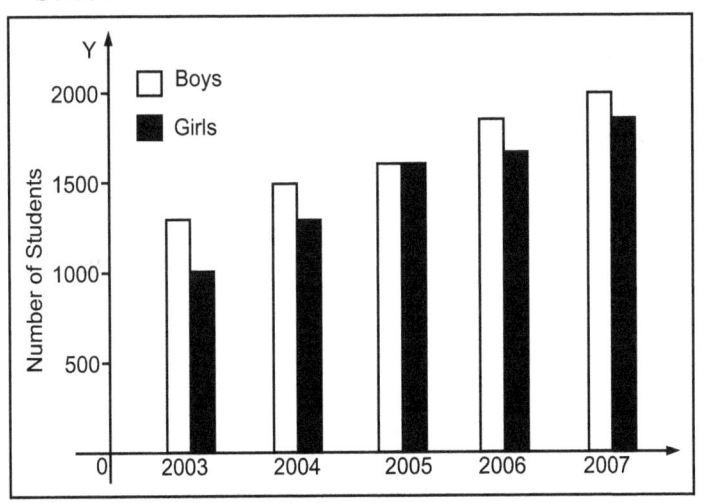

Fig. 2.12

(iii) Subdivided bar diagram : When a single variable involves two or more components, subdivided, bar diagram is used. A bar representing the total value is divided into several parts. Those parts represent the different components. The parts are chosen such that the height is proportional to the respective component. These parts are displayed in different colours or shades.

Illustration 14 : Following is a table showing faculty wise strength for 4 year :

Year	No. of Students			
	Arts	Science	Commerce	Total
1982 - 83	800	800	1400	3000
1983 - 84	750	1000	1750	3500
1984 - 85	700	1100	1800	3600
1985 - 86	900	1200	1900	4000

Represent the data by subdivided bar diagram.

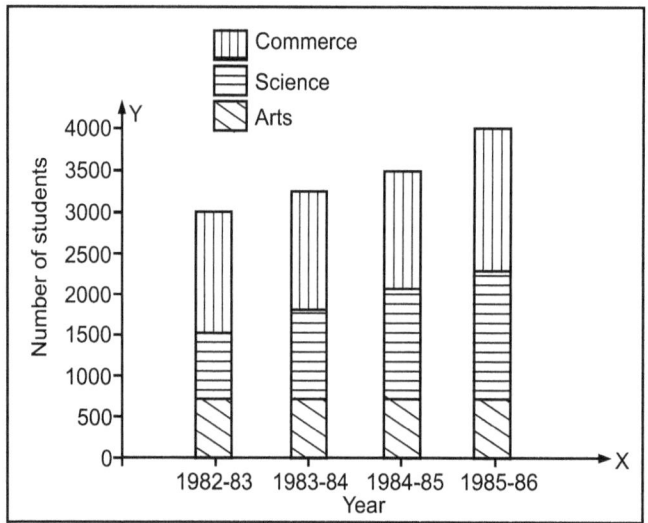

Fig. 2.13 : Sub-divided bar diagram

Illustration 15 : Present the following data using a suitable diagram.

Class	F. Y.	S. Y.	T. Y.
Pass	300	325	210
Fail	100	125	90
Total	400	450	300

Solution : In this case subdivided bar diagram is suitable because along with total components are also known.

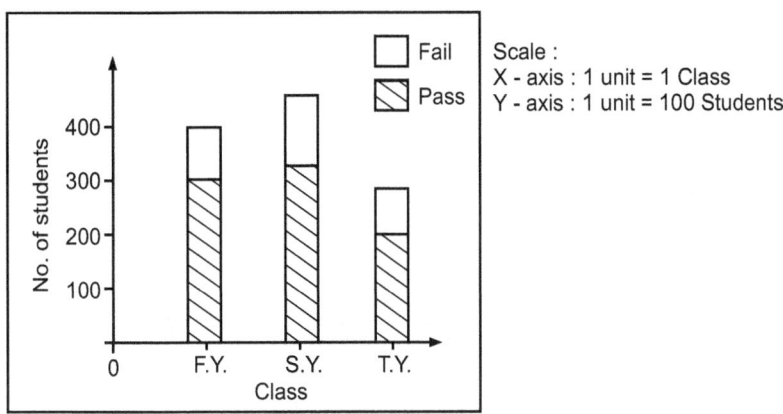

Fig. 2.14 : Sub-divided bar diagram

(iv) Pie diagram : When a variable is expressed as a sum of several components we use subdivided bar diagram. Such data can also be represented by pie diagram. In this diagram a circle is divided into several sectors as shown in illustration (by radial lines). Sectors have area proportional to the value of the component. Clearly number of sectors is same as number of components.

In order to draw pie diagram we express the data component wise in terms of percentage of total. Since 100 % corresponds to angle 360°, we take 3.6° for 1 %. Thus, we obtain angle for each sector and divide the corresponding circle into several sectors. We take angle for the sector proportional to the percentage which keeps area proportional to the value of the component.

Percentage for component $= \dfrac{\text{Component magnitude}}{\text{Total magnitude}} \times 100$

Angle for component = (Percentage for component) × 3.6°

Illustration given below will clarify the procedure.

Illustration 16 : Draw a pie diagram to represent the following data :

Group of Item	Average monthly expenses (in ₹) of a family
Food	2400
Clothing	1400
House rent	1600
Fuel and lighting	600
Miscellaneous	2000

Solution : Here the total of expenses is ₹ 8000. We express the values of components in terms of percentage. Then we obtain angle for sector by taking product of percentage and 3.6.

Item	Percentage	Angle in degrees
Food	$\frac{2400}{8000} \times 100 = 30.0$	$30 \times 3.6 = 108°$
Clothing	$\frac{1400}{8000} \times 100 = 17.5$	$17.5 \times 3.6 = 63°$
House rent	$\frac{1600}{8000} \times 100 = 20.0$	$20 \times 3.6 = 72°$
Fuel and lighting	$\frac{600}{8000} \times 100 = 7.5$	$7.5 \times 3.6 = 27°$
Miscellaneous	$\frac{2000}{8000} \times 100 = 25.0$	$25 \times 3.6 = 90°$
Total	100.0	360°

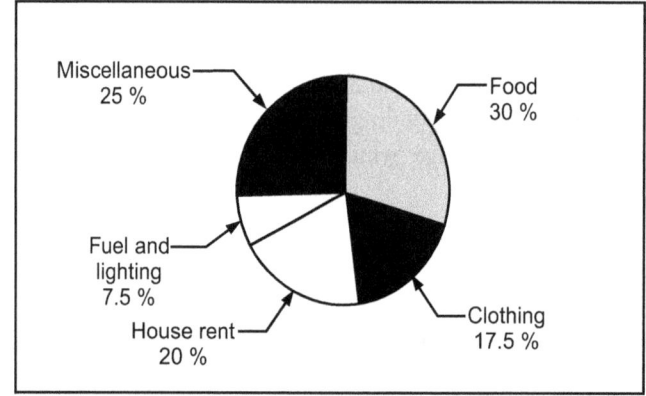

Fig. 2.15

Illustration 17 : The table below gives data relating education, obtained from census 1971 of India. Represent the data by pie diagram and percentage bar diagram.

Education level	Percentage
Illiterate	70.60 %
Literate	10.85 %
Primary	9.26 %
Non-S.S.C.	5.29 %
S.S.C.	2.23 %
Others	01.77 %

Solution : Angle in degrees obtained from percentage for different educational levels are calculated below :

Education	Illiterate	Literate	Primary	Non-S.S.C.	S.S.C.	Others	Total
Angle	70.6 × 3.6 = 254.16°	10.85 × 3.6 = 30.06°	9.26 × 3.6 = 33.34°	5.29 × 3.6 = 19.04°	2.23 × 3.6 = 8.03°	1.77 × 3.6 = 6.37°	360°

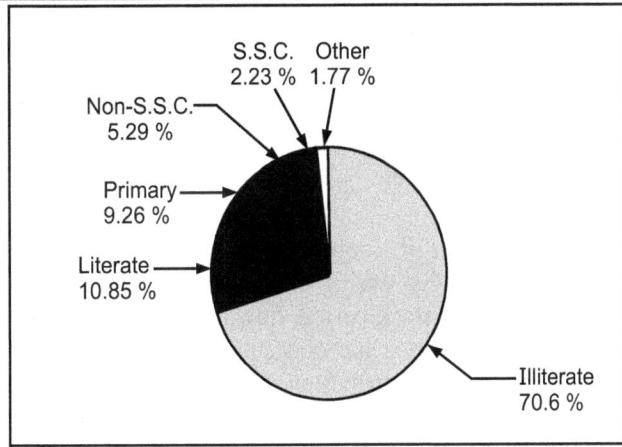

Fig. 2.16

Note :
1. In order to compare two phenomena using pie diagrams, we draw two separate pie diagrams such that their radii are taken proportional to the square root of total value.
2. If there are more components, percentage bar diagram or subdivided bar diagram does not remain effective. In such cases pie diagram is preferable.

2.10 Choice of Diagram

We give below the basis for the choice of suitable diagram.
(i) When we study the changes in totals related to a single variable, bar diagram is used.
(ii) When we study the changes in totals for several variables together, multiple bar diagram is used.
(iii) When we study the changes in the components and changes in totals, subdivided bar diagram or percentage bar diagram or pie diagram is used.

2.11 Advantages and Limitations of Graphs

Advantages :
1. Information is presented in condensed form.
2. Facts are presented in more effective and impressive manner as compared to tables.
3. Easy to understand for a layman.
4. Create effect which lasts for longer time.
5. Facilitate the comparison.
6. Help in revealing patterns.

Limitations :

1. Using graphs we find the values approximately, while, tables give exact values.
2. Graphs give only a general idea about the phenomenon, which is not sufficient for further satistical analysis.

2.12 General Rules for Construction of Graphs

Following are the general rules which should be observed while constructing diagrams.
1. Height and width of bars in histogram should be properly chosen, so that graph looks attractive.
2. A suitable scale should be chosen to occupy the available space properly.
3. Index should be provided, if essential.
4. Graphs should be neat and clean.
5. Scale should be mentioned.

Case Study : (1) The manager of a departmental store would like assign different work at different period of time to salesmen during the day. Particularly salesman required during peak hour is more, where as during slack period, how many will be made free for other work such as to main inventory, attach price bar code, packaging, sorting removing the spoiled material etc. He obtained frequency distribution of customers during every hour. He could make available proportionate and adequate number of salesmen as well he could open the additional counters. He had prepared work shedule based upon the frequency distribution of customer.

(2) The owner of the perfect shoes manufacturing company wants to prepare production schedule according to the various sizes of shoes.

He prepared the sales frequency distribution according to size of shoes. It helped him a lot to prepare the manufacturing schedule.

Illustrative Examples

Example 2.1 : *Find more than cumulative distribution for the following frequency distribution :*

Class	11-15	16-20	21-25	26-30	31-35
Frequency	8	12	15	10	5

Solution :

Class	11-15	16-20	21-25	26-30	31-35
More than cummulative frequency	50	42	30	15	5

Example 2.2 : *The frequency distribution of daily expenditure of 100 college students is given below :*

Daily Expenditure (₹)	50-59	60-69	70-79	80-89	90-99	100-109	110-119	120-129
Number of Students	3	10	18	25	24	10	6	4

Obtain :
(i) Class Boundaries of fourth class.
(ii) Class Width of any class.

(iii) Modal class.
(iv) Class Mark of last class.
(v) Number of students having expenditure less than ₹89.

Solution :

(i) Class boundaries of 4th class = Class boundaries of (80 – 89) : (79.5 – 89.5)

(ii) Class width = Upper limit of class under consideration
− Upper limit of preceeding class
= 10

All classes are of equal width 10.

(iii) Modal class = Class with maximum frequency
= 80 – 89

(iv) Class mark of last class = Mid-point of (120 – 129)
= 124.5

(v) Number of students having expenditure
less than ₹ 89 = Less than cumulative frequency of class (80-89)
= 3 + 10 + 18 + 25 = 56

Example 2.3 : *Draw histogram for the following frequency distribution.*

Marks	0-10	10-20	20-30	30-40	40-50	50-60
Number of Students	15	25	60	40	35	25

Solution :

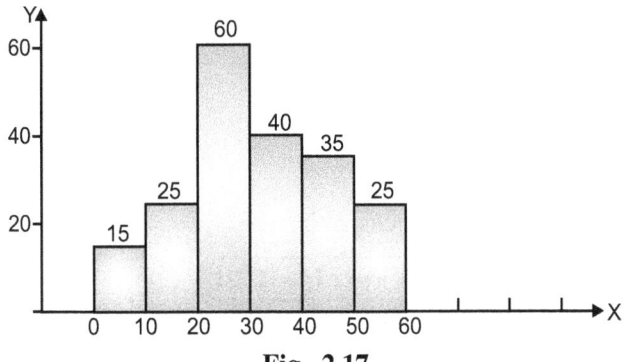

Fig. 2.17

Points to Remember

1. There are two data types : variables and attributes. The attributes are qualitative where as variables are numerical quantities.

2. Inclusive classification : classification with classes which include both the limits. Exclusive classification : classification with classes which exclude the upper limits of classes.

3. Class mark is the mid-point of class internal.
4. Class frequency is the number of observations in a class.
5. To make the classes continuous, we obtain class boundaries.
6. Histogram gives the idea of symmetry, spread and central value of frequency distribution.
7. Relative frequency = class frequency ÷ Total frequency.
8. Class width = Upper limit of succeeding class – Upper limit of the class.

Exercise 2.1

A. Theory Questions :
1. Explain the need of classification.
2. Explain the different methods of classification briefly.
3. Explain the following terms with illustrations :
   (i) attribute (ii) variable (iii) discrete variable (iv) continuous variable (v) raw data.
4. Explain the following terms :
   (i) class limits (ii) class boundaries (iii) class width (iv) class frequency (v) less than type cumulative frequency (vi) more than type cumulative frequency (vii) relative frequency (viii) open end class.
5. Explain the general guidelines or principles of choosing the classes.
6. What do you mean by classification ?
7. Discuss the importance of classification in statistical analysis.
8. (a) State the advantages of graphical presentation of data.
   (b) State the limitations of graphical presentation of data.
9. Explain the construction of the following graphs along with the rough sketches :
   (i) histogram (ii) frequency polygon (iii) frequency curve (iv) ogives.
10. What are the uses of histogram and ogives ?
11. (A) Discuss the importance of graphs in presentation of statistical data.
12. (B) Distinguish between :
    (a) Inclusive method of classification and exclusive method of classification.
    (b) Variable and attribute.
    (c) Raw data and classified data.
    (d) Discrete variable and continuous variable.

Exercise 2.2

B. Frequency Distribution :
12. Heights in cm of 50 students in a class are given below :

   168.9 163.1 161.5 168.0 167.1 157.5 163.9 168.9
   166.7 160.8 161.3 161.5 162.0 166.3 162.6 168.0
   170.1 165.8 165.2 164.5 171.3 158.0 158.7 159.6
   167.4 162.1 166.7 169.0 167.0 160.3 167.7 157.7
   164.9 168.3 164.0 157.6 172.5 171.1 168.2 172.6
   169.3 159.2 171.7 163.7 162.3 171.9 169.7 167.7
   170.2 169.0

Classify the above data by using 'exclusive method' of classification. Take the first class interval as 157–160.

13. The marks out of 100 scored by 40 students in the subject statistics are given below :

56	78	62	37	54	39	62	60	47	41
28	82	38	72	62	44	54	42	50	52
42	55	57	65	68	47	42	56	47	48
56	56	55	66	42	52	48	48	53	68

Classify the data by using 'inclusive method' of classification. Take the starting class to be 25 - 29.

14. Following is a frequency distribution of 95 shops according to daily shops in a super market on a particular day.

Daily sales (in '000 ₹)	No. of Shops
10 – 20	12
20 – 30	23
30 – 40	47
40 – 50	*
50 – 60	3
60 and above	2

(i)   Find the missing frequency.

(ii) Form the less than type cumulative frequency distribution.

(iii) Is the classification exclusive ?

(iv) How many shops have sales less than or equal to ₹ 50,000 ?

(v)   Obtain the more than cumulative frequency distribution.

(vi) How many shops have sales more than ₹ 40,000 ?

(vii) Is there any open end class ? If yes, state those.

(viii) Obtain the width of class and class mark of the classes for which it is possible.

15. Following is a frequency distribution of number of students according to marks scored in a certain examination.

Marks	0-19	20-39	40-59	60-79	89-99
No. of students	8	26	24	12	5

(i)   State whether the classification is inclusive.

(ii) Obtain class-boundaries of each class. Are the class boundaries and limits same ?

(iii) Find width and class-mark of each class.

(iv) Obtain the less than cumulative frequency distribution, hence obtain the number of students scoring marks less than or equal to 59.

(v)   Obtain the more than cumulative frequency distribution and hence find the number of students scoring marks more than or equal to 60.

16. The following is the distribution of the height of students in a class of secondary school.

Height (in cm)	Number of students
130 – 134	5
135 – 139	15
140 – 144	28
145 – 149	24
150 – 154	17
155 – 159	10
160 – 164	1

Find : (i) class mark of 3rd class.
   (ii) class width of any class.
   (iii) class boundaries of 5th class.
   (iv) class limits of 6th class.
   (v) number of students whose height is less than 149 cm.

17. Answer the following questions for the given frequency distribution :

I.Q.	60-69	70-79	80-89	90-99	100-109	110-119	120-129
Number of students	21	37	51	49	21	13	4

(i) State the type of classification.
(ii) State the class mark of 4th class.
(iii) State the class-boundaries of 5th class.
(iv) How many students have I.Q. less than 99 ?
(v) How many students have I.Q. more than 80 ?

18. The frequency distribution of marks obtained by 100 students in F.Y.B. Com. is given below :

Marks	0-9	10-19	20-29	30-39	40-49
No. of students	10	24	30	20	16

Answer the following questions :
(i) State the type of classification.
(ii) Find the class-mark of 3rd class.
(iii) State the class boundaries of 5th class.
(iv) Find the class width of 2nd class.
(v) Find the number of students getting marks less than 30.

19. Answer the questions using following frequency distribution of age of 50 citizens :

(B.B.A. Oct. 2014)

Age (years)	Below 30	31-40	41-50	51-60	61-70	Above 71
Frequency	3	7	–	16	8	2

(i) State type of classification.
(ii) Identify open end classes and state them.
(iii) Find missing frequency.
(iv) Find class-mark of fifth class.
(v) Obtain class boundaries of fourth class.

20. Following is the frequency distribution of number of students according to marks scored in a certain examination :

Marks	0-19	20-39	40-59	60-79	80-99
No. of students	8	26	24	12	5

   (i) State the type of classification.
   (ii) Obtain the class boundaries of the third class.
   (iii) Class width of the fourth class.
   (iv) Class-mark of second class.
   (v) How many students getting the marks less than 79 ?

21. Answer questions using the following frequency distribution of 100 companies :

Profit (00,000) ₹	No. of companies
0-100	09
100-200	15
200-300	18
300-400	21
400-500	–
500-600	14
600-700	05

   (i) State type of classification.
   (ii) Find missing frequency.
   (iii) Find class-mark of fifth class.
   (iv) Identify median class.
   (v) Find class width of third class.

22. The frequency distribution of daily expenditure of 100 college students is given below :

Daily Expenditure (₹)	50-59	60-69	70-79	80-89	90-99	100-109	110-119	120-129
Number of Students	3	10	18	25	24	10	6	4

   Obtain :
   (i) Class boundaries of fourth class.
   (ii) Class width of any class.
   (iii) Modal class.
   (iv) Class-mark of last class.
   (v) Number of students having expenditure less than ₹ 89.

23. The following data relate to the income of 90 persons :

Income (₹)	500-999	1000-1499	1500-1999	2000-2499
Number of Persons	15	22	45	8

   Answer the following questions :
   (i) Find class-mark of 3rd class.
   (ii) Find class width of 2nd class.
   (iii) Find number of persons having income less than ₹ 1,500.
   (iv) Find percentage of persons earning more than ₹ 1,500.
   (v) State the modal class.

C. Cumulative Frequency Distribution :

24. Obtain less than cumulative frequency distribution for the following data. Also represent it graphically.

Class	100-150	150-200	200-250	250-300	300-350
Frequency	12	15	08	03	01

25. Find less than cumulative frequencies and more than cumulative frequencies for the frequency distribution given below :

Class	100-150	150-200	200-250	250-300	300-350
Frequency	12	15	30	8	2

Also draw ogive curves.

26. Find more than cumulative distribution for the following frequency distribution and represent it by suitable graph.

Class	11-15	16-20	21-25	26-30	31-35
Frequency	8	12	15	10	5

27. Can the following be a less than type cumulative frequency distribution ?

Upper limit	10	20	30	40
Less than cumulative frequency	2	18	12	50

Justify your answer.

28. Obtain the frequency distribution from the following, cumulative frequency distributions :

(a)
Marks below	Number of stuents
10	1
20	8
30	35
40	46
50	50

(b)
Age in years	No. of persons
Less than 20	15
Less than 30	35
Less than 40	72
Less than 50	108
Less than 60	120
Less than 70	124

Also find greater than cumulative frequencies.

29. Prepare the frequency distribution from the following cumulative frequency distribution :

Income more than ₹	No. of persons
500	100
1000	96
1500	92
2000	59
2500	28
3000	2

30. Convert the following less than cumulative frequency distribution to usual frequency distribution. Also find more than cumulative frequencies.

Waiting time in minutes at octri check post	No. of vehicles
less than 1	12
less than 3	58
less than 5	206
less than 8	372
less than 12	500
less than 16	520

31. Convert the frequency distribution from the following more than cumulative frequency distribution. Also obtain the less than type cumulative frequency distribution.

Height of students	No. of students
More than 145 cm.	130
More than 150 cm.	123
More than 155 cm.	111
More than 160 cm.	89
More than 165 cm.	51
More than 170 cm.	21
More than 175 cm.	0

D. Graphical Presentation :

32. Draw the histogram, frequency polygon and ogive curves for the following frequency distribution. :

Weight in *lb*	80-89	90-99	100-109	110-119	120-129	130-139	140-149
Frequency	8	16	20	26	50	13	5

33. Draw a histogram for the following income distribution :

Monthly income	1000-2000	2000-2500	2500-3500	3500-5000
Frequency	120	125	180	150

34. Draw less than cumulative frequency curve for frequency distribution of intelligence quotient given below. Also obtain number of candidates having intelligence quotient between 105 and 125.

I.Q.	60-69	70-79	80-89	90-99	100-109	110-119	120-129
Frequency	21	37	51	49	21	13	4

35. Draw a frequency curve, frequency polygon and histogram for the following data :

Mid-values	25	35	45	55	65
Frequencies	5	12	33	13	7

36. Draw less than cumulative frequency curve and more than cumulative frequency curve for the following frequency distribution of marks in statistics :

Marks	0-20	20-40	40-60	60-80	80-100
No. of students	2	18	42	28	5

37. Draw histogram for the following data :

Weight (kg)	30 - 40	40 - 50	50 - 60	60 - 70	70 - 80
Number of Students	40	50	70	30	10

38. Draw histogram, frequency polygon and ogives for the following frequency distribution.

Class	0 – 10	10 – 20	20 – 30	30 – 40	40 – 50
Frequency	4	12	18	16	3

39. From the following frequency distribution of weights of 50 students, draw less than ogive curve :

Weight (kg)	10-15	15-20	20-25	25-30	30-35
Number of Students	5	12	15	10	8

E. Miscellaneous Problems :

40. Among a group of students, 10% scored marks below 20, 20% scored marks between 20 and 40, 35% scored marks between 40 and 60, 20% scored marks between 60 and 80, and the remaining 30 students scored marks between 80 and 100.
    (a) Using the information prepare a frequency distribution of marks of students.
    (b) If minimum 40 marks are required for passing, how many students have passed the examination ?
    (c) If maximum 60 marks are required for getting first class, how many students secured first class ?

41. Prepare a frequency distribution for each of the following :
    (a) Mid-value   :   47.5   52.5   57.5   62.5
        Frequency   :   4   9   17   10
    (b) Class-mark :   4   8   12   16   20
        Frequency   : 24 45   20   10   1

42. Following is a frequency distribution of heights in cm.

Classes	150-154	55-159	160-164	165-169	170-174
Frequency	2	17	29	21	1

   (a) Obtain class boundaries of each of the classes.
   (b) Determine the class width.

43. Present the following information in a frequency distribution.
    In a branch of a certain co-operative bank, 50 % fixed deposits are less than ₹ 5000. Thirty percent fixed deposits are of the amount ₹ 5,000 to ₹ 10,000. The number of fixed deposits of amount in between ₹ 10,000 to ₹ 20,000 is 150. It is 15 % of total deposits. The remaining 5 % deposits are of amount more than ₹ 20,000.

44. Find the frequencies a, b, c, d in the following frequency distribution.

Class	0 – 10	10 – 20	20 – 30	30 – 40	Total
Frequency	a	b	c	d	100

   Given that : (i) d = 3 a (ii) b : c = 7 : 3 (iii) c : d = 3 : 5

F : Diagrams :

45. Represent the following data by a suitable diagram :

Year	No. of students admitted
1991	1200
1992	1500
1993	1800

46. Represent the following data by a suitable diagram.

Country	India	Shri Lanka	U. S. A.	U. K.	Mexico
Population growth rate	2.5 %	1.8 %	2.0 %	1.8 %	3.2 %

47. Using a suitable diagram represent the following data :

Year	Birth rate (per thousand)	Death rate (per thousand)
1921 - 30	46.4	36.3
1931 - 40	45.2	31.2
1941 - 50	39.9	27.4
1951 - 60	41.7	22.8
1961 - 70	41.1	18.9
1971 - 80	37.0	14.0
1981 - 90	32.5	11.4
1991 - 00	26.0	9.0

48. Draw a pie diagram and percentage bar diagram to represent the following data :

Components	Cost of construction of a house
Labour	25 %
Bricks	15 %
Cement	20 %
Steel	15 %
Timber	10 %
Supervision	15 %

49. Draw a suitable diagram to represent the following data :

Year	Exports (crores ₹)	Imports (crores ₹)
1983 - 84	430	260
1984 - 85	350	300
1985 - 86	360	290
1986 - 87	400	300

50. Draw a bar diagram and pie diagram to represent following data :

Gas	Oxygen	Nitrogen	Carbon dioxide	Others
Percentage in atmosphere	21	78	0.03	0.97

51. Draw a pie diagram and subdivided bar diagram to represent the following data :

Country	Percentage of population in the world in 1980 - 81
India	15.53
China	21.72
Russia	6.05
U.S.A.	5.04
Others	23.69

52. Represent the following data by a suitable diagram :

Census year	Urban population in India
1931	12.18 %
1941	14.10 %
1951	17.62 %
1961	18.26 %
1971	20.22 %
1981	23.73 %

53. Draw a bar diagram to represent the following data related to the capacity of production of electricity (in crores kilowatt).

Year	Total
1975 - 76	7920
1976 - 77	8850
1977 - 78	9130
1978 - 79	9790
1979 - 80	10560

54. Draw a pie diagram for the following data :

Items	Food	House rent	Clothing	Education	Saving	Miscellaneous
Expenditure	300	200	125	110	90	75

55. Draw a bar diagram for the data in problem No. 34.

56. Present the following information using suitable diagram : **(B.B.A. April 2015)**

Mode of transport	Bus	Train	Aeroplane	Private vehicle	Own vehicle	Total
No. of passengers	1250	2250	100	600	500	5000

57. Draw a suitable diagram and represent the following data of ABC steel company.

Year	1994 – 95	1995 – 96	1996 – 97	1997 – 98	1998 – 99
Iron production	2100	2140	2200	2300	2500
Saleable steel production	1800	1830	1850	1900	1900

58. Draw a suitable diagram to represent the following data of a company.

Year	1994 – 95	1995 – 96	1996 – 97	1997 – 98	1998 – 99
Gross assets (in crores)	1900	2000	2200	3000	4000
Net assets (in crores)	900	1000	1050	2000	3000

59. The data given below relates to export performance in crores of ₹ of a company.

Year	Total
1995 – 96	93
1996 – 97	145
1997 – 98	210
1998 – 99	450

Draw a suitable diagram to represent the above data.

60. Distribution of revenue of a certain company for the year 1998 – 99 is given below, represent it by pie diagram.

Government taxes : 14 %	Material consumed : 20 %
Interest : 5 %	Repairs renewals : 7 %
Operation and other expenses : 27 %	Depreciation : 5 %
Reserves : 4 %	Dividends : 2 %
Employees : 16 %	

61. Represent the following data by a suitable diagram

Date (July 1999)	1	2	5	6	7	8	9
Stock Exhange Index	4140	4140	4194	4306	4322	4321	4326

62. Following data are regarding cashewnut export by Indian market, represent the same by a suitable diagram.

Year	92-93	93-94	94-95	95-96	96-97	97-98	98-99
Export (tons)	0.58	0.74	0.80	0.71	0.70	0.77	0.75
Revenue (crores ₹)	749	1048	1253	1241	1288	1396	1610

63. Transmission and distribution (T&D) losses in electricity occurring in various countries are as follows :

Country	Bangladesh	Pakistan	Thailand	Philippines	India	USA	Japan
T & D losses	40 %	28 %	22 %	22 %	21 %	8 %	7 %

Draw a suitable diagram and represent the above data.

64. The following is information regarding port traffic at Mumbai Port Trust, represent it by a suitable diagram. (Figures are in million tonnes)

Year	Total
1995 – 96	34
1996 – 97	34
1997 – 98	32
1998 – 99	31

65. Represent the following data expressing yearly values in thousand ₹ by suitable diagram.

Year	Expenditure	Income
1980	63	70
1985	84	96
1990	105	125

66. Represent the cost of per article by pie diagram and percent diagram.
   Manufacturing cost : 85 %
   Taxes : 8 %
   Packing and transportation expenses : 7 %

67. Represent the following information by suitable diagram.

Age group	Urban population	Rural population
0 - 5	13 %	10 %
5 - 15	25 %	22 %
15 - 35	32 %	38 %
35 - 65	20 %	20 %
above 65	10 %	10 %

68. Represent the following data by suitable diagram :

Country	Death rate per 1000 persons	Birth rate per 1000 persons
India	10.3	20.9
Pakistan	10.7	39.1
China	6.7	21.1
Sri Lanka	5.8	21.2
Japan	6.7	9.9

69. Answer the questions based on the following diagram

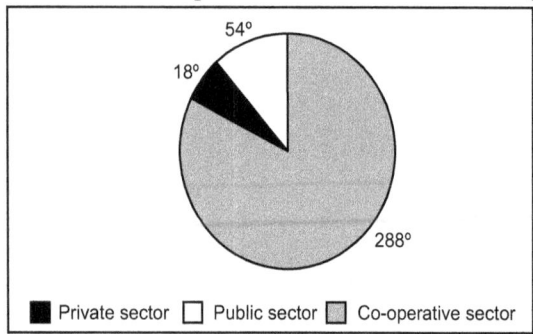

Sectorwise direct loans given by a nationalised bank in 1997–98.

Index

Fig. 2.18

(a) What is the type of diagram ?
(b) State the sector taking maximum loan amount.
(c) State the sector taking minimum loan amount among all the sectors.

70. Following diagram shows industrywise direct loans given by a industrial development bank, using the diagram answer the questions given below the diagram.

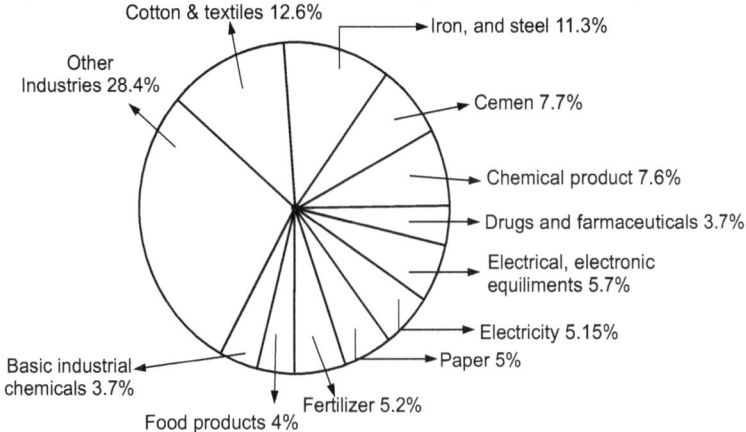

Fig. 2.19

(a) State the type of diagram.
(b) State the sector which is allotted maximum loan amount.
(c) State the industrial sectors receiving loan amount less than 5 %.

71. composition of port folio of a industrial development bank is given by the following data draw a suitable diagram.

Rupee loans : 56 %
Foreign currency loans : 11 %
Investment in Industry : 8 %
Bills finance : 7 %
Refinance : 6 %
SIDBI : 5 %
Investment in financial institutions : 5 %
Equipment leasing : 2 %

72. Marks scored by Sunil in the annual examination are given below :

Fig. 2.20

(a) Which is the type of diagram ?
(b) State the subject in which he has scored maximum marks.
(c) State the subject in which he has scored least marks.

Answers 2.1

12.

Class	157-160	160-163	163-166	166-169	169-172	172-174
Frequency	7	9	8	14	10	2

13.

Class	25-29	30-34	35-39	30-44	45-49	50-54	55-59
Frequency	1	0	3	6	6	6	7

Class	60-64	65-69	70-74	75-79	80-84
Frequency	4	4	1	1	1

14. (i) 8
 (ii) Less than cumulative frequencies 12, 35, 82, 90, 93, 95.
 (iii) yes (iv) 90 (v) more than cumulative frequencies 95, 83, 60, 13, 5, 2
 (vi) 13 (vii) 60 and above (viii) except the last class all have same width, which is 10
 Class marks : 15, 25, 35, 45, 55, not defined.
15. (i) yes (ii) class boundaries 0 – 19.5, 19.5 – 39.5, 39.5 – 59.5, 59.5 – 79.5, 79.5 – 99.5.
 Class boundaries are not same as class limits.
 (iii) Class marks 9.5, 29.5, 49.5, 69.5, 89.5.
 All classes have same width which is 20.
 (iv) Less than cumulative frequencies 8, 34, 58, 70, 75.
 No. of students having marks less than or equal to 59 is 58.
 (v) More than cumulative frequencies 75, 67, 41, 17, 5.
 No. of students having marks more than or equal to 60 is 17.
16. (i) 142 (ii) 5 (iii) 149.5 – 154.5 (iv) 155 – 159 (v) 72
17. (i) inclusive (ii) 94.5 (iii) 99.5 – 105.5 (iv) 158 (v) 138.
18. (i) inclusive (ii) 24.5 (iii) 39.5 – 49.5 (iv) 90 (v) 64.
19. (i) inclusive (ii) Below 30, Above 71 (iii) 14 (iv) 65.5 (v) 50.5 – 60.5.
20. (i) inclusive (i) 39.5 – 59.5 (iii) 20 (iv) 29.5 (v) 75.
21. (i) exclusive (ii) 18 (iii) 450 (iv) 300 – 400 (v) 100.
22. (i) 79.5 – 89.5 (ii) 10 (iii) 80 – 89 (iv) 56.

23. (i) 1749.5 (ii) 500 (iii) 37 (iv) 53 (iv) 1500 – 1999.

24. 12, 27, 35, 38, 39.

25. Less than cumulative frequencies : 12, 27, 57, 65, 67.

    More than cumulative frequencies : 67, 55, 40, 10, 2.

26. 50, 42, 30, 15, 5.

27. No, less than cumulative frequency cannot be decreasing.

28. (a)

Class	0-10	10-20	20-30	30-40	40-50
Frequency	1	7	27	11	4

(b)

Class	01-20	20-30	30-40	40-50	50-60	60-70
Frequency	15	20	37	36	12	4

29.

Class	Frequency
500 – 1000	4
1000 – 1500	4
1500 – 2000	33
2000 – 2500	31
2500 – 3000	26
above 3000	2

30.

Class	0-1	1-3	3-5	5-8	8-12	12-16
Frequency	12	46	148	166	128	20
More than cum. frequency	520	508	462	314	148	20

31.

Class	145-150	150-155	155-160	160-165	165-170	170-175
Frequency	7	12	22	38	30	21
More than cum. frequency	7	19	41	79	109	130

40. (a)

Class	0-20	20-40	40-60	60-80	80-100
Frequency	20	40	70	40	30

(b) 140 (c) 70.

41.

(a)
Class	Frequency
45-50	4
50-55	9
55-60	17
60-65	10

(b)
Class	Frequency
2-6	24
6-10	45
10-14	20
14-18	10

42. (a) 149.5 – 154.5, 154.5 – 159.5, 159.5 – 164.5, 164.5 – 169.5, 169.5 – 174.5
    (b) Classes are of same width, class width = 5.

43.
Class	Below 5000	5000-1000	10000-20000	Above 20000
Frequency	500	300	150	50

44.
Class	0-10	10-20	20-30	30-40
Frequency	10	42	18	30

45. Bar diagram
46. Bar diagram
47. Multiple bar diagram or several bar diagrams
49. Multiple Bar diagram or several bar diagrams
52. Bar diagram
56. Pie diagram
57. Multiple bar diagram or several bar diagrams
58. Multiple bar diagram or several bar diagrams
59. Bar diagram
61. Bar diagram
62. Multiple bar diagram or several bar diagrams
63. Bar diagram
64. Bar diagram.
65. Several bar diagram or multiple bar diagram
67. Bar diagram
68. Multiple bar diagram or several bar diagrams.
69. (a) Pie diagram, (b) private, (c) co-operative.
70. (a) Pie, (b) other industries, (c) chemical, food, drug.
71. Pie diagram.
72. (a) Bar diagram, (b) Mathematics, (c) Hindi.

Chapter 3...
Measures of Central Tendency

Contents ...
3.1 Introduction
3.2 Objectives or Requisites of Ideal Average
3.3 Arithmetic Mean (A.M.)
3.4 Merits and Demerits of Arithmetic Mean (A.M.)
3.5 Mean of Combined Groups
3.6 Median
3.7 Median by Graph
3.8 Merits and Demerits of Median
3.9 Mode

Key Words :
Central Tendency, Average, Arithmetic Mean, Deviation, Combined Mean, Median, Deciles, Percentiles, Box Plot, Cumulative Frequency, Mode, Empirical Relation.

Objectives :
Averages are tools of summarizing data, finding representative. It also facilitates the comparison. The methods of determining averages are illustrated in this chapter. The third and fourth aspects of statistics are analysis and interpretation. Averages help in both analysis and interpretation.

3.1 Introduction

We have studied in the previous chapters the various methods of summarizing data and its graphical representation. However it becomes essential to condense the data into a single value. Such a single value is treated as a representative of data and it is referred to an **average** or **central value** or measure of **central tendency**. It is desired that all the important properties of the observations in the data should be represented in the average. The word average is very commonly used in day-to-day life,

For example : Average marks, average profit, average run-rate of a team in one day. A single value is suitable for comparison. Therefore, average is essential quantity. Average is a value around which most of the observations are clustered, hence this single value itself gives clear idea regarding phenomenon under study.

There are several types of averages used in practice according to the type of data and purpose. In this chapter we study three important averages viz. mean, median and mode.

3.2 Objectives or Requisites of Ideal Average

The following are the objectives of average :

1. To obtain a single representative quantity for the entire data.
2. To facilitate comparison.

There are several averages in use, hence it is necessary to discuss the requisites of good or ideal average. **The following are requisites of good average :** (B.B.A. April 2015)

1. It should be simple to understand and easy to calculate.
2. It should be rigidly defined.
3. It should be based on all observations in the data.
4. It should be capable of further mathematical treatment.
5. It should be least affected by extreme observations.

3.3 Arithmetic Mean (A.M.)

This is very commonly used and widely applicable average.

Definition : Arithmetic mean (A.M.) or mean is a sum of observations divided by number of observations i.e.

$$A.M. = \frac{\text{Sum of the observations}}{\text{Number of observations}}$$

According to the different types of data calculation of A.M. differs slightly. We consider these cases as given below :

Case (i) Individual Observations or Ungrouped Data :

Suppose $x_1, x_2, \ldots, x_n$ is a set of n observations by definition, arithmetic mean will be

$$A.M. = \frac{x_1 + x_2 + \ldots + x_n}{n} \qquad \ldots (3.1)$$

Numerator of right side of (3.1) can be symbolically written as $\sum x$ i.e. $x_1 + x_2 + \ldots + x_n$.

Symbol $\sum$ (sigma) represents the sum. Further it is a customary to denote A.M. by $\bar{x}$. Hence

$$A.M. = \bar{x} = \frac{\sum x}{n}$$

Case (ii) Discrete Frequency Distribution :

Suppose $x_1, x_2, \ldots, x_n$ are values with $f_1, f_2, \ldots, f_n$ as the corresponding frequencies. Clearly to find the sum of observations we need to add observation x_1, f_1 times, observation

x_2, f_2 times and so on. Hence sum of observations will be $f_1x_1 + f_2x_2 + \ldots + f_nx_n$ and total number of observations will be $f_1 + f_2 + \ldots + f_n$. Hence,

$$\bar{x} = \frac{f_1x_1 + f_2x_2 + \ldots + f_nx_n}{f_1 + f_2 + \ldots + f_n}$$

Using $\sum$ notation we get

$$\bar{x} = \frac{\sum f\, x}{\sum f}$$

Case (iii) Continuous Frequency Distribution :

In this case, frequency is associated to the entire class and not to any specific single value. This creates difficulty in choosing $x_1, x_2, \ldots, x_n$.

For calculation purpose we make a reasonable assumption that the frequency is associated with mid-point of class or equivalently the frequency is distributed over the respective class uniformly. Thus, taking $x_1, x_2, \ldots, x_n$ as the mid-values of class intervals we calculate mean by the same formula discussed in case (ii), i.e.

$$\bar{x} = \frac{\sum f \cdot x}{\sum f} = \frac{\sum f \cdot x}{N}$$

Illustration 1 : *Calculate the arithmetic mean of marks scored by a student in 7 subjects given below : 61, 68, 69, 63, 70, 60, 78.*

Solution :

$$\bar{x} = \frac{\text{Total marks scored}}{\text{Number of subjects}}$$

$$\bar{x} = \frac{61 + 68 + 69 + 63 + 70 + 60 + 78}{7} = \frac{469}{7} = 67$$

Fig. 3.1

It can be noticed in the above illustration that the observations are nearer to 60, so for convenience we assume the mean to be 60 and obtain the sum of excess of marks. It will be $1 + 8 + 9 + 3 + 10 + 10 + 18 = 49$. We find the average of excess and add in the assumed mean. Thus mean will be $60 + 49/7 = 67$.

The above discussion leads to a short-cut method of finding arithmetic mean.

Short-cut Method or Derivation Method or Assumed Mean Method :

This method reduces the calculations involved in finding mean. Following are the steps in the computational procedure of mean.

(1) Decide a suitable figure 'a' which is referred as assumed mean.

(2) Subtract 'a' from each observation, the difference so calculated is called deviation from 'a', we denote deviation by 'd'.

(3) Find sum of deviations

$\sum d$ in case of individual observations.

$\sum fd$ in case of frequency distribution.

(4) Use the following formula and find the mean :

$$\bar{x} = a + \frac{\sum d}{n}$$ in case of individual observations

and

$$\bar{x} = a + \frac{\sum fd}{N}$$ in case of frequency distribution.

Illustration 2 : *Calculate arithmetic mean for the following frequency distribution :*

Observation (x)	103	110	112	118	95
Frequency (f)	4	6	10	12	3

Solution : We solve the problem by both the methods.

1. **Direct method :**

x	f	f.x
103	4	103 × 4 = 412
110	6	110 × 6 = 660
112	10	112 × 10 = 1120
118	12	118 × 12 = 1416
95	3	95 × 3 = 285
Total	N = 35	$\sum fx$ = 3893

$$\therefore \quad \bar{x} = \frac{\sum fx}{\sum f} = \frac{3893}{35} = 111.2286$$

2. **Deviation method :**

Taking assumed mean a = 100, we prepare the following table and use deviation method.

x	Deviations d = x − a d = x − 100	f	f·d
103	3	4	12
110	10	6	60
112	12	10	120
118	18	12	216
95	− 5	3	− 15
	Total	N = 35	$\sum fd$ = 393

Thus $\bar{x} = a + \dfrac{\Sigma fd}{N} = 100 + \dfrac{393}{35} = 100 + 11.2286 = 111.2286$

Step-deviation method : We have seen that deviation method reduces the calculations when the observations are large in magnitude. Sometimes the observations or deviations are multiples of some number. Especially when we deal with frequency distribution of continuous variables, deviations are found to be multiple of class width. In this situation step-deviation method is advisable.

Steps in the computational procedure are given below :

(1) Decide a suitable figure 'a'. (assumed mean a).

(2) Subtract 'a' from each observation and find deviation d (or class mark) i.e.

$$d = x - a.$$

(3) Divide d, obtained in (2) by convenient figure 'h' (or by class width).

This figure is called as step-deviation.

i.e. $d' = \dfrac{d}{h}$

(4) Find sum of step deviations

$\Sigma d'$ in case of individual observations

$\Sigma fd'$ in case of frequency distribution.

(5) Use the following formula to find the mean

$\bar{x} = a + \left(\dfrac{\Sigma d'}{n} \times h\right)$ in case of individual observations

and

$\bar{x} = a + \left(\dfrac{\Sigma fd'}{N} \times h\right)$ in case of frequency distribution.

Illustration 3 : The following is a distribution of monthly salaries of the employees of a firm.

Salaries in ₹	No. of employees
0 – 500	2
500 – 1000	8
1000 – 1500	12
1500 – 2000	23
2000 – 2500	25
2500 – 3000	20
3000 – 3500	9
3500 – 4000	1

Compute arithmetic mean of salaries.

Solution : We use step-deviation method to find the mean.

Class	Mid-values	d = x − 1750	$d' = \dfrac{d}{500}$	f	fd'
0 − 500	250	− 1500	− 3	2	− 6
500 − 1000	750	− 1000	− 2	8	− 16
1000 − 1500	1250	− 500	− 1	12	− 12
1500 − 2000	1750	0	0	23	0
2000 − 2500	2250	500	1	25	25
2500 − 3000	2750	1000	2	20	40
3000 − 3500	3250	1500	3	9	27
3500 − 4000	3750	2000	4	1	4
Total	−	−	−	100	62

$$\bar{x} = a + \left(\dfrac{\sum fd'}{N} \times h\right)$$

Note that a = 1750, $\sum fd' = 62$, N = 100 and h = 500.

Hence, $\bar{x} = 1750 + \dfrac{62}{100} \times 500$

∴ $\bar{x} = 1750 + 310 = 2060$

Thus average salary is ₹ 2,060.

Effect of change of origin and Scale on Arithmetic mean :

Change of origin means to add or to subtract a constant from each observation. Thus, if the original variable is denoted by x than x − a or x + a is a variable obtained by shifting the origin (where a is a constant). The new variable x − a is also referred as deviation. In this situation arithmetic mean need not be obtained again however from the earlier mean we can determine the mean after the change of origin.

(1) If y = x − a then $\bar{y} = \bar{x} - a$.

(2) If y = x + a then $\bar{y} = \bar{x} + a$.

Similarly, changing of scale means to multiply or to divide the observations by a constant. Thus, if x is the variable x/c or cx is a variable obtained by changing the scale, c being constant. In this case also we need not find the arithmetic mean once again due to change in scale. The change of scale is similar to step deviation. However the same relation is observed between old variable and the variable after changing the scale. We summarize the rules below :

(3) If $y = \dfrac{x}{c}$ then $\bar{y} = \dfrac{\bar{x}}{c}$.

(4) If $y = cx$ then $\bar{y} = c\bar{x}$.

(5) If $y = ax + b$ then $\bar{y} = a\bar{x} + b$.

(6) If $y = \dfrac{x-a}{c}$ then $\bar{y} = \dfrac{\bar{x}-a}{c}$.

Illustration 4 : Suppose the arithmetic mean of 50 observations is 120. Find the arithmetic mean if each observation is

(i) increased by 10

(ii) decreased by 5

(iii) doubled

(iv) reduced to one third

(v) doubled and then increased by 5

(vi) increased by 5 and then doubled.

Solution : This illustration explains the change of origin and scale (or linear transformations). Let x = Original variable = y = New variable.

(i) $y = x + 10$, $\bar{y} = \bar{x} + 10 = 120 + 10 = 130$

(ii) $y = x - 5$, $\bar{y} = \bar{x} - 5 = 120 - 5 = 115$

(iii) $y = 2x$, $\bar{y} = 2\bar{x} = 2 \times 120 = 240$

(iv) $y = \dfrac{x}{3}$, $\bar{y} = \dfrac{\bar{x}}{3} = \dfrac{120}{3} = 40$

(v) $y = 2x + 5$, $\bar{y} = 2\bar{x} + 5 = 2 \times 120 + 5 = 245$

(vi) $y = 2(x+5)$, $\bar{y} = 2(\bar{x} + 5) = 2(120 + 5) = 250$.

3.4 Merits and Demerits of Arithmetic Mean

Arithmetic mean possesses most of the requisites of good average. Hence it is widely used. We state below its merits and demerits :

Merits : (B.B.A. April 2015)

1. It is easy to calculate and simple to follow.
2. It is based on all observations.
3. It is rigidly defined.
4. It possesses sampling stability.
5. It is capable of further mathematical treatment. Given the means and sizes of two or more groups we can find mean of combined group. We can find the total given the mean and number of observations.

Demerits : (B.B.A. April 2015)

1. It is applicable only for quantitative data.
2. It is unduly affected by extreme observations.
3. It cannot be computed for frequency distribution with open end class.
4. It cannot be determined graphically.
5. Sometimes arithmetic mean may not be an observation in a data. *For example,* arithmetic mean of number of T.V. sets sold daily is 5.25.

3.5 Mean of Combined Groups

Many times it is required to compute mean of two groups combined together. If means and sizes of groups are known we can determine the combined mean i.e. mean of combined group.

Let $\bar{x}_1$ be the arithmetic mean of first group of size n_1. Similarly $\bar{x}_2$ be mean of second group of size n_2, then the combined mean is derived as follows :

$$\bar{x}_1 = \frac{\text{(Sum of observations in first group)}}{n_1}$$

hence, $n_1 \bar{x}_1$ = Sum of observations in first group

Similarly $n_2 \bar{x}_2$ = Sum of observations in second group.

Thus, the combined mean $\bar{x}_c$ is

$$\bar{x}_c = \frac{\begin{pmatrix}\text{Sum of the observations in} \\ \text{first group}\end{pmatrix} + \begin{pmatrix}\text{Sum of the observations} \\ \text{in second group}\end{pmatrix}}{\text{(Size of first group)} + \text{(Size of second group)}}$$

$$\bar{x}_c = \frac{n_1 \bar{x}_1 + n_2 \bar{x}_2}{n_1 + n_2}$$

Illustration 5 : *Arithmetic mean of weight of 100 boys is 50 kg and the arithmetic mean of 50 girls is 45 kg. Calculate the arithmetic mean of combined group of boys and girls.*

Solution : Let $\bar{x}_1$ and n_1 be the mean and size of group of boys and $\bar{x}_2$ and n_2 be the mean and size of group of girls. So that $n_1 = 100$, $\bar{x}_1 = 50$, $n_2 = 50$, $\bar{x}_2 = 45$. Hence, combined mean is

$$\bar{x}_c = \frac{n_1 \bar{x}_1 + n_2 \bar{x}_2}{n_1 + n_2} = \frac{(100 \times 50) + (50 \times 45)}{100 + 50}$$

$$= \frac{7250}{150} = 48.3333$$

Illustration 6 : *The mean weekly salary paid to 300 employees of a firm is 1,470 ₹ There are 200 male employees and the remaining are females. If mean salary of males is 1,505 ₹ Obtain the mean salary of females.*

Solution : Suppose $\bar{x}_1$ and n_1 are mean and group size of males. $\bar{x}_2$ and n_2 are mean and size of group of females, $\bar{x}_c$ is mean of all the employees considered together.

Now,
$$\bar{x}_c = \frac{n_1 \bar{x}_1 + n_2 \bar{x}_2}{n_1 + n_2}$$

∴ $$1470 = \frac{(200 \times 1505) + (100 \times \bar{x}_2)}{200 + 100}$$

∴ $$1470 = \frac{301000 + 100 x_2}{300}$$

∴ $$441000 = 301000 + 100 \bar{x}_2$$

∴ $$4410 = 3010 + \bar{x}_2$$

∴ $$\bar{x}_2 = 1,400 ₹$$

3.6 Median

We have seen that arithmetic mean cannot be calculated for qualitative observations like beauty, debating skill, honesty, blindness. Moreover if a frequency distribution includes open end class, mean does not exist and it is unduly affected by extreme observations. In order to overcome these drawbacks, other measures of central tendency, median or mode are used.

Illustration : The arithmetic mean of 38, 43, 41, 39, 52, 48, 60, 167 is 61. This cannot be the representative value of the data, because among 8 observations, 7 are smaller than arithmetic mean. Thus incase extreme observations are widely separated from most of the observations, arithmetic mean does not remain suitable, whereas median is suitable.

Definition : Median is the value of middle most observation in the data when the observations are arranged in increasing (or decreasing) order of their values.

Thus, median is the central observation. It divides the data into two equal parts. There are equal number of observation above as well as below the median. It is also called as **positional average**.

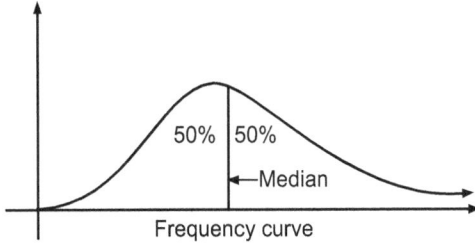

Fig. 3.2

(i) Computation of Median for Ungrouped data :

It may be noticed that in case of individual observations or ungrouped data computation of median does not require any formula. It can be determined by inspection.

Suppose n is the number of observations in the data. If n is odd then there is only one middle most observation which is $\frac{(n+1)^{th}}{2}$ observation. On the other hand if n is even then there are two middle most observations which are $(n/2)^{th}$ and $(n/2 + 1)^{th}$. In this case we take median to be mean of these two middle most observations. We follow the procedure described below for calculating median.

Step 1 : Arrange the observations in increasing (or decreasing) order.

Step 2 : Compute the median by the following criteria :

Median = The value of $(n + 1)/2$ th observation if n is odd.

$$\text{Median} = \frac{\left(\text{The value of } (n/2)^{th} \text{ observation}\right) + \left(\text{The value of } (n/2 + 1)^{th} \text{ observation}\right)}{2} \text{ if n is even}$$

Illustration 7 : *Following are the temperatures recorded in a certain city, observed in a certain week.*

$$35,\ 38,\ 40,\ 39,\ 35,\ 36,\ 37$$

Obtain the median temperature.

Solution : The ordered arrangement of 7 observations is

$$35,\ 35,\ 36,\ \boxed{37},\ 38, 39,\ 40$$

Since, n = 7 is odd we get,

Median = The value of $(n + 1)/2^{th}$ observation

= The value of 4th observation = 37.

Illustration 8 : *The following are the sales in ₹ for 6 days in a certain week.*

$$3020,\ 4120,\ 3600,\ 3250,\ 3830,\ 4000$$

Obtain the median sale.

Solution : The ordered arrangement of 6 observations is

$$3020,\ 3250,\ \boxed{3600,\ 3830}\ ,\ 4000,\ 4120$$

Since n = 6 is even we get two middle observations. Hence

$$\text{Median} = \frac{\left(\text{The value of } (n/2)^{th} \text{ observation}\right) + \left(\text{The value of } (n/2+1)^{th} \text{ observation}\right)}{2}$$

$$\text{Median} = \frac{\left(\text{The value of } 3^{rd} \text{ observation}\right) + \left(\text{The value of } 4^{th} \text{ observation}\right)}{2} = \frac{3600 + 3830}{2} = 3715\ ₹$$

(ii) Computation of Median for Continuous frequency distribution : Suppose N is the total frequency. Since the variable under consideration is continuous we can estimate the value of (N/2)th observation. Hence regardless of N whether it is even or odd in continuous frequency distribution we take median to be the value of (N/2)th observation.

Computational procedure :

Step 1 : Obtain the class boundaries.

Step 2 : Obtain less than cumulative frequencies.

Step 3 : Locate the median class. Where median class is the class in which median i.e. (N/2)th observation falls. In other words, it is in a class where less than cumulative frequency is equal to or exceeds N/2 for the first time.

Step 4 : Apply the formula and find the median.

$$\text{Median} = l + \left(\frac{N/2 - c.f.}{f} \times h \right)$$

where,

l = Lower boundary (extended class limit) of the median class

N = Total frequency

c.f. = Less than cumulative frequency of the class just **preceding** to median class.

f = Frequency of median class

h = Class width

Illustration 9 : *Calculate median for the following frequency distribution :*

(B.B.A. April 2015)

Marks	below 20	21-40	41-60	61-80	81-100
No. of students	1	9	32	16	7

Solution :

Class boundaries	Frequency	Less than cumulative frequency
0 – 20.5	1	1 < N/2
20.5 – 40.5	9	c.f. = 10 < N/2
40.5 – 60.5 Median class	f = 32	42 > N/2
60.5 – 80.5	16	58
80.5 – 100	7	65 = N

Median = The value of N/2 i.e. 32.5th observation.

Median class : 40.5 – 60.5,

because N/2 exceeds less than cumulative frequency for the first time in this class.

Therefore, l = 40.5, N/2 = 32.5, c.f. = 10, f = 32, h = 20.

Hence,

$$\text{Median} = l + \left(\frac{N/2 - c.f.}{f}\right) \times h$$

$$= 40.5 + \frac{32.5 - 10}{32} \times 20$$

$$= 54.5625$$

3.7 Median – by Graphical Method

Median can be obtained graphically by means of ogive curve. Plot less than cumulative frequency curve taking upper boundaries on x-axis, and less than cumulative frequency on y-axis. Draw a line parallel to x-axis passing through point N/2 on y-axis. From the point of intersection of the line and ogive curve, draw a perpendicular to x-axis. The value at the foot of perpendicular is the median.

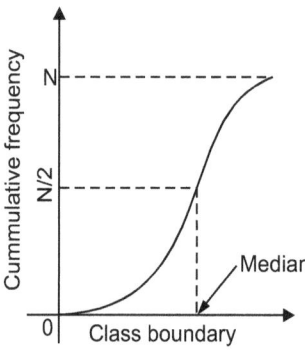

Fig. 3.3

Illustration 10 : *Obtain the median, from the following frequency distribution using formula and also graphically.*

Monthly Salary (₹)	1400-1600	1600-1800	1800-2000	2000-2200	2200-2400	2400-2600
Frequency	12	30	55	40	35	28

Solution : Here the classes are continuous, hence they can be used as they are :

Class	Frequency	Less than type cumulative frequency
1400 – 1600	12	12
1600 – 1800	30	42
1800 – 2000	55	97
2000 – 2200	40	137
2200 – 2400	35	172
2400 – 2600	28	200 = N

$$\text{Median} = \left(\frac{N}{2}\right)^{th} \text{observation}$$

$$= \left(\frac{200}{2} = 100\right)^{th} \text{observation}$$

Median lies in the (2000 – 2200) class, since 100 lies between less than cumulative frequencies 97 and 137,

$$\text{Median} = l + \left(\frac{N/2 - c.f.}{f}\right) \times h$$

$$= 2000 + \left(\frac{100 - 97}{40}\right) \times 200$$

$$= 2015$$

To obtain median graphically we use less than type cumulative frequency curve.

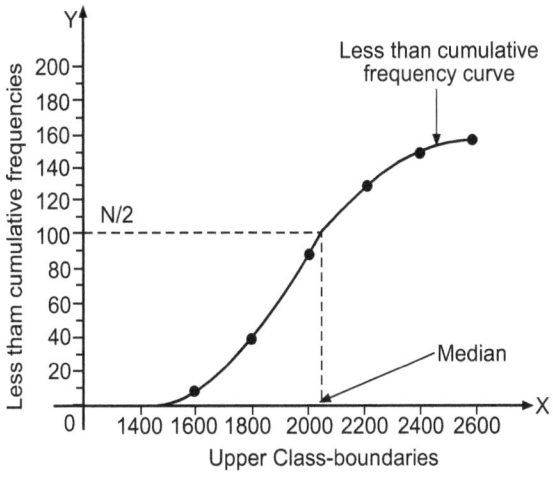

Fig. 3.4

3.8 Merits and Demerits of Median

Merits :
1. It is easy to understand and easy to calculate.
2. It is not affected due to extreme observations.
3. It can be computed for a distribution with open end classes.
4. It can be determined graphically.
5. It is applicable to qualitative data also. In this case observations are arranged in order according to the quality and the middle most observation can be obtained. The quality of this item is taken to be average quality or median quality.

Demerits :
1. It is not based on all the observations, hence it is not proper representative.
2. It is not capable of further mathematical treatment.
3. It is not as rigidly defined as the arithmetic mean.

3.9 Mode

It is yet another measure of central tendency developed to overcome the drawbacks of arithmetic mean. Apart from this, in some situations mode is the proper average.

Definition : The observation with maximum frequency or the most repeated observation is called as mode.

It is clear from earlier discussion that the general nature of frequency curve is bell shaped in majority of situations. Thus initially frequency is small, it increases and reaches the maximum and then it declines. The value on x-axis at which the maxima or the peak of the frequency curve appears is a mode.

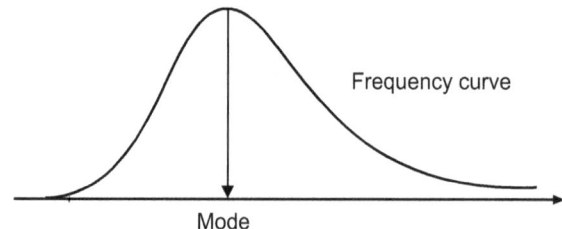

Fig. 3.5

In case of election results, a political party with largest votes (i.e. maximum frequency) is considered as representative. Thus, it is mode or modal opinion. In this situation, mode is the appropriate average. Similarly, to estimate the crop yield, too good quality or too poor quality crop is not considered. A quality of crop most commonly found is taken into account, which is nothing but mode. In titration experiment, out of three readings a repeated reading is taken to be final reading. It is mode and not the arithmetic mean. Thus in number of situations mode is appropriate.

(i) Computation of mode for Individual observations and Discrete frequency distribution : In this case we can find the observation with the largest frequency just by inspection. If the largest frequency occurs twice (or more), then we say there are two (or many) modes.

Illustration 11 : *Find the mode of the following frequency distribution :*

x	10	11	12	13	14	15
f	2	5	10	21	12	13

Solution : Since maximum frequency is associated with observation 13, the mode is 13.

(ii) Computation of mode for Continuous frequency distribution :

Step 1 : Obtain the class – boundaries.

Step 2 : Locate the modal class. Modal class is class in which mode lies or a class with the largest frequency.

Step 3 : Apply the formula and find the mode.

$$\text{Mode} = l + \left(\frac{f_m - f_1}{2f_m - f_1 - f_2}\right) \times h$$

where,

l = Lower boundary (or extended class limit) of modal class

f_m = Frequency of (or extended class limit) modal class

f_1 = Frequency of pre-modal class

f_2 = Frequency of post-modal class

h = Width of modal class

Illustration 12 : *Calculate modal income from the following income distribution :*

Daily income (₹)	30 and below	31-60	61-90	91-120	121-150	above 150
No. of Persons	22	198	110	95	42	33

Solution :

Class boundaries	Frequency
below 30.5	f_1 = 22
30.5 – 60.5	f_m = 198 Modal class
60.5 – 90.5	f_2 = 110
90.5 – 120.5	95
120.5 – 150.5	42
above 150.5	33

Modal class is 31–60. Since the corresponding frequency is the highest.

Here we get l = 30.5, f_m = 198, f_1 = 22, f_2 = 110, h = 30

$$\text{Mode} = l + \left(\frac{f_m - f_1}{2f_m - f_1 - f_2}\right) \times h$$

$$= 30.5 + \frac{198 - 22}{2 \times 198 - 22 - 110} \times 30 = 50.5$$

Note :

1. If the maximum frequency is repeated, to find the mode uniquely, a method of grouping is adopted and a modal class is determined. The method of grouping is beyond the scope of book.

2. Mode cannot be determined if modal class is at the extreme. (i.e. the maximum frequency occurs at the beginning or at the end of the frequency distribution.)

3. Modal, pre-modal and post-modal classes should be of the same width.

4. If $f_1 = f_2$ then mode is the class-mark of modal class.

(iii) Computation of mode – by Empirical relation : Arithmetic mean, mode and median are averages, hence we expect that those should be identical in value. However, this is true only in ideal situation. It is true whenever the frequency curve is perfectly symmetric and bell-shaped. For a moderately asymmetric unimodal frequency distribution the following empirical relationship holds approximately.

Mean – Mode ≈ 3 (Mean – Median) ... (3.2)

In some situations mode is ill-defined (see notes 1, 2 stated above). To overcome this difficulty in computing mode, the empirical relation (1) is used. If any two averages included in (3.2) are known, the remaining third can be computed. Therefore, if mean and median are known, then mode can be determined.

The empirical relation cannot be theoretically proved. Karl Pearson has stated it on the basis of vast experience. This relationship is observed to be valid for number of data sets after actual computations.

(iv) Computation of mode – by graphical method : Mode can be obtained graphically with the help of histogram. Mode is the x-co-ordinate of point P or the value at foot of perpendicular from P to x-axis, shown in Fig. 3.6.

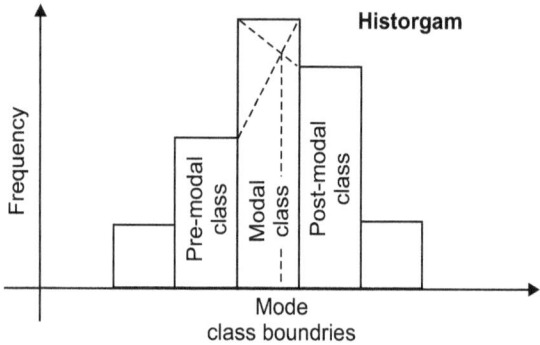

Fig. 3.6 : Histogram

Merits and Demerits of mode :
Merits :
1. It is simple to understand and easy to compute.
2. It is applicable for qualitative and quantitative data.
3. It is not affected by extreme observations.
4. It can be computed for distribution with open end classes.
5. It can be determined graphically.

Demerits :
1. It is not based on all the observations.
2. It is not capable of further mathematical treatment.
3. It is not rigidly defined like arithmetic mean.
4. It is indeterminate if the modal class is at the extreme of the distribution.

Note : It is possible to have two modes, such frequency distribution is called as bimodal frequency distribution. Sometimes bimodal frequency distribution is an indication of mixture of two frequency distributions.

For example, operator or machine is changed in manufacturing process. In medical sciences, two types of anaemia viz. microcytic and macrocytic are found in same population which give bimodal frequency curve.

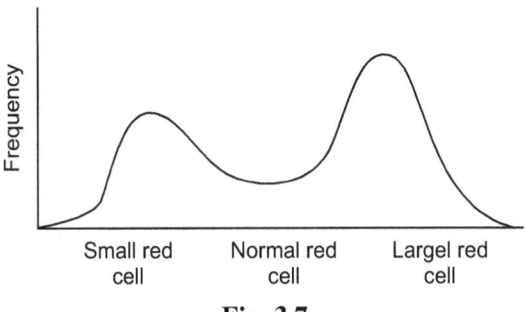

Fig. 3.7

Illustration 13 : *Calculate arithmetic mean and mode for the following data :*

Monthly salary (₹)	Number of workers
Below 400	0
Below 600	4
Below 800	14
Below 1000	33
Below 1200	45
Below 1400	49
Below 1600	50

Solution : We need to prepare frequency distribution from the given cumulative frequency distribution.

Class	Frequency	Mid-values x	$u = \dfrac{x - 900}{200}$	fu
400 - 600	4 – 0 = 4	500	– 2	– 8
600 - 800	14 – 4 = 10	700	– 1	– 10
800 - 1000	33 – 14 = 19	900	0	0
1000 - 1200	45 – 33 = 12	1100	1	12
1200 - 1400	49 – 45 = 4	1300	2	8
1400 - 1600	50 – 49 = 1	1500	3	3
Total	50	–	–	5

$$\text{Mean} = a + \frac{\Sigma fu}{N} \times h, \text{ where, } a = 900, \Sigma fu = 5, N = 50, h = 200$$

$$= 900 + \frac{5}{50} \times 200 = 920 \text{ ₹}$$

Modal class : 800 – 1000

$$\text{Mode} = l + \left(\frac{f_m - f_1}{2f_m - f_1 - f_2}\right) \times h$$

Here $l = 800$, $f_m = 19$, $f_1 = 10$, $f_2 = 12$, $h = 200$

$$\therefore \text{Mode} = 900 + \left(\frac{19 - 10}{38 - 10 - 12}\right) \times 200 = 912.5$$

Illustrative Examples

Example 3.1 : *From the following data find the missing frequencies, it is given that mean is 15.3818 and total frequency is 55.*

Class	9-11	11-13	13-15	15-17	17-19	19-21
Frequency	3	7	–	20	–	5

Solution : Let the missing frequencies be a and b

Class	Mid-value x	Frequency f	f · x
9 - 11	10	3	30
11 - 13	12	7	84
13 - 15	14	a	14a
15 - 17	16	20	320
17 - 19	18	b	18b
19 - 21	20	5	100
Total	–	35 + a + b = N = 55	534 + 14a + 18b = Σfx

We get two equations from the given information

i.e. $\quad 35 + a + b = 55 \qquad (\because \text{Total frequency } N = 55)$

$\therefore \quad a + b = 20 \qquad \ldots (1)$

$\bar{X} = \frac{\Sigma fx}{N}$ gives

$$15.3818 = \frac{534 + 14a + 18b}{55}$$

$\therefore \quad 845.999 = 534 + 14a + 18b$

$\therefore \quad 14a + 18b = 311.999 \qquad \ldots (2)$

Solving (1) and (2) we get, a = 12.0002, b = 7.9998.

After rounding-off the values, a = 12 and b = 8.

Thus, frequency of the class 11-13 is 12 and that of 17-19 is 8.

Example 3.2 : *Find the arithmetic mean given that $\sum (x - 10) = 230$ and $n = 50$.*

Solution : Let $d = x - 10$, $a = 10$, hence $\sum d = 230$

∴ $\quad$ Mean $= a + \dfrac{\sum d}{n} = 10 + \dfrac{230}{50} = 14.6$

Example 3.3 : *Arithmetic mean of 50 items is 104. While checking, it was noticed that observation 98 was misread as 89. Find the correct value of mean.*

Solution :

$\quad$ Incorrect mean $= 104 = \dfrac{\text{Incorrect sum}}{n}$

∴ $\quad$ Incorrect sum $= 104 \times 50 = 5200$

$\quad$ Correct sum $=$ Incorrect sum + Correct observation − Incorrect observation

$\quad\quad\quad\quad\quad\quad = 5200 + 98 - 89 = 5209$

∴ $\quad$ Correct mean $= \dfrac{\text{Correct sum}}{n}$

$\quad\quad\quad\quad\quad = \dfrac{5209}{50} = 104.18.$

Example 3.4 : *The number of washing machines sold in a shop per day are distributed as follows. Find median*

No. of machines sold	0	1	2	3	4	5
No. of days	6	10	4	3	3	1

Solution : Let X = No. of machines sold, f = No. of days.

X	f	Less than type cumulative frequency
0	6	6
1	10	16
2	4	20
3	3	23
4	3	26
5	1	27 = n

$\quad$ Median $=$ The value of $\left(\dfrac{n+1}{2} = \dfrac{27+1}{2} = 14\right)^{th}$ observation in the ordered arrangement

$\quad\quad\quad\quad = 1$

Example 3.5 : *A salesman has given a target to complete average daily sales of ₹1000. In a particular week, average sales of first 6 days is ₹980. What should be his sales on seventh day in order to make-up the target ?*

Solution : Here we use average as arithmetic mean

$$\bar{X} = \frac{\Sigma x}{n} = \frac{\Sigma x}{7} = 1000$$

∴ Total sales for 7 days $= \Sigma x = n\bar{X} = 7 \times 1000 = 7000$ ₹

The average of first 6 days $= \frac{\Sigma x}{6} = 980$.

Total sales for 6 days $= 6 \times 980 = 5880$ ₹

Sales required on 7th day $= 7000 - 5880 = 1120$ ₹

Example 3.6 : *The median of a group of 100 observations is computed to be 70. While verifying, it was found that the observation 13 was misread as 31. Find the correct median.*

Solution : Note that the median is 70. The observation 31 is to be replaced by correct observation as 13. This change does not affect the middle most observation in the ordered arrangement, hence median will remain same. Thus the median after correction is 70.

Note : *However, arithmetic mean will change.*

Example 3.7 : *Calculate mode of the following frequency distribution*

Class	50–100	100–150	150–200	200–250	250–300	300–350	350–400
Frequency	5	15	25	18	12	3	2

Solution : Modal class $= (150–200)$

$$\text{Mode} = l + \left(\frac{f_m - f_1}{2f_m - f_1 - f_0}\right) \times h = 150 + \left(\frac{25 - 18}{50 - 18 - 15}\right) \times 50$$

$$= 150 + \left(\frac{7}{17}\right) \times 50 = 170.5882$$

Example 3.8 : *Following is a frequency distribution regarding the number of family members, number of earning members in a certain locality.*

Income per month	No. of families	No. of family members	
		Earners	Non-earners
0 – 2000	22	25	40
2000 – 3000	59	75	143
3000 – 4000	70	91	179
4000 – 6000	25	57	136
6000 – 10000	15	42	85
10000 – 14000	9	30	17
Total	200	320	600

Calculate :

1. Average monthly income per family
2. Average monthly income per earning member
3. Per capita income
4. Average family size
5. The median family income.

Solution :

Income	Mid-point (x)	No. of families (f)	f.x	Less than cumulative frequency
0 – 2000	1000	22	22000	22
2000 – 3000	2500	59	147500	81
3000 – 4000	3500	70	245000	151
4000 – 6000	5000	25	125000	176
6000 – 10000	8000	15	120000	191
10000 – 14000	12000	9	108000	200
	Total	200	767500	–

1. Average monthly income per family $= \dfrac{\Sigma fx}{\Sigma f} = \dfrac{767500}{200} = 3837.5$ ₹

2. Average monthly income per earning member $= \dfrac{\text{Total income}}{\text{No. of earning members}}$

$$= \dfrac{767500}{320} = 2398.44 \text{ ₹}$$

3. Per capita income $= \dfrac{\text{Total income}}{\text{Total population}} = \dfrac{7675000}{320 + 600} = 834.24$ ₹

   (Total population = No. of earners + No. of non-earners.)

4. Average family size $= \dfrac{\text{Total number of earners and non-earners}}{\text{Total number of families}}$

$$= \dfrac{320 + 600}{200} = \dfrac{920}{200} = 4.6$$

5. The median of family income.

   Median = The value of $\left(\dfrac{N}{2} = \dfrac{200}{2} = 100\right)^{th}$ observation

$$= l + \left(\dfrac{\dfrac{N}{4} - C.F.}{f}\right) h = 3000 + \left(\dfrac{100 - 81}{70}\right) \times 1000 = 3271.43 \text{ ₹}$$

Example 3.9 : *The monthly income (₹) of 10 families in a village is as follows :*

1200, 1000, 1100, 1250, 950, 1300, 1350, 1150, 1200, 1050.

Find Mean, Median and Mode of this Income Distribution.

Solution :
$$\text{Mean} = \frac{\Sigma x}{n} = \frac{11550}{10} = 1155$$

The ordered arrangement to find the median is as follows :

950, 1000, 1050, 1100, $\boxed{1150, 1200}$, 1200, 1250, 1300, 1350.

$$\text{Median} = \text{The value of } \left(\frac{n+1}{2} = \frac{11}{2} = 5.5\right)^{th} \text{ observation}$$

$$= \frac{5^{th} \text{ observation} + 6^{th} \text{ observation}}{2}$$

$$= \frac{1150 + 1200}{2}$$

$$= 1175 ₹$$

Mode = Observation with maximum frequency

= 1200 ₹

Thus, Mean = ₹ 1155, Median = ₹ 1175, mode = 1200 ₹

Example 3.10 : *The following data relates to age distribution of 50 persons :*

Age (years)	Frequency
20-30	3
30-40	7
40-50	14
50-60	16
60-70	8
70-80	2

Find mode of above distribution

Solution : Modal class : 50–60

$$\text{Mode} = l + \frac{f_m - f_0}{2f_m - f_0 - f_1} \times h$$

$l = 50$, $f_m = 16$, $f_0 = 14$, $f_1 = 8$, $h = 10$.

$$\therefore \quad \text{Mode} = 50 + \left(\frac{16 - 14}{32 - 14 - 8}\right) \times 10$$

$$= 52 \text{ years}$$

Case study : Shriram Oxygen Ltd. is a company in a manufacturing of industrial oxygen based in a industrial area of Washi, Navi Mumbai. There are in all about 1000 employees in this company. They are of various grades.

For example, there is a managing director, about 10 directors, 30 senior general managers, about 200 managers, 150 officers and rest are workers of different grades. Company's monthly salary budget is about ₹ 30 lac.

Management of this company is of the opinion to increase the productivity by not increasing the man power but through increasing the salary of existing employees.

Existing salary of managing director is approximately ₹ 1 lacs per month, directors get around ₹ 75,000/- per month, general manager gets around ₹ 50,000. Whereas workers salary varies from ₹ 20,000 to ₹ 50,000 as per their grades.

Company has a revised budget of ₹ 40 lac per month. Company would like to know about what is the average salary per month. Whether to find mean would be appropriate or should median be used. What would be average revised salary per month ?

Points to Remember

1. Arithmetic mean $(\bar{X}) = \dfrac{\sum x}{n}$ for ungrouped data

    $= \dfrac{\sum fx}{\sum f}$ for frequency distribution.

2. Median $= l + \left(\dfrac{\dfrac{N}{2} - Cf}{f}\right) \times h$.

3. Mode $= l + \left(\dfrac{f_m - f_1}{2f_m - f_1 - f_2}\right) \times h$

4. If $y = ax + b$ then $\bar{y} = a\bar{x} + b$, $y = \dfrac{x - c}{d}$ then $\bar{y} = \dfrac{\bar{x} - c}{d}$

5. Combined arithmetic mean $= \dfrac{n_1 \bar{x} + n_2 \bar{y}}{n_1 + n_2}$

6. Median can be obtained graphical using ogive curves.
7. Mode can be obtained graphically using histogram.
8. Arithmetic mean is the best average.
9. Arithmetic mean cannot be determined by graph.

Exercise 3.1

A. **Theory Questions :**
 1. What do you mean by central tendency ? Explain the purpose of measures of central tendency.

2. State the requisites of an ideal average.

3. Define mean, median, mode and state the formula for each, in case of (i) individual observations (ii) frequency distributions.

4. Discuss merits and demerits of (i) mean, (ii) median, (iii) mode.

5. Explain graphical method of determination of (i) median (ii) mode.

Exercise 3.2

B. Discrete Series :

6. Monthly consumption of electricity in units of a certain family in a year is given below :

    210, 207, 315, 250, 240, 232, 216, 208, 209, 215, 300, 290.

    Compute the mean, median and modal consumption of electricity.

7. The marks obtained by 12 students are given below :

    30, 55, 50, 40, 50, 60, 55, 62, 55, 45, 61, 65

    Calculate mean, median and mode for the above data.

8. Compute the mean, mode and median for the following data : **(P.U. 2011)**

    68, 49, 38, 41, 49, 54, 89, 99, 67

9. Find the mean, median and mode of the following observations : **(Oct. 2014)**

    61, 62, 63, 62, 63, 62, 64, 64, 60, 65.

10. In a set of 50 items, arranged in ascending order of magnitude the values of 24th, 25th and 26th items are 40, 42 and 45 respectively. Find the median. Also find the median if the number of observations was 51.

11. Calculate mean and median weight of the group of students with weights (in kg) given below :

    51, 52, 53, 51, 53, 54, 54, 50, 55, 53.

    If a new group of students with weights in kg as 50, 56, 58, 57, 60 is added to the original group, find mean and median of combined group.

12. Compute median of the following series

    5, 20, 18, 12, 0, 21, 18, 26, 5, 15, 20.

13. The following figures represent the number of books issued at the counter of commerce college library on 8 different days.

    96, 98, 75, 80, 102, 100, 94, 75.

    Calculate the median and mode of the data.

14. Compare the average runs scored by cricters A and B using arithmetic mean.

Cricketer	Runs scored				
A	5	20	90	75	100
B	40	35	60	65	50

15. The weekly income of 10 families in a village is as follows :

    1200, 1000, 1100, 1250, 950, 1300, 1350, 1150, 1200, 1050.

    Find the mean, mode, median of the income distribution.

C. Frequency Distribution :

16. Find the mean, mode and median of the following data.

X	5	6	7	8	9	10	11	12
Frequency	8	10	9	6	5	4	4	1

17. Find the mean, median and mode of the following frequency distribution.

Marks	0-20	20-40	40-60	60-80	80-100
No. of frequency	5	12	32	40	11

18. Find arithmetic mean, mode and median of following frequency distribution.

Marks	0-20	20-40	40-60	60-80	80-100
No. of students	4	8	9	20	9

19. Compute arithmetic mean, mode and median of the following frequency distribution.

Weight in kg.	30-40	40-50	50-60	60-70	70-80
No. of students	3	5	12	20	10

20. Determine arithmetic mean, mode and median of marks from the data given below :

Marks	0-10	10-20	20-30	30-40	40-50
No. of students	1	3	10	4	2

21. The monthly profit in rupees of 100 shops are distributed as follows :

Profit (in ₹) per shop	0-100	100-200	200-300	300-400	400-500	500-600
No. of shops	12	18	27	20	17	6

    (i) Calculate the mode for above data. (ii) Find mode graphically.

22. A study of a certain operation shows the following distribution for 180 workers. Calculate the median. Also find it graphically.

Class interval (in seconds)	10-30	30-50	50-70	70-90	90-110
Frequency	10	40	80	35	15

23. Find the mean, mode and median for the following data :

Class	100-200	200-300	300-400	400-500
Frequency	15	20	10	5

24. Compute the median for the following frequency distribution. Also find it graphically.

Dividend (%)	0-20	20-40	40-60	60-80	80-100
No. of companies	20	35	15	8	2

25. Find the mean, mode and median of the following frequency distribution.

Weight (kg)	30-40	40-50	50-60	60-70	70-80
No. of students	4	5	7	3	1

26. Find mode for the following frequency distribution of income of 70 workers :

Income (₹)	Less than 1000	1000-2000	2000-3000	3000-4000	4000-5000	Above 5000
No. of Workers	08	14	13	25	07	03

27. The following data relates to age distribution of 50 persons :

Age (Years)	Frequency
20-30	3
30-40	7
40-50	14
50-60	16
60-70	8
70-80	2

Find mode of above distribution.

28. Following is the frequency distribution of sales of companies :

Sale (00,000 ₹)	0-20	20-40	40-60	60-80	80-100
No. of companies	05	18	20	12	05

Find the mode.

29. Following is the frequency distribution of percentage of dividend declared by companies :

Dividend %	10-15	15-20	20-25	25-30	30-35
No. of companies	15	20	35	10	5

Find the mode.

30. Calculate median for the following distribution :

Class	5-15	15-25	25-35	35-45	45-55
Frequency	5	15	20	15	5

31. Draw the histogram for the following frequency distribution :

Sales (in thousand ₹)	0-20	20-40	40-60	60-80	80-100
No. of companies	5	18	20	12	5

Hence locate the mode.

D. Missing Values :

32. If mean of the following frequency distribution is 15.82 find the missing value of ∗.

X	10	12	13	17	∗	25	18	30
Frequency	25	17	13	15	14	8	6	2

33. Find the missing frequency of the following frequency distribution if the arithmetic mean is 26.90.

Class	10-15	15-20	20-25	25-30	30-35	35-40	40-45
Frequency	5	6	8	∗	7	5	4

34. You are given the following complete frequency distribution. It is known that the total frequency is 100 and the median is 44. Find the missing frequencies. Also compute the mean after finding missing frequencies.

Class	Frequency	Class	Frequency
10-20	5	50-60	–
20-30	12	60-70	10
30-40	–	70-80	4
40-50	20		

35. Mean daily salary of 50 employees in a firm is ₹ 188.40. Frequency distribution of salaries of these employees in which some frequencies are missing is given below :

Salary	140-160	160-180	180-200	200-220	220-240
Frequency	6	–	17	–	5

Find the missing frequencies.

36. The daily expenditure of 100 families is given below :

Expenditure	20-29	30-39	40-49	50-59	60-69
No. of families	14	–	27	–	15

If the mode of the distribution is 43.5, find the missing frequencies.

E. Combined Mean :

37. Find the combined mean of the following data : **(B.B.A. April 2015)**

    Group I $\bar{x}_1 = 2100$ $n_1 = 100$

    Group II $\bar{x}_2 = 1500$ $n_2 = 200$

38. Average monthly sale of certain departmental store for first 11 months was ₹ 56000. Due to repairs and renewal of shop in the last month the sales dropped down to ₹ 8000. Find the average monthly sales in the year.

39. Obtain the combined mean profit per salesman from the following data

	Mean profit per salesman	No. of salesman
Shop 1	2000	5
Shop 2	3000	12
Shop 3	5000	3

40. Find the combined arithmetic mean and salary given that :

Group	Male	Female
No. of employees	100	50
Arithmetic mean of salary	6000 ₹	5100 ₹

41. Given   Group 1   Group 2

                 $n_1 = 100$ $n_2 = 100$

                 $\Sigma x = 600$ $\Sigma y = 800$

    Find $\bar{x}$, $\bar{y}$ and combined mean of the two groups.

F. Miscellaneous Problems :

42. A set of 10 values has arithmetic mean 20. Find the arithmetic mean if, (i) each value is doubled and then increased by 2 (ii) each value is increased by 5 and then doubled. (iii) each value is decreased by 5 (iv) each value is increased by 3.

43. The arithmetic mean of 10 items is 30. What will be mean, if each item is doubled ?

44. If $n = 10$ and $\Sigma (x - 5) = 90$ find the mean.

45. Obtain the average bonus per employee for the following frequency distribution.

Salary Group (₹)	1000-2000	2000-4000	4000-6000	above 6000
Bonus (₹)	300	400	450	500
Frequency	5	12	5	3

46. Calculate median and mode wage from the following data : (i) by using the formula (ii) by graphical method :

Wages in ₹	No. of workers
above 130	520
above 140	470
above 150	399
above 160	210
above 170	105
above 180	45
above 190	7

47. Find the median and mode of the following data by computational method and graphical method :

No. of days absent	No. of students
less than 5	29
less than 10	224
less than 15	465
less than 20	582
less than 25	634
less than 30	644
less than 35	650
less than 40	653
less than 45	655

48. Obtain the mean, median and mode from following data :

Monthly Rent (in ₹)	No. of families
221-240	6
241-260	9
261-280	11
281-300	14
301-320	20
321-340	15
341-360	10
361-380	8
381-400	7

49. Average of marks of 30 candidates was 40. Later on it was found that a score of 47 was misread as 74. Find the correct average. **(B.B.A. April 2015) (P.U. 2011)**

50. The mean weight of 98 students as calculated from a frequency distribution is 50 kg. It was later found that the frequency of the class 30-40 was wrongly taken as 8 instead of 10. Calculate the correct arithmetic mean. **(P.U. 2011)**

51. A salesman has given a target to complete average daily sales of ₹ 5000. In a particular week average of first 6 days is ₹ 4990. What should be his sales on seventh day in order to make-up the target ?

Answers 3.2

6. Mean = 241, Median = 224, No mode.
7. Mean = 52.33, Mode = Median = 55.
8. Mean = 61.56, Mode = 49, Median = 54.
9. Mean = 62.6, Median = 62.5, Mode = 62
10. 43.5, 45
11. Original data : Mean = 52.6, Median = 53, Combined data : Mean = 53.8, Median = 53
12. 18
13. Mode = 75, Median = 95
14. $\bar{X}_A = 58 > \bar{X}_B = 50$.
15. Mean = 1155, mode = 1200, Median = 1175.
16. Mean = 7.4894, Mode = 6, median = 7.
17. Mean = 58, Median = 60.2857, Mode = 64.32
18. Mean = 58.8, Median = 64, Mode = 65,
19. Mean = 60.8, Mode = 64.44, Median = 62.5,
20. Mean = 26.8, Mode = 25.3846, Median = 26,
21. 256.25
22. 60
23. Mean = 260, Mode = 233.33, Median = 250,
24. Median = 25.7142
25. Mean = 51, Mode = 53.3333, Median = 53.333.
26. 3400
27. 52
28. 42.

29. 21.875.
30. 30
31. By histogram 42
32. 24
33. 15
34. Missing frequencies 25, 24, Mean = 44.2
35. 12, 20
36. 23, 21
37. 1700
38. 52,000
39. 3050
40. ₹ 5700
41. $\bar{X} = 6$, $\bar{Y} = 8$, Combined mean = 7.
42. (i) 45 (ii) 50 (iii) 15 (iv) 23
43. 60
44. 14
45. 402
46. Median = 157.3545, Mode = 155.8416
47. Median = 12.1473, Mode = 11.35
48. Mean = Median = 310.5, Mode = 311.409
49. 39.5
50. 49.7
51. ₹ 5600

Objective Questions

1. Arithmetic mean of a group is 20. If each observation is increased by 5, find the mean of new observations.
2. State the imperical relation between mean, mode and median.
3. If n = 10, $\Sigma (x - 6) = 30$, find $\bar{x}$.
4. State the mode of following frequency distribution :

Class	0-10	10-20	20-30	30-40	40-50
Frequency	7	10	22	10	8

5. If each frequency is doubled, then what will happen to the arithmetic mean.

6. If frequency distribution has open end class, which average will be possible to compute.

7. Individual observations are not known but the total of 10 observations is known. Suggest the average which can be computed.

8. Suggest the average which you can compute if all the observations except the largest and smallest are known.

Answers

1. 25
2.
3. 9
4. 25
5. Will not change
6. Mode, Median
7. Mean
8. Median

Chapter 4

Measures of Dispersion

Contents ...

4.1 Introduction
4.2 Measures of Dispersion (Relative and Absolute)
4.3 Range and Coefficient of Range
4.4 Quartiles and Quartile Deviation
4.5 Standard Deviation and Coefficient of Variation
4.6 Standard Deviation of Combined Group

Key Words :

Dispersion, Deviation, Relative Dispersion Absolute Dispersion, Maximum, Minimum, Range, Coefficient Of Range, Standard Deviation (S.D.), Coefficient of Variation (C.V.), Variance.

Objectives :

The reliability of average is more if dispersion is less. Measures of dispersion is a tool which summarizes the internal variation or variation within the observations. The techniques of measurement of dispersion are discussed in this chapter. Statistics is in existence because of variation. Statistician has to talk in terms of S.D. and C.V. There are some situations such as genetics, biodiversity etc. where larger S.D. or C.V. has its importance.

4.1 Introduction

We have seen that, average condenses information into a single value. However, average alone is not sufficient to describe the frequency distribution completely. There may be two frequency distributions or data sets with same means but those may not be identical.

Illustration : Marks of students A, B, C in 5 subjects are as follows :

Student	Marks					A.M.
A	51	52	50	48	49	50
B	30	35	50	65	70	50
C	0	15	45	95	95	50

Notice that the average marks of all students are the same but they differ in variation. Clearly we can say that A is more consistent than B and B is more consistent than C.

For further study and analysis it becomes essential to measure the extent of variation. Observations are scattered or dispersed from central value. This variation is called as *dispersion*. Thus, next important aspect of comparison or study of frequency distribution or data sets is dispersion. Moreover it plays very important role in further analysis.

Average remains good representative, if dispersion is less (i.e. if the observations are close to it). Thus, dispersion decides the reliability of average.

4.2 Measures of Dispersion (B.B.A. April 2015)

In this chapter we study the following measures of dispersion : (i) range and (ii) standard deviation. These measures have the same units as that of the observation, for example, ₹, cm., hours, etc., and the measures are called as **absolute measures of dispersion**.

Absolute and Relative Measures of Dispersion (B.B.A., B.B.M. April 2015)

It can be very well seen that absolute measures possess units and hence create difficulty in comparison of dispersion for two or more frequency distributions or data sets. *For example :* For a group of persons, variation in height and variation in weight is to be compared. Height may be in cm and weight may be in kg. Therefore, comparison is not possible until a unitless quantity is available. Therefore, with respect to every absolute measure of dispersion, relative measure of dispersion is defined. Relative measure can be obtained by dividing the absolute measure by corresponding average. Such a relative measure is called as coefficient of the respective absolute measure.

4.3 Range and Coefficient of Range

Range is a crude measure of dispersion. However, it is the simplest measure and suitable if the extent of variation is small.

Definition : If L is the largest observation and S is the smallest observation then range is the difference between L and S. Thus,

$$\text{Range} = L - S$$

and the corresponding relative measure is

$$\text{Coefficient of range} = \frac{L - S}{L + S}$$

In case of frequency distribution lower limit of first and upper limit of last class intervals are taken to be the smallest and the largest observations respectively.

Note : Requisites of good measures of dispersion are same as those of average.

Merits of Range : (1) It is simple to understand and easy to calculate.

(2) It is rigidly defined.

Demerits of Range : (1) It is not based on all observations. It does not give proper idea regarding variation between the extreme observations.

For example : Range of 0, 3, 5, 200 is same as that of 0, 50, 100, 150, 200, however, variation patterns are different.

(2) It cannot be determined for frequency distribution with open end class.

Applications of Range :

Range is suitable measure of dispersion in case of small group with less variation. (i) It is widely used in the branch of statistics known as Statistical Quality Control. (ii) The changes in prices of shares lowest and highest observations are used. (iii) Temperature at a certain place is recorded using maximum and minimum value. (iv) Range used in medical sciences to check whether blood pressure, hemoglobin count etc. is normal.

Illustration 1 : *Compute range and coefficient of range for the following data :*

100, 24, 14, 105, 21, 35, 106.

Solution : Here,

Smallest observation (S) = 14

Largest observation (L) = 106

Range = L – S = 106 – 14 = 92

Coefficient of range = $\dfrac{L-S}{L+S} = \dfrac{92}{106+14}$

$= \dfrac{92}{120} = 0.7667$

Illustration 2 : *Determine the range and the coefficient of range for the following data :*

Electricity consumption per month	100-150	150-300	300-450	450-600
No. of families	28	56	43	23

Solution :

Range = Largest observation (L) – Smallest observation (S)

= 600 – 100 = 500

Coefficient of range = $\dfrac{L-S}{L+S} = \dfrac{500}{700} = \dfrac{5}{7}$.

4.4 Quartile Deviation or Semi-interquartile Range

The range uses only two extreme items. Hence, any change in the inbetween observations is not going to affect the range. This is a main drawback of range. Moreover in many situations extreme items are widely separated from remaining items. In this situation range will overestimate the dispersion. Thus, range fails to give true picture of dispersion. In order to overcome these drawbacks range of middle 50% items is computed.

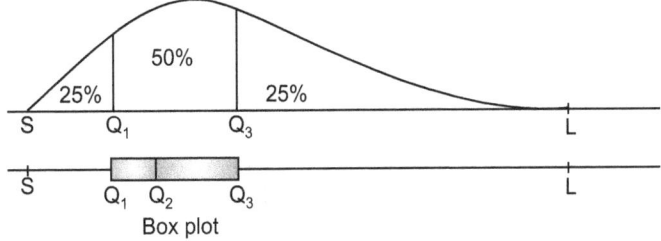

Fig. 4.1

Partition Values : Quartiles

Quartiles, Deciles and Percentiles : Earlier we have seen that median divides the total number of observations into two equal parts. Similarly in order to make four equal parts we use quartiles, for making 10 equal parts we use deciles and for making 100 equal parts we use percentiles, when the observations are ordered.

Definitions : The observations Q_1, Q_2, Q_3 which divide the total number of observations into 4 equal parts are called *quartiles*.

Median, quartiles, deciles and percentiles are called **partition values** in common. The procedure of obtaining median is used to compute other partition values with appropriate changes. To obtain the partition values of series of individual observations, tedious calculations or formulae are not required. However, to compute partition values of a continuous frequency distribution, corresponding formula of median is suitably modified. In this case, first of all less than cumulative frequency is determined. Using these cumulative frequencies a class in which partition value lies is decided and then using the formula, partition value is determined.

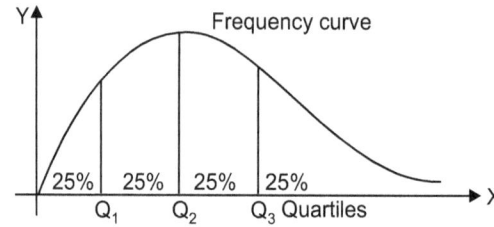

Fig. 4.2

$$\text{First quartile } (Q_1) = l + \left(\frac{\frac{N}{4} - \text{C.F.}}{f}\right) \times h$$

$$\text{Second quartile } (Q_2) = \text{Median} = l + \left(\frac{\frac{N}{2} - \text{C.F.}}{f}\right) \times h$$

$$\text{Third quartile } (Q_3) = l + \left(\frac{\frac{3N}{4} - \text{C.F.}}{f}\right) \times h$$

Note :
1. Median = Q_2.
2. The area between any two successive quartiles in 25% of the total area under the frequency curve.
3. Quartiles can be determinal graphically using less than cumulative frequency curve.
4. Minimum < Q_1 < Q_2 < Q_3 < Maximum.

Illustration 3 : Compute the quartiles for the following series of observations.

26, 30, 35, 5, 6, 7, 9, 20, 40, 45, 11, 18, 15, 49, 60.   **(B.B.A. April 2015)**

Solution : To find the quartiles first we arrange the observations in increasing (or decreasing) order of their magnitudes. Ordered arrangement will be

5, 6, 7, 9 , 11, 15, 18, 20 , 26, 30, 35, 40 , 45, 49, 60.

First quartile or lower quartile Q_1

$$= \left(\frac{n+1}{4}\right)^{\text{th}} \text{observation} = \left(\frac{15+1}{4} = 4\right)^{\text{th}} \text{observation} = 9$$

Second quartile or median Q_2

$$= \left(\frac{n+1}{2}\right)^{th} \text{ observation} = \left(\frac{15+1}{2} = 8\right)^{th} \text{ observation} = 20$$

Third quartile or upper quartile Q_3

$$= \left(\frac{3(n+1)}{4}\right)^{th} \text{ observation}$$

$$= \left(\frac{3(15+1)}{4} = 12\right)^{th} \text{ observation} = 40.$$

Illustration 4 : Obtain the quartiles from the following frequency distribution using formula and also graphically.

Weekly Salary (₹)	1400-1600	1600-1800	1800-2000	2000-2200	2200-2400	2400-2600
Frequency	12	30	55	40	35	28

Solution : Here the classes are continuous, hence they can be used as they are :

Class	Frequency	Less than type cumulative frequency
1400–1600	12	12
1600–1800	30	42
1800–2000	55	97
2000–2200	40	137
2200–2400	35	172
2400–2600	28	200 = N

$$Q_1 = \left(\frac{N}{4}\right)^{th} \text{ observation} = \left(\frac{200}{4} = 50\right)^{th} \text{ observation.}$$

First quartile (Q_1) $= l + \left(\dfrac{\frac{N}{4} - \text{C.F.}}{f}\right) \times h$

Since we have to consider 50th observation, and from less than cumulative frequencies we obsere that $42 < 50 < 97$, we have to consider the class of less than cumulative frequency in which partition value lies. Therefore, 1800 – 2000 is the first quartile class.

∴ Q_1 lies in (1800 – 2000) class

∴ $Q_1 = 1800 + \dfrac{50 - 42}{55} \times 200$

$= 1800 + 29.0909 = 1829.0909$ ₹

$Q_2 = \left(\dfrac{N}{2}\right)^{th}$ observation $= \left(\dfrac{200}{2} = 100\right)^{th}$ observation

$= l + \left(\dfrac{N/2 - \text{C.F.}}{f}\right) \times h$

Note that 100th observation lies in class (2000–2200).

Since we get from less than cumulative frequency that 97 < 100 < 137. Hence, (2000–2200) is a Q_2 class.

$$\therefore \quad Q_2 = 2000 + \left(\frac{100-97}{40}\right) \times 200 = 2015$$

Similarly, $Q_3 = \left(\frac{3N}{4}\right)^{th}$ observation $= \left(\frac{3 \times 200}{4} = 150\right)^{th}$ observation.

Since 150th observation lies in class 2200–2400, it is Q_3 class (137 < 150 < 172).

$$Q_3 = l + \left(\frac{3N/4 - C.F.}{f}\right) \times h$$

$$= 2200 + \left(\frac{150-137}{35}\right) \times 200 = 2274.2857 \text{ ₹}$$

To obtain Q_1, Q_2, Q_3 graphically we use less than type cumulative frequency curve.

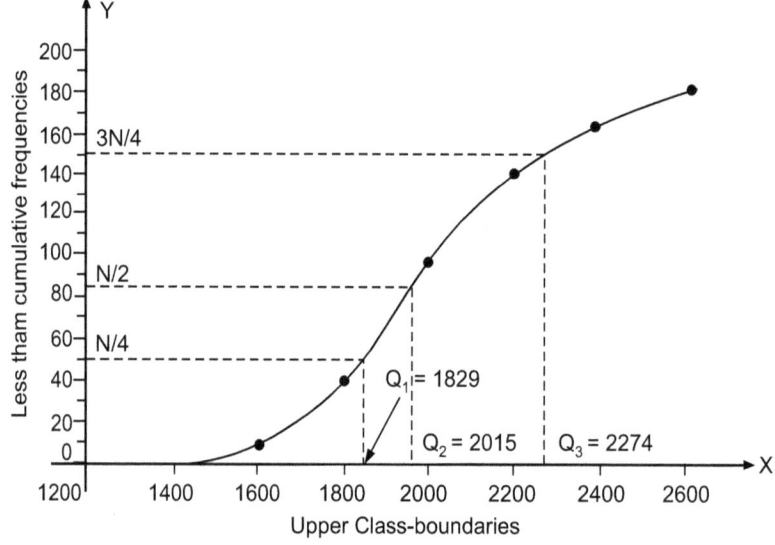

Fig. 4.3

BOX AND WHISKER PLOT

There is one more way of graphical representation of data known as box and whisker plot.

To draw box plot we find the three quartiles and the extreme observations. We illustrate the procedure by the following example.

Illustration 5 : Construct box plot to represent the data given below

26, 30, 35, 5, 6, 7, 9, 20, 40, 45, 11, 18, 15, 49, 60.

Solution : Clearly the ordered arrangement is

5, 6, 7, $\boxed{9}$, 11, 15, 18, $\boxed{20}$, 26, 30, 35, $\boxed{40}$, 45, 49, 60.

Note that the minimum is 5, maximum is 60 and the three quartiles are respectively 9, 20, 40. We take observations from minimum to maximum on line and put the rectangular box to include the first quartile and the third quartile. Thus the length of box is $Q_3 - Q_1$. In this case it is $40 - 9 = 31$. We divide the box in two boxes by putting horizontal line at median. The box plot is drawn below :

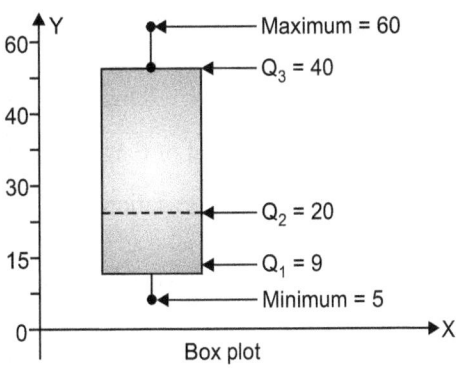

Fig. 4.4

Uses of box plot :

1. It gives the idea about the spread of data.
2. The box represents the interquartile range $Q_3 - Q_1$ of the data. In other words it gives the range in which middle 50% observations lie.
3. It gives the idea about the symmetry of the data around the median.
4. Median divides the data in two equal parts, box plot gives idea about how the observations are clustered or spread in each part of data.
5. The box plot facilitates the comparison of the aspects (i) central tendency, (ii) spread, (iii) symmetry.

Note : Box plot can also be drawn horizontally.

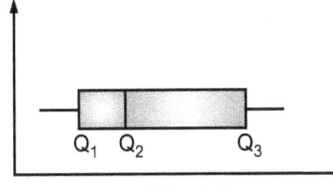

Fig. 4.5

Clearly the middle 50% items lie inbetween the two quartiles Q_1 and Q_3. The measure of dispersion based on these quartiles is given below :

Quartile Deviation (Q.D.) or Semi-Interquartile Range $= \dfrac{Q_3 - Q_1}{2}$.

And the corresponding measure of comparison is

Coefficient of Quartile Deviation $= \dfrac{Q_3 - Q_1}{Q_3 + Q_1}$

Illustration 6 : Compute (i) range and coefficient of range (ii) quartile deviation and coefficient of quartile deviation for the following data :

100, 24, 14, 105, 21, 35, 106, 16, 100, 72, 68, 103, 61, 90, 20.

(B.B.M. April 2010, B.B.A. Oct. 2010)

Solution : (i) Here, Smallest observation (S) = 14
Largest observation (L) = 106
$$\text{Range} = L - S = 106 - 14 = 92$$
$$\text{Coefficient of range} = \frac{L - S}{L + S} = \frac{92}{106 + 14} = \frac{92}{120} = 0.7667$$

(ii) To find quartile deviation, we arrange the observations in ascending order as follows :

14, 16, 20, $\boxed{21}$, 24, 35, 61, 68, 72, 90, 100, $\boxed{100}$, 103, 105, 106

Q_1 = The value of $\left(\frac{n+1}{4} = \frac{15+1}{4} = 4\right)^{th}$ item in the ordered arrangement
= 21

Q_3 = The value of $\left(\frac{3(n+1)}{4} = \frac{3 \times 16}{4} = 12\right)^{th}$ item in the ordered arrangement
= 100

$\therefore \quad$ Q.D. $= \frac{Q_3 - Q_1}{2} = \frac{100 - 21}{2} = 39.5$

Coefficient of Q.D. $= \frac{Q_3 - Q_1}{Q_3 + Q_1} = 0.6529$

Illustration 7 : Compute Q.D. and Coefficient of Q.D. for the following frequency distribution.

Daily Wages (in ₹)	below 35	35–40	40–45	45–50	50–55	55–60	60–65	above 65
No. of workers	12	18	22	26	36	23	19	8

Solution :

Class	Frequency	Less than type cumulative frequency	
below 35	12	12	
35–40	18	30	
40–45	22	52	→ Q_1 class
45–50	26	78	
50–55	36	114	
55–60	23	137	→ Q_3 class
60–65	19	156	
above 65	8	164 = N	

$$Q_1 = \text{The value of } \left(\frac{N}{4} = \frac{164}{4} = 41\right)^{st} \text{ observation}$$

Therefore, (40–45) is Q_1 class

$$\therefore \quad Q_1 = l + \frac{N/4 - C.F.}{f} \times h = 40 + \frac{41 - 30}{22} \times 5 = 42.5$$

$$Q_3 = \text{The value of } \left(\frac{3N}{4} = \frac{3 \times 164}{4} = 123\right)^{rd} \text{ observation}$$

Therefore, Q_3 lies in (55–60)

$$\therefore \quad Q_3 = l + \frac{3N/4 - C.F.}{f} \times h = 55 + \frac{123 - 114}{23} \times 5 = 56.9565$$

$$\therefore \quad Q.D. = \frac{Q_3 - Q_1}{2} = \frac{56.9565 - 42.5}{2} = 7.2283$$

$$\text{Coefficient of Q.D.} = \frac{Q_3 - Q_1}{Q_3 + Q_1} = \frac{55.9565 - 42.5}{55.9565 + 42.5} = 0.1454$$

Remark : One of the requisites of a good measure is that, it should be based on all the observations. However, Q.D. depends upon only two partition values. Therefore, it is not affected by any changes except the upper and lower quartile.

4.5 Standard Deviation and Coefficient of Variation

Here we discuss a measure of dispersion which satisfies most of the requisites of good measure and free from the drawbacks present in the other measures of dispersion.

Definition : The positive square root of mean of squares of the deviations taken from arithmetic mean is called as **standard deviation** (S.D.)

It is denoted by σ (read as sigma, a lower case Greek letter).

Therefore, $\quad \sigma = \sqrt{\dfrac{\sum (x - \bar{x})^2}{n}} \quad$ for individual observations

$$= \sqrt{\dfrac{\sum f (x - \bar{x})^2}{N}} \quad \text{for frequency distributions}$$

After simplification we can have computational formula for σ in more suitable form as follows :

$$\sigma = \sqrt{\dfrac{\sum x^2}{n} - \bar{x}^2} \quad \text{for individual observations}$$

$$= \sqrt{\dfrac{\sum fx^2}{N} - \bar{x}^2} \quad \text{for frequency distribution.}$$

where, $\bar{x}$ is a arithmetic mean.

Note : The quantity σ^2 is called as **variance.** Prof. R. A. Fisher has suggested the term variance.

Relative measure of S.D. is called coefficient of variation.

Coefficient of Variation : Prof. Karl Pearson suggested the relative measure of standard deviation. It is called as coefficient of variation (C.V.)

It is given by $\text{C.V.} = \dfrac{\text{S.D}}{|\text{A.M.}|} \times 100 = \dfrac{\sigma}{|\bar{x}|} \times 100\%$ ... (4.1)

Coefficient of variation is always expressed in percentage.

Remarks : (1) R.H.S. of (4.1) includes the multiplier 100, because $\dfrac{\sigma}{|\bar{x}|}$ is too small in many cases. Thus, for convenience it is multiplied by 100.

2. Frequently we need to compare dispersions of two or more groups. If the values in data set are large in magnitude, naturally variation among them will be proportionately larger.

For example, S.D. of weights of a group of elephants will be larger than that of a group of human beings. Suppose S.D. of weights of a group of elephants is 15 kg and that of human beings is also 15 kg. In this case we cannot say, both the groups have identical variation. This is because average weight of a group of elephants is larger than that of the average weight of a group of persons. Therefore for comparing variations between two different data sets, a measure based on the ratio of σ and $\bar{x}$ would be appropriate. This is achieved in coefficient of variation. It measures variation in all data sets using a common yard stick; moreover it is free from units.

3. According to Prof. Karl Pearson, C.V. is the percentage variation in mean whereas S.D. gives the total variation in the mean.

Uses of Coefficient of Variation :

It is already discussed that for comparison of variability, homogeneity, stability, uniformity, consistency, a unitless measure of dispersion is coefficient of variation (C.V.).

In manufacturing process C.V. is very important quantity. Larger the C.V., larger is the variation and poorer is the quality. In quality control section every effort is made to improve upon the quality, which means the items to be manufactured as per specifications. The extent of deviation from specifications can be measured by C.V. Thus, C.V. is unit of measurement of variation.

Almost all industries reduced the C.V. of their goods to considerable extent in last 50 years. This was due to competition. In pharmaceutical industries C.V. is as low as 1 or less than 1. The variation in weight of tablets is almost negligible.

Earlier the Japanese industrial product and American industrial product have same average quality, however, there was considerable difference in C.V. C.V. of Japanese goods was less than 5 times than that of American goods.

As a result of low C.V. the Japanese goods were more popular.

If C.V. is increased how it affects is explained below with the following example. Suppose we purchase a bag or pauch of edible oil packed by a automatic filling machine. Suppose the volume of oil is expected to be 1 litre. If the machine is set for C.V. = 1, (since

C.V. = 0 is impossible). Using statistical laws we can conclude that approximately 99.73% of the bags filled by machine will contain oil in the range 970 ml to 1030 ml. This range is reasonable for user. Instead if the machine is set to C.V. = 5, then 14% bags will found to contain 900 ml to 950 ml oil, another 2.1% will found to contain oil between 850 ml to 900 ml. Approximately 16% bags will contain 900 ml or less oil. Thus alongwith average one have take extreme care to reduce C.V.

Let us discuss an example from automobile industry. Suppose company A and B manufacture scooters which give 50 km per litre. Suppose C.V. of company A is 1 and that of company B is 5.

Among the scooters manufactured by company A, 99.73% will run 48.5 to 51.5 per litre. On the other hand among the scooters manufactured by company B, 14% will run 45 to 47.5 km per litre and 2.1% will run 42.5 to 45 km per litre. Thus, in case of C.V. = 5 about 16.1% customers will be unhappy. Although averages are same, they differ in C.V. which has considerable effect.

C.V. of industrial product depends upon raw material. Hence, a good quality of raw material ultimately give homogeneous end product.

In chemical and pharmaceutical industries C.V. is reduced by thorough mixing, pounding to convert raw material into homogeneous end product.

C.V. and Least Count :

Use of proper measuring instrument is also a way to check whether C.V. is maintained properly. If appropriate instrument is not used, C.V. will be inflated. As a thumb rule in industry.

Least count $\approx \frac{1}{10}$ specified range.

For example, if the inner diameter of cylinder is required to be between 0.95 cm and least count of the instrument should be $\left(\frac{1}{10}\right)^{th}$ of the specified range which $\frac{1}{10}(1.05 - 0.95)$ = 0.01 cm = 0.1 mm.

Illustration 8 : *Compute S.D. and C.V. for the following data :*

36, 15, 25, 10, 14.

Solution :

						Total
x	36	15	25	10	14	100
x^2	1296	225	625	100	196	2442

$$\bar{x} = \frac{\Sigma x}{n}$$

$$= \frac{100}{5} = 20$$

$$\sigma = \sqrt{\frac{\Sigma x^2}{n} - \bar{x}^2}$$

$$= \sqrt{\frac{2442}{5} - 20^2}$$

$$= \sqrt{88.4} = 9.4021$$

$$\text{C.V.} = \frac{\sigma}{|\bar{x}|} \times 100$$

$$= 47.0106\,\%$$

In order to reduce the bulk of calculation similar to mean we can use 'deviation method' and 'step deviation method' to calculate S.D.

S.D. by Deviation Method :

Step 1 : Decide assumed mean 'a'.

Step 2 : Let $d = x - a$. Compute deviation 'd'.

Step 3 : Find sum of deviations and sum of squares of deviations

$\Sigma d, \Sigma d^2,$ for individual observations.

$\Sigma fd, \Sigma fd^2,$ for frequency distribution.

Step 4 : Apply formula and find S.D. as follows :

$$\sigma = \sqrt{\frac{\Sigma d^2}{n} - \left(\frac{\Sigma d}{n}\right)^2} \qquad \text{for individual observations}$$

$$\sigma = \sqrt{\frac{\Sigma fd^2}{N} - \left(\frac{\Sigma fd}{N}\right)^2} \qquad \text{for frequency distribution}$$

Illustration 9 : *Compute S.D. and C.V. of marks scored by 10 candidates given below :*
54, 61, 64, 69, 58, 56, 49, 57, 55, 50.   **(B.B.A. April 2015)**

Solution : Let $a = 57$, $d = x - 57$

x	54	61	64	69	58	56	49	57	55	50	Total
d	−3	4	7	12	1	−1	−8	0	−2	−7	3
d²	9	16	49	144	1	1	64	0	4	49	337

$$\sigma = \sqrt{\frac{\Sigma d^2}{n} - \left(\frac{\Sigma d}{n}\right)^2} = \sqrt{\frac{337}{10} - \left(\frac{3}{10}\right)^2}$$

$$= \sqrt{33.61} = 5.7974$$

C.V. requires $\bar{x}$, hence $\bar{x} = a + \frac{\Sigma d}{n} = 57.3$

$$\text{C.V.} = \frac{\sigma}{|\bar{x}|} \times 100 = \frac{5.7974}{57.3} \times 100 = 10.1176\,\%$$

S.D. by Step Deviation Method :

Step 1 : Decide assumed mean 'a'.

Step 2 : Find the deviations, $d = x - a$.

Step 3 : Find the step deviations, $d' = \dfrac{d}{h}$.

Step 4 : Find the sum of d' and d'².

$\sum d', \sum d'^2$ for individual observations

$\sum fd', \sum fd'^2$ for frequency distribution

Step 5 : Apply the formula.

$$\sigma = \sqrt{\dfrac{\sum d'^2}{n} - \left(\dfrac{\sum d'}{n}\right)^2} \times h \quad \text{for individual observations.}$$

$$\sigma = \sqrt{\dfrac{\sum fd'^2}{N} - \left(\dfrac{\sum fd'}{N}\right)^2} \times h \quad \text{for frequency distribution.}$$

Illustration 10 : *Calculate the standard deviation and coefficient of variation for the frequency distribution of marks of 100 candidates given below :*

Marks	0–20	20–40	40–60	60–80	80–100
Frequency	5	12	32	40	11

Solution : We use step-deviation method to find σ.

Class	Mid-values x	Freq. f	$d' = \dfrac{x-50}{20}$	f × d'	f × d'²
00-20	10	5	− 2	− 10	− 10 × − 2 = 20
20-40	30	12	− 1	− 12	− 12 × − 1 = 12
40-60	50	32	0	0	0
60-80	70	40	1	40	40 × 1 = 40
80-100	90	11	2	22	22 × 2 = 44
Total	−	100	−	40	$\sum fd'^2 = 116$

Here, $a = 50, h = 20, N = 100$

$$\text{Mean} = a + \dfrac{\sum fd'}{N} \times h$$

$$= 50 + \dfrac{40}{100} \times 20 = 58$$

$$\text{S.D.} = \sqrt{\dfrac{\sum fd'^2}{N} - \left(\dfrac{\sum fd'}{N}\right)^2} \times h$$

$$\sigma = \sqrt{\dfrac{116}{100} - \left(\dfrac{40}{100}\right)^2} \times 20 = 20$$

$$\text{C.V.} = \frac{\sigma}{|\bar{x}|} \times 100$$

$$= \frac{20}{58} \times 100 = 34.4828\ \%$$

Merits of S.D. :
1. It is based on all observations.
2. It is rigidly defined.
3. It is capable of further mathematical treatment.
4. It does not ignore algebraic signs of deviations.
5. It is not much affected by sampling fluctuations.

Demerits of S.D. :
1. It is difficult to understand and to calculate.
2. It cannot be computed for a distribution with open end class.
3. It is unduly affected due to extreme deviations.
4. It cannot be calculated for qualitative data.

Important Notes :
1. If all the observations are increased (or decreased) by a constant, S.D. remains the same.
2. If each of the observation is multiplied by constant K, then S.D. is K times the original S.D.
3. If all the observations are equal, S.D. is zero (why ?).
4. If data contains only one observation, S.D. is zero (why ?)

As far as variance is concerned smaller variance is better in many situations. However there are some situations in genetical sciences where larger variance is better.

Variance and standard deviation are used in number of situations. Some of them are discussed below :

(a) Precision of an instrument is inversely proportional to variance. Therefore precision = k/variance.

(b) In portfolio analysis, risk is described in terms of variance of prices of shares.

(c) For the comparison of performance of two or more instruments, machines, coefficient of variation is used.

(d) The spread of variable is approximately taken as $(\bar{x} - 3\sigma, \bar{x} + 3\sigma)$.

Thus standard deviation helps in estimating lower limit and upper limit of the items.

4.6 Standard Deviation of Combined Group

Suppose there are two groups with sizes n_1, n_2 having arithmetic means $\bar{x}_1$, $\bar{x}_2$; standard deviations σ_1, σ_2 respectively. Then the mean of combined group is

$$\bar{x}_c = \frac{n_1 \bar{x}_1 + n_2 \bar{x}_2}{n_1 + n_2}$$

Let $d_1 = \bar{x}_1 - \bar{x}_c$ and $d_2 = \bar{x}_2 - \bar{x}_c$. Then S.D. of combined group is given by.

$$\sigma_c = \sqrt{\frac{n_1(\sigma_1^2 + d_1^2) + n_2(\sigma_2^2 + d_2^2)}{n_1 + n_2}}$$

Illustration 11 : *A group of 50 items have mean and standard deviation 61 and 8 respectively. Another group of 100 observations has mean and standard deviation 70 and 9 respectively. Find mean and standard deviation of combined group.*

Solution : We are given that : $n_1 = 50$, $\bar{x}_1 = 61$, $\sigma_1 = 8$, $n_2 = 100$, $\bar{x}_2 = 70$ and $\sigma_2 = 9$. Therefore combined mean

$$\bar{x}_c = \frac{n_1 \bar{x}_1 + n_2 \bar{x}_2}{n_1 + n_2}$$

$$= \frac{(50 \times 61) + (100 \times 70)}{50 + 100} = 67$$

∴ $d_1 = \bar{x}_1 - \bar{x}_c = 61 - 67 = -6$ and $d_2 = \bar{x}_2 - \bar{x}_c = 70 - 67 = 3$.

∴ Combined S.D. is

$$\sigma_c = \sqrt{\frac{n_1(\sigma_1^2 + d_1^2) + n_2(\sigma_2^2 + d_2^2)}{n_1 + n_2}}$$

$$\sigma_c = \sqrt{\frac{50(64 + 36) + 100(81 + 9)}{150}}$$

$$= 9.6609$$

Illustration 12 : *The mean weight of 150 students is 60 kg. The mean weight of boys is 70 kg, with standard deviation of 10 kg. For girls the mean weight is 55 kg with standard deviation of 15 kg. Find the number of boys and combined standard deviation.*

Solution : Let there be n_1 boys with mean $\bar{x}_1$ and S.D. σ_1. Similarly, there be n_2 girls with mean $\bar{x}_2$ and standard deviation σ_2. Hence, we get : $n_1 + n_2 = 150$, $\bar{x}_c = 60$, $\bar{x}_1 = 70$, $\bar{x}_2 = 55$, $\sigma_1 = 10$, $\sigma_2 = 15$.

$$\bar{x}_c = \frac{n_1 \bar{x}_1 + n_2 \bar{x}_2}{n_1 + n_2}$$

∴ $$60 = \frac{70 n_1 + 55 n_2}{n_1 + n_2}$$

$$60 n_1 + 60 n_2 = 70 n_1 + 55 n_2$$

$$n_2 = 2 n_1 \qquad \qquad \dots (1)$$

Note that

$$n_1 + n_2 = 150$$

$$\therefore \quad n_1 + 2n_1 = 150 \quad \ldots \text{from (1)}$$

$$n_1 = 50$$

∴ Number of boys = 50.

We get $d_1 = \bar{x}_1 - \bar{x}_c = 70 - 60 = 10$ and

$$d_2 = \bar{x}_2 - \bar{x}_c = 55 - 60 = -5$$

∴ Combined standard deviation

$$\sigma = \sqrt{\frac{n_1\left(\sigma_1^2 + d_1^2\right) + n_2\left(\sigma_2^2 + d_2^2\right)}{n_1 + n_2}}$$

$$\therefore \quad \sigma = \sqrt{\frac{50\,(100 + 100) + 100\,(225 + 25)}{150}}$$

$$= 15.2753 \text{ kg.}$$

Illustration 13 : *The mean and standard deviation of 10 observations were 9.5 and 2.5 respectively. If one more observation with value 15 is included in the group, obtain the mean and standard deviation of these 11 observations.*

Solution : Let there be two groups, first group of original 10 observations and second group of new single observation. Hence,

$$n_1 = 10, \quad n_2 = 1$$

$$\bar{x}_1 = 9.5, \quad \bar{x}_2 = 15 \text{ (why ?)}$$

$$\sigma_1 = 2.5, \quad \sigma_2 = 0 \text{ (why ?)}$$

Combined mean

$$\bar{x}_c = \frac{n_1 \bar{x}_1 + n_2 \bar{x}_2}{n_1 + n_2}$$

$$= \frac{10 \times 9.5 + 15}{11} = 10$$

$$\therefore d_1 = \bar{x}_1 - \bar{x}_c = -0.5 \text{ and } d_2 = \bar{x}_2 - \bar{x}_c = 5$$

$$\therefore \quad \sigma_c = \sqrt{\frac{10\,(6.25 + 0.25) + (25 + 0)}{11}}$$

$$= 2.8604$$

Illustrative Examples

Example 4.1 : *The number of runs scored by cricketers A and B in 5 test matches are shown below :*

| A | 5 | 20 | 90 | 76 | 102 | 90 | 6 | 108 | 20 | 16 |
| B | 40 | 35 | 60 | 62 | 58 | 76 | 42 | 30 | 30 | 20 |

Find (i) which cricketer is better in average ? (ii) which cricketer is more consistent ?

Solution :

$$\text{Mean of A} = \frac{\Sigma x}{n} = \frac{533}{10} = 53.3$$

$$\text{S.D. of A} = \sqrt{\frac{\Sigma x^2}{n} - \left(\frac{\Sigma x}{n}\right)^2}$$

$$= \sqrt{\frac{45161}{10} - (53.3)^2}$$

$$= 40.9293$$

∴ C.V. of A = 76.79%

$$\text{Mean of B} = \frac{\Sigma y}{n} = \frac{453}{10} = 45.3$$

$$\text{S.D. of B} = \sqrt{\frac{\Sigma y^2}{n} - \left(\frac{\Sigma y}{n}\right)^2} = \sqrt{\frac{23373}{10} - (45.3)^2}$$

$$= 16.8882$$

∴ C.V. of B = 37.28%

(i) A gives better average runs (mean A > mean B).

(ii) B is more consistent (C.V. of B < C.V. of A).

Example 4.2 : *Arithmetic mean and standard deviation of 12 items are 22 and 3 respectively. Later on it was observed that the item 32 was wrongly taken as 23. Compute correct mean, standard deviation and coefficient of variation.*

Solution :

Incorrect sum (Σx) = n × Incorrect mean = 12 × 22 = 264

Correct Σx = Incorrect Σx + Correct item – Incorrect item

Σx = 264 – 23 + 32 = 273

Correct mean = $\frac{273}{12}$ = 22.75

$$\sigma^2 = \frac{\Sigma x^2}{n} - (\bar{x})^2$$

$\therefore \quad n\left[\sigma^2 + (\bar{x})^2\right] = \Sigma x^2$

$\therefore \quad$ Incorrect $\Sigma x^2 = n\left[\sigma^2 + (\bar{x})^2\right]$ with σ and $\bar{x}$ incorrect.

$= 12(9 + 484) = 5916$

Correct $\Sigma x^2 =$ Incorrect $\Sigma x^2 +$ (Correct item)$^2 -$ (Incorrect item)^2

$= 5916 + 32^2 - 23^2 = 6411$

Correct $\sigma = \sqrt{\dfrac{\Sigma x^2}{n} - \left(\dfrac{\Sigma x}{n}\right)^2}$ with correct Σx^2 and Σx

$= \sqrt{\dfrac{6411}{12} - (22.75)^2}$

$= \sqrt{16.6875} = 4.0850$

Correct C.V. $= \dfrac{\sigma}{|\bar{x}|} \times 100 = 17.9562\%$

Example 4.3 : *For a set of 90 items the mean and standard deviation are 59 and 9 respectively. For 40 items selected from those 90 items the mean and standard deviation are 54 and 6 respectively. Find the mean and standard deviation of the remaining items.*

Solution : We have

Group 1	Group 2	Combined Group
$n_1 = 40$	$n_2 = 50$	$n = 90$
$\bar{x}_1 = 54$	$\bar{x}_2 = ?$	$\bar{x}_c = 59$
$\sigma_1 = 6$	$\sigma_2 = ?$	$\sigma_c = 9$

To find $\bar{x}_2$ we use $\bar{x}_c$.

$$\bar{x}_c = \dfrac{n_1 \bar{x}_1 + n_2 \bar{x}_2}{n_1 + n_2} \text{ gives}$$

$$59 = \dfrac{40 \times 54 + 50\,\bar{x}_2}{90}$$

$\therefore \quad \bar{x}_2 = 63.$

$\therefore \quad d_1 = \bar{x}_1 - \bar{x}_c = -5, \; d_2 = \bar{x}_2 - \bar{x}_c = 4$

$$\sigma_c^2 = \dfrac{n_1(\sigma_1^2 + d_1^2) + n_2(\sigma_2^2 + d_2^2)}{n_1 + n_2}$$

$$81 = \dfrac{40(36 + 25) + 50(\sigma_2^2 + 16)}{90}$$

$\therefore \quad \sigma_2 = 9.$

Example 4.4 : Given that : $n = 10$, $\sum(x - 20) = 8$, $\sum(x - 20)^2 = 762$. Find mean and S.D.

Solution : Let $d = x - 20$, Hence $\bar{x} = 20 + \dfrac{\sum d}{n} = 20.8$

$$S.D. = \sqrt{\dfrac{\sum d^2}{n} - \left(\dfrac{\sum d}{n}\right)^2} = \sqrt{\dfrac{762}{10} - \left(\dfrac{8}{10}\right)^2} = 8.6925$$

Example 4.5 : Compute standard deviation of the following frequency distribution :

Weight (in Kg)	30–40	40–50	50–60	60–70	70–80
No. of standards	3	5	12	20	10

Solution :

Class	mid point (x)	frequency (f)	$d' = \dfrac{x-55}{10}$	fd'	fd'^{2}
30–40	35	3	–2	–6	12
40–50	45	5	–1	–5	5
50–60	55	12	0	0	0
60–70	65	20	1	20	20
70–80	75	10	2	20	40
Total		50	–	29	77

$$\sigma = h \cdot \sqrt{\dfrac{\sum fd'^2}{\sum f} - \left(\dfrac{\sum fd'}{\sum f}\right)^2} = 10\sqrt{\dfrac{77}{50} - \left(\dfrac{29}{50}\right)^2} = 10.9709$$

Example 4.6 : The following data represents the goals scored by two teams in foot ball matches. **(B.B.A. April 2015)**

Number of goals scored	0	1	2	3	4
No. of matches by Team A	20	12	8	3	2
No. of matches by Team B	18	10	7	6	4

Which team scores more goal in a average ? Which team is more consistent ?

Solution : In order to test the consistency, we have to determine coefficient of variation.

Let   X = Number of goals scored.
   f = Number of matches played.

Team A					Team B			
X	f	fx	fx²		X	f	fx	fx²
0	20	0	0		0	18	0	0
1	12	12	12		1	10	10	10
2	8	16	32		2	7	14	28
3	3	9	27		3	6	18	54
4	2	8	32		4	4	16	64
Total	45	45	103		Total	45	58	156

$$\bar{X} = \frac{\Sigma fx}{\Sigma f} = \frac{45}{45} = 1 \qquad\qquad \bar{X} = \frac{\Sigma fx}{\Sigma f} = \frac{58}{45} = 1.2889$$

$$\sigma = \sqrt{\frac{\Sigma fx^2}{\Sigma f} - \bar{X}^2} \qquad\qquad \sigma = \sqrt{\frac{\Sigma fx^2}{\Sigma f} - \bar{X}^2}$$

$$= \sqrt{\frac{103}{45} - \left(\frac{45}{45}\right)^2} \qquad\qquad = \sqrt{\frac{156}{45} - 1.2889^2}$$

$$= 1.13529 \qquad\qquad\qquad\qquad = 1.3437$$

$$\text{C.V. (A)} = \frac{\sigma}{\bar{X}} \times 100 \qquad\qquad \text{C.V. (B)} = \frac{\sigma}{\bar{X}} \times 100$$

$$= 113.529\ \% \qquad\qquad\qquad = 104.25\ \%$$

Conclusion :

1. Since $\bar{X}_B > \bar{X}_A$, team B is better in average performance.
2. Since C.V. (B) < C.V. (A), team B is more consistent than A.

Example 4.7 : The following is information regarding portfolios A and B.

Portfolio	Average return	Risk (variance)
A	10 % ($\bar{X}$)	15 (σ_1^2)
B	20 % ($\bar{Y}$)	30 (σ_2^2)

We assume that the portfolios are independent, find the average return and combined risk if (i) equal investment in both portfolios is considered (ii) 25% of the shares are from portfolio A and the remaining from portfolio B.

Case (i) : If we invest 50 % amount of total in each portfolio then

$$\text{Average return (R)} = 0.5\ \bar{X} + 0.5\ \bar{Y} \qquad (\textbf{Result : If } Z = ax + by, \text{ then } \bar{Z} = a\bar{x} + b\bar{y})$$
$$= 0.5 \times 10 + 0.5 \times 20 \qquad\qquad\qquad\qquad \text{Here } a = b = 0.5$$
$$= 15$$

$$\text{Combined risk} = 0.5^2\ \sigma_1^2 + 0.5^2\ \sigma_2^2 \qquad (\textbf{Result : } \sigma_{ax+by}^2 = a^2\ \sigma_x^2 + b^2\ \sigma_y^2)$$
$$= 11.25$$

Thus the combined risk reduces.

Case (ii) : If we invest 25 % in portfolio A and 75 % in portfolio B then

$$\text{Average return} = 0.25\ \bar{X} + 0.75\ \bar{Y} \qquad (a = 0.25,\ b = 0.75,\ \bar{z} = a\bar{x} + b\bar{y})$$
$$= 17.5\ \%$$

$$\text{Combined risk} = 0.25^2\ \sigma_1^2 + 0.75^2\ \sigma_2^2 \qquad\qquad (a^2 \sigma_1^2 + b^2 \sigma_2^2)$$
$$= 17.81$$

Note : One can determine the percentage of investment in each portfolio so that the total risk is minimum, similarly one can find investment pattern that will maximise the total return. The details are beyond the scope of book.

Example 4.8 : *Compute Range and Coefficient of Range for the daily wages (₹) of 8 workers in a factory : 90, 120, 150, 80, 120, 125, 105, 75.*

Solution : Largest observation (L) = 150
Smallest observation (S) = 75
Range = L − S = 150 − 75 = 75

$$\text{Coefficient of range} = \frac{L-S}{L+S} = \frac{75}{150+75} = \frac{75}{225} = \frac{1}{3}$$

Example 4.9 : *Compute Standard Deviation for the following data :*
15, 18, 22, 25, 10.

Solution :

						Total
x	15	18	22	25	10	90
x²	225	324	484	625	100	1758

Standard deviation $(\sigma) = \sqrt{\dfrac{\Sigma x^2}{n} - \bar{X}^2}$

$n = 5, \bar{X} = \dfrac{\Sigma x}{n} = \dfrac{90}{5} = 18$

∴ $\sigma = \sqrt{\dfrac{1758}{5} - 18^2} = \sqrt{351.6 - 324} = \sqrt{27.6}$
= 5.2536

Example 4.10 : *Two workers on the same job show the following results over long period of time :*

	Worker 'A'	Worker 'B'
Mean time of completing the job (in minutes)	30	25
Standard deviation	6	4

(i) Which worker appears to be more consistent in the time he requires to complete the job ? Why ?

(ii) Which worker is faster in completing the job ? Why ?

Solution : (i) Consistency is compared by coefficient of variation (C.V.).

$$\text{C.V. (A)} = \frac{\sigma_A}{\bar{X}_A} \times 100 = \frac{6}{30} \times 100 = 20\%$$

$$\text{C.V. (B)} = \frac{\sigma_B}{\bar{X}_B} \times 100 = \frac{4}{25} \times 100 = 16\%$$

Since C.V. (B) < C.V. (A), where B is more consistent.

(ii) Worker is faster if the mean time required is smaller, since $\bar{X}_B = 25 < \bar{X}_A = 30$, Worker B is more faster.

Case Study

Parag Infotech Pvt. Ltd. is a company to provide a software solutions. Directors of the company have taken a decision to double the capital and expand it in a big way. In view of this company decides to recruit at least 50 computer engineers. Company invited applications from fresh computer engineering graduates having at least 70% marks at their final examination. Company also expected furnish details of marks obtained from their SSC examination onwards.

Company received 200 applications. Most of the applications have secured marks between 70% to 73% in their final examination. Due to short time to recruit, company is not interested to conduct personal interview of all the applicants but to select 70 of the best applicants for personal interview of the final selection. Company feels that 2% to 3% variation in final examination marks may be due to chance and has no effect in the performance.

Statisticians have advised to company to use the concept of measures of dispersion. Discuss the use of range and standard deviation in this regard to take the proper decision.

Points to Remember

1. Range = Largest observations – Smallest observation.

   $$\text{Coefficient of range} = \frac{\text{Largest observation} - \text{Smallest observation}}{\text{Largest observation} + \text{Smallest observation}}$$

2. Standard deviation (S.D.) $= \sigma = \sqrt{\frac{\sum x^2}{n} - \bar{X}^2}$ for discrete series

   $= \sqrt{\frac{\sum fx^2}{\sum f} - \bar{X}^2}$ for frequency distribution

3. Coefficient of variation (C.V.) $= \frac{\sigma}{\bar{X}} \times 100\%$.

4. C.V. is used for the comparison of variation.

Exercise 4.1

A. Theory Questions :

1. What is dispersion ? What purpose does it serve in the study of distribution ?
2. What type of measures will you use for comparison of dispersion in different distributions ? Mention any two of such measures.
3. Explain relative measure of dispersion and state its utility.
4. Define : Range, quartile deviation and standard deviation. State the formula for each incase of ungrouped data and frequency distribution.
5. Compare critically the two measures of dispersion : range and standard deviation.

6. State the merits and demerits of each of the following measures of dispersion : range and S.D.
7. Explain why S.D. is the best measure of dispersion.
8. What is utility of C.V. ?
9. Write a note on dispersion.
10. Write a note on measures of dispersion.

Exercise 4.2

B. Discrete Series :

1. Find the standard deviation of the following data : 2, 3, 5, 2, 7, 5, 7, 6, 11, 12.
2. Find the arithmetic mean and standard deviation of the following series
    14, 8, 11, 10, 13, 16, 5, 9, 12, 2.
3. Monthly consumption of electricity in units of a certain family in a year is given below :
    210, 207, 315, 250, 240, 232, 216, 208, 209, 315, 300, 200.
    Compute (i) range and coefficient of range
             (ii) standard deviation and coefficient variation.
4. Calculate the range and coefficient of range for the following data :
    88, 52, 67, 38, 59, 46. Also compute standard deviation.
5. Monthly consumption of electricity in units of six families in a city is given below. Compute coefficient of variation.
    210, 207, 315, 320, 250, 240.
6. Compute the (i) range and the coefficient of range (ii) quartile deviation and coefficient of quartile deviation for the following data :
    8, 12, 10, 18, 28, 17, 20, 22, 12, 9, 16.
    Also find the new range and coefficient of range in which each observation is doubled.
7. Calculate the range and the coefficient of range for the following data :
    125, 140, 110, 105, 130, 95, 115, 125, 80.
8. Compute the range and coefficient of range for the data given below :
    52, 45, 60, 53, 48, 65, 42, 45, 60.
9. The prices of shares of a company from Monday to Friday are as follows :

Days	Mon.	Tues.	Wed.	Thur.	Fri.
Price (₹)	524	502	544	519	558

   Calculate the range and the coefficient of range.
10. Compute the standard deviation for the following data :
    15, 18, 22, 25, 10.
11. Calculate the coefficient of variation for the following series :
    12, 18, 15, 20, 16.

12. Find the standard deviation and coefficient of variation for the following data :

    6, 4, 5, 3, 12, 10.

13. Which of the following two series A and B is more stable ? Why ?

A	4	4	2	3	6	8	2	0	1	−1
B	8	7	5	5	6	7	4	3	4	1

14. Using coefficient of variation find which of the following batsman is more consistent in scoring :

Score of A	42	115	6	73	7	19	119	36	84	29
Score of B	47	12	76	42	4	51	37	48	13	0

15. Compare the variation between the weight and the height of a group of 10 persons using coefficient of variation.

Sr. No.	1	2	3	4	5	6	7	8	9	10
Weight (kg)	70	65	65	64	69	63	65	70	71	62
Height (cm)	170	140	151	145	165	167	156	160	153	168

C. Frequency Distribution :

16. A survey conducted to determine distance travelled (in kms) per litre of petrol by newly introduced motorcycle gives the following distribution :

Distance (km)	40-45	45-50	50-55	55-60	60-65
No. of Motorcycles	10	17	23	40	10

    Find the (i) standard deviation (ii) quartile deviation, (iii) coefficient of quartile deviation.

17. Find the variance for the following frequency distribution :

Class	5-15	15-25	25-35	35-45	45-55
Frequency	05	15	12	18	08

18. Compute the standard deviation for the following data :

Marks	0.-10	10-20	20-30	30-40	40-50
No. of Students	3	7	25	20	5

19. Calculate the coefficient of variation (C.V.) for the following data :

Class	0-10	10-20	20-30	30-40	40-50	50-60
Frequency	5	9	15	21	6	4

20. Calculate the standard deviation and coefficient of variation for the following frequency distribution :

X	2	4	6	8	10
Frequency	2	4	14	8	2

21. Find the standard deviation and quartile deviation from the following data :

Marks	0 - 10	10 - 20	20 - 30	30 - 40	40 - 50
Frequency	10	16	30	32	12

22. Find the standard deviation and coefficient of variation and quartile deviation of distribution of daily wages.

Daily wages	1 - 20	21 - 40	41 - 60	61 - 80	81 - 100
Frequency	5	32	45	17	1

23. Compute the coefficient of variation and coefficient of quartile deviation for the following data :

Class	0 - 20	20 - 40	40 - 60	60 - 80	80 - 100
Frequency	6	32	45	17	0

24. Obtain the standard deviation for the following data :

Class	20 - 40	40 - 60	60 - 80	80 - 100
Frequency	6	8	4	2

25. Compute the standard deviation of the following frequency distributions :

Marks	0 - 10	10 - 20	20 - 30	30 - 40	40 - 50
No. of students	1	3	10	4	2

26. Find the coefficient of variation, quartile deviation and coefficient of quartile deviation for the following data :

Size of item	2	4	6	8	10	12
No. of items	6	10	20	24	12	8

27. A share broker studied 100 companies and obtained the following data for the year 2012-13.

Divident declared (%)	0 - 8	8 - 16	16 - 24	24 - 32	32 - 40
No. of companies	15	30	40	10	5

Calculate the mean and the standard deviation of the above data and obtain the coefficient of variation.

28. (a) Two automatic tea filling machines A and B tested for the performance. Machines are supposed to fill 500 gm. tea in each packet. A random sample of 100 filled packets on each machine showed the following distribution.

Weight in gm.	Frequency A	Frequency B
485–490	12	10
490–495	18	15
495–500	20	24
500–505	22	20
505–510	24	18
510–515	4	13

Which machine is more consistent ? Why ?

(b) Find the quartile deviation and its coefficient for the following frequency distribution. (P.U. 2011)

Class	0-20	20-40	40-60	60-80	80-100
Frequency	3	12	20	10	5

D. Combined Standard Deviation :

29. Find combined deviation from the following data :

Workers	Number	Average Salary	Standard Deviation
Male	80	1520	06
Female	20	1420	05

30. Two workers on the same job show the following results over long period of time :

	Worker 'A'	Worker 'B'
Mean time of completing the job (in minutes)	30	24
Standard Deviation	6	4
Number of jobs	10	10

   (i) Which worker appears to be more consistent in the time he requires to complete the job ? Why ?
   (ii) Which worker is faster in completing the job ? Why ?
   (iii) Find the combined mean and standard deviation of the two workers together.

31. For a set of 50 items, the mean and standard deviation are 60 and 3 respectively. For another set of 100 items, the mean and standard deviation are 63 and 4 respectively. Find the mean and the standard deviation of combined group.

32. Information about the daily salaries of employees in firms A and B is stated below :

Firm	No. of employees	Mean Salary	S.D. of Salary
A	60	₹ 400	₹ 10
B	40	₹ 500	₹ 11

   (i) Which firm gives more amount as salary ?
   (ii) Which firm has smaller variation in salary ?
   (iii) Find the combined mean and S.D. of two firms.

33. Information regarding daily salaries of two companies A and B is given below :

	Company A	Company B
No. of workers	600	400
Mean salary	₹ 180	₹ 200
S.D. of salary	₹ 9	₹ 10

   (i) Which company pays larger salary ?
   (ii) Which company has less variation in salaries ?
   (iii) Find combined mean and S.D. of two firms A and B.

34. Find the combined standard deviation of groups A and B taken together given that :

Group	Size	Arithmetic mean	Standard deviation
A	100	60	6
B	200	63	4

35. Find the combined mean and standard deviation from the following data.

Group	Arithmetic mean	S.D.	Size
A	50	10	100
B	55	11	150

36. Find the arithmetic means of each group from the following data :

Group	S.D.	C. V.
1	16	40%
2	20	50%

37. The arithmetic mean and standard deviation of a group of 50 items are 61 and 8 respectively. In a second group of 100 items they are 70 and 9 respectively. Find the combined mean and S.D. of the two groups.

38. The means of two samples of sizes 50 and 100 are 40 and 25 respectively. The standard deviations of those samples are 10 and 8 respectively. Obtain the combined standard deviation.

39. The arithmetic mean and the standard deviation of the values of 100 items in a group are 80 and 5 respectively. In a second group of 25 items, each item has a value equal to 60. Find the combined standard deviation of two groups taken together.

40. Calculate the combined variance of the two groups of items.

	Group I	Group II
No. of observations	40	60
Arithmetic mean	25	30
Standard deviation	6	4

E. Miscellaneous Problems :

41. The arithmetic mean and standard deviation of 20 observations are 10 and 2 respectively. Later on it was noticed that item 8 taken was incorrect. Calculate arithmetic mean and standard deviation if

    (i) the wrong item is omitted.

    (ii) the wrong item is replaced by 12.

42. The mean and standard deviation of 100 observations are 40 and 5.1 respectively. It was later discovered that an observation 40 was misread as 50. Calculate correct mean and standard deviation.

43. If $n = 10$, $\Sigma (x - 120) = 20$, $\Sigma (x - 120)^2 = 200$. Find the mean and the standard deviation.

44. If $n = 100$, $\Sigma x = -20$, $\Sigma x^2 = 220$, find standard deviation and coefficient of variation.

45. Find the standard deviation of set A, Set B, Set C and Set D and comment on findings.

Set A :	1	2	3	4	5
Set B :	11	12	13	14	15
Set C :	10	20	30	40	50
Set D :	4	4	4	4	4

46. The range, arithmetic mean and standard deviation of 10 items are 20, 62, 10 respectively. If each observation is increased by 5, what will be the range, arithmetic mean and standard deviation.

Answers 4.2

1. 3.2558.
2. $\bar{X} = 10$, $\sigma = 4$
3. (i) 115, 0.2233 (ii) 41.95, 17.35%
4. Range = 50, Coefficient of range = 0.3968, $\sigma = 16.1314$
5. 45.4239%
6. Range = 20, Coefficient of range = 0.5555
   New range = 40, $Q_1 = 10$, $Q_3 = 20$, Q.D. = 5,
   Coefficient of quartile deviation = 0.3333. New coefficient of range = 0.5555
7. Range = 60, Coefficient of range = 0.2727
8. Range = 23, Coefficient of range = 0.215.
9. Range = 56, Coefficient of range = 0.0528
10. 5.2536
11. 16.75%
12. $\sigma = 3.2489$, C.V. = 48.73%
13. Series B more stable, C.V. (A) = 89.1898% C.V. (B) = 40%
14. B is more consistent C.V. (A) = 75.54 %, C.V. (B) = 70.82 %
15. C.V. (weight) = 4.67 % < C.V. (height) = 6.18 %
16. C.V. = 5.7383, $Q_1 = 19.375$, $Q_3 = 35.9375$, Q.D. = 16.5625,
    Coefficient of Q.D. = 0.2994.
17. 144.14

18. 9.5029
19. $\sigma = 12.8279$, C.V. 43.73%
20. $\sigma = 1.9137$, C.V. = 30.5378
21. S.D. = 11.4891, $Q_1 = 33$, $Q_3 = 57.3889$, Q.D. = 12.19445,
    Coefficient of Q.D. = 0.2698.
22. S.D. = 16.4572, C.V. = 35.85 %
23. C.V. = 36.3505, $Q_1 = 31.875$, $Q_3 = 56.444$, Q.D. = 12.293,
    Coefficient of Q.D. = 0.2782
24. S.D. = 18.8680, $Q_1 = 26$, $Q_3 = 12$, Q.D. = 6, Coefficient of Q.D. = 1/3
25. 9.6307
26. 37.3625 %
27. $\bar{x} = 16.8$, $\sigma = 8.1584$, C.V. = 48.56 %
28. (a) C.V. (A) = 1.4294 % C.V. (B) = 1.5084 %, Machine A is more consistent.
    (b) $Q_1 = 35.8333$, $Q_2 = 65$, Q.D. = 14.5834, Coefficient of Q.D. = 0.2893.
29. 40.42029
30. (i) C.V. (A) = 20% > C.V. (B) = 16.6667%, B is more consistent
    (ii) B (iii) Combined mean = 27, Combined S.D. = 5.9161
31. Combined mean = 62, Combined S.D. = 3.9581
32. (i) B (ii) C.V. (A) = 2.5% > C.V. (B) = 2.2%, B has smaller variation
    (iii) Combined mean = 440, Combined S.D. = 50.0839
33. (i) B (ii) Both name same C.V. = 5%, both are equal in variation
    (iii) Combined mean = 188, Combined S.D. = 14.2969%
34. 4.97
35. $\bar{x}_c = 53$, $\sigma_c = 10.8904$
36. 40, 40
37. $\bar{x}_c = 67$, $\sigma_c = 9.6605$
38. 11.225
39. $\sigma_c = 9.1651$
40. $\sigma_c = 5.477$
41. (i) Mean = 10.1053, S.D. = 1.9922 (ii) Mean = 10.2, S.D. = 1.99
42. Mean = 39.9, S.D. = 5
43. Mean = 116, S.D. = 22.9783
44. S.D. = 1.4697, C.V. = 734.8469%
45. $\sigma_A = \sigma_B = \sqrt{2}$, $\sigma_C = 10\sqrt{2}$, $\sigma_D = 0$.
46. Range = 20, $\bar{x} = 67$, $\sigma = 10$.

Objective Questions

1. Find the standard deviation of 2, 2, 2, 2, 2.
2. If the standard deviation of 1, 2, 3, 4, 5 is $\sqrt{2}$ then state the standard deviation of
   (a) 11, 12, 13, 14, 15 (b) 10, 20, 30, 40, 50 (c) $-1, -2, -3, -4, -5$.
3. If each observation is doubled what will be the standard deviation ?
4. If each observation is increased by 5, what will be the standard deviation ?
5. Suppose there are two groups with following details :

Group	A	B
Size	10	10
Arithmetic mean	50	50
Standard deviation	4	6

Find the standard deviation of the combined groups.

Answers

1. 0   2. (a) $\sqrt{2}$ (b) $10\sqrt{2}$ (c) $\sqrt{2}$
2. S.D. will be doubled.
3. S.D. will be change.
5. $\sigma_c = \sqrt{26}$.

Chapter 5...
Correlation and Regression

Contents ...

5.1 Introduction

5.2 Types of Correlation

5.3 Scatter Diagram

5.4 Merits and Demerits of Scatter Diagram

5.5 Covariance

5.6 Karl Pearson's Coefficient of Correlation

5.7 Computational Procedure of Correlation Coefficient

5.8 Merits and Demerits of Karl Pearson's Coefficient of Correlation

5.9 Regression Lines

5.10 Interpretation of Regression Coefficient

5.11 Applications of Correlation and Regression

5.12 Linear Regression Causes and Effect

5.13 Properties of Regression Coefficient

5.14 Properties of Regression Lines

5.15 Standard Error or Regression Estimate

5.16 Correlation and Regression Analysis.

Key Words :

Bivariate Data, Correlation, Scatter Diagram, Covariance, Karl Pearson's Coefficient of Correlation, Ranks, Rank Correlation, Regression Lines, Regression Coefficients, Coefficient of Determination, Standard Error of Regression Estimate.

Objectives :

In this chapter we study the technique to bivariate data to know whether there is any interrelationship between them. A particular type of relationship viz. the extent of linear relationship is being measured using correlation. Such measure is developed for quantitative and qualitative data.

The relation between correlated variables can be established using regression analysis. It is useful in forecasting or prediction of one variable when the value of other variable is known. The estimates are more reliable if the r^2 is larger.

5.1 Introduction

Many a times we come across situations where two variables are interrelated. For example : (i) Marks and intelligence quotient of students. (ii) Rainfall and agricultural production. (iii) Demand and price of a certain commodity. (iv) Income and expenditure of a family. (v) Height of son and that of father. In these situations we may be interested in examining the relation between the two variables. Such interrelated variables are called as *correlated variables.* The extent of linear relation between the two variables is called as *correlation.*

Bivariate Data :

In order to determine correlation, we require data regarding two concerned variables. These data are called as *bivariate data.* Suppose X and Y are the variables under consideration.

Whenever the variables X and Y are the variables measured on the same item, they are likely to be correlated. For example, the income of family (X) and the expenditure of family (Y). We record the values of X and Y for each of the families under study. Suppose it gives a set of n pairs $(x_1, y_1); (x_2, y_2); \ldots ; (x_n, y_n)$ where x is income and y is the expenditure of the family. This set of n pairs is a **bivariate data.** When n is large, for convenience the data are expressed in bivariate frequency distribution or two-way frequency distribution. In this case we make m classes of X and n classes of Y. Like univariate classification, pairs (x, y) are classified by using tally marks (i, j)th class. Number of tally marks is denoted by f_{ij}.

Remark : Note that (x_i, y_i) is an ordered pair. First component in every pair is observation on variable X and second component is on variable Y. In the further analysis the components X_i and Y_i are inseparable, i.e. we cannot rearrange the pairs as (x_1, y_{10}) or (x_3, y_4) etc.

5.2 Types of Correlation (B.B.A. April 2015, Oct. 2014)

Positive Correlation, Negative Correlation, No Correlation

It may be noticed that in some cases, increase in value of one variable is associated with increase in value of other variable or decrease in value of one variable is associated with decrease in value of other variable. Correlation between these variables is said to be **positive**.

For example : Marks and intelligence quotient. In this case, there is a positive correlation between these variables.

On the other hand in some other situations increase in value of one variable is accompanied by decrease in value of other variable and vice-versa. Here the changes in values of two variables are in opposite direction. Correlation between these variables is said to be **negative**. **(April 2010)**

For example : Consider supply and price of commodity. Clearly if supply of commodity is more, price falls down and if there is a scarcity of a commodity, then price goes up. Hence, there is a negative correlation between supply and price of a commodity.

Soimetimes, change in one variable is not related to change in other variable then we say that there is **no correlation**.

For example : Height of student and his examination score.

There are several measures of correlation of which three are in general used :
(i) Scatter diagram, (ii) Product moment correlation coefficient and (iii) Rank correlation.

5.3 Scatter Diagram

In order to visualise the correlation between two variables, the first step is scatter diagram.

Suppose $\{(x_i, y_i); i = 1, 2, \ldots, n\}$ are bivariate data on two variables x and y.

If these n pairs are plotted on a graph paper, taking one of the variable on X axis and other on Y axis, we get a diagram called as *Scatter diagram*. With the help of scatter diagram we get a general idea about the existence of correlation and the type of correlation. However, it fails to give correct numerical value of correlation. It is easy but crude and approximate method of measuring correlation. In this method we need to find out correlation by visual judgement only. We classify scatter diagrams broadly into 5 categories which are depicted below in Fig. 5.1 to Fig. 5.8.

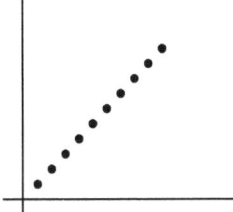

Fig. 5.1 : Positive perfect correlation

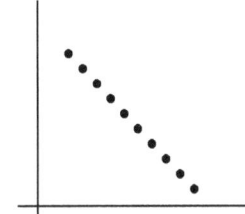

Fig. 5.2 : Negative perfect correlation

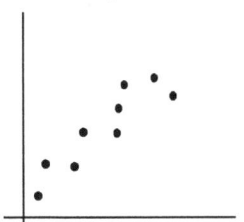

Fig. 5.3 : Positive correlation

Fig. 5.4 : Negative correlation

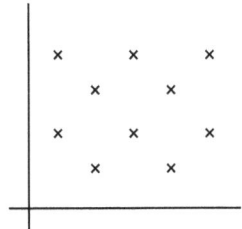

Fig. 5.5 : No correlation

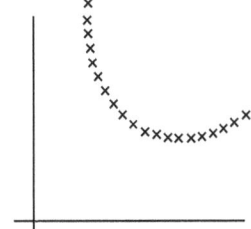

Fig. 5.6 : Non-linear correlation

Fig. 5.7 : No Correlation   Fig. 5.8 : No Correlation

In Fig. 5.1 and Fig. 5.3 we see that the changes in value of one variable and changes in value of other variable are in the same direction. Hence, the correlation is positive or direct. Moreover in Fig. 5.1 all the points lie on the same line, hence correlation is perfect positive.

In Fig. 5.2 and Fig. 5.4 we see that changes in values of one variable and those of other variable are in opposite direction. Hence, the correlation is negative or inverse. Specifically in Fig. 5.2 we observe that points fall on the same line. This is an indication of negative perfect correlation. In Fig. 5.5 we see that the points are scattered in a haphazard manner without showing any particular pattern. This is an indication of almost no correlation. In Fig. 5.6 points show non-linear pattern.

In Fig. 5.7 and 5.8 one of the variables is not really a variable. It is a constant. It does not increase or decrease for any type of change in the other variable. Thus, change in one variable is not at all associated with that of in the other variable. Hence, in this situation, there is no correlation between the two variables. This type of scatter diagram will be observed in the following situations. For example : Suppose X is Interest on debenture, Y is Dividend paid on shares. X is fixed, whereas Y depends upon company's profit. Clearly there is no correlation between X and Y.

Thus, we can draw conclusions regarding correlation between two variables by means of scatter diagram.

5.4 Merits and Demerits of Scatter Diagram

Merits :

1. Scatter diagram is the simplest method of studying correlation.
2. It is easy to understand.
3. It is not influenced by extreme values.

Demerits :

1. It does not give a numerical measure of correlation.
2. It is a subjective method.
3. It cannot be applied to qualitative data.

Illustration 1 : *Following table gives aptitude score (X) and creativity (Y).*

X	63	61	62	52	69	72	55	67	80	73
Y	69	65	67	60	72	86	62	75	82	83

Draw scatter diagram and comment on the type of correlation between X and Y.

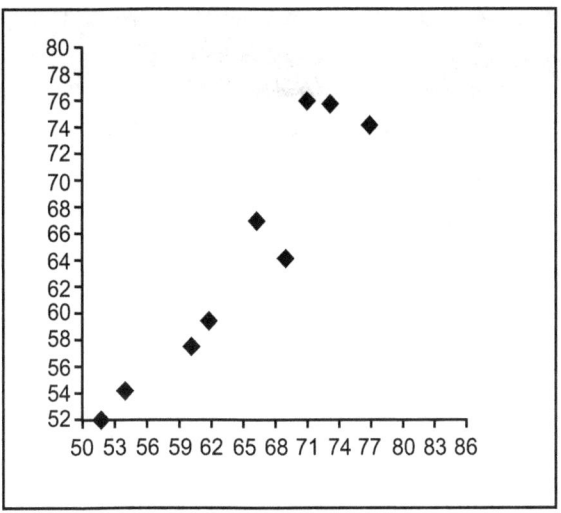

Fig. 5.9

Interpretation : There exist positive correlation of high degree between X and Y.

5.5 Covariance

We introduce the concept of covariance. It will be required to study correlation and regression critically. The drawbacks of scatter diagram as a measure of correlation can be overcome by covariance. The covariance is the joint mutual variation between two variables.

Covariance : The covariance between X and Y is denoted by Cov (X, Y) and is defined as

$$\text{Cov}(X, Y) = \frac{\sum (x - \bar{x})(y - \bar{y})}{n}$$

The computational formula after simplification will be

$$\text{Cov}(X, Y) = \frac{\sum xy}{n} - \bar{x}\bar{y}$$

Remark : (1) Cov (X, Y) is similar to variance.

Note that Var $(X) = \frac{\sum x^2}{n} - \bar{x}^2$ can be expressed as Var $(X) = \frac{\sum x \cdot x}{n} - \bar{x} \cdot \bar{x}$. Here replacing the second x by y and second $\bar{x}$ by $\bar{y}$ we get, $\frac{\sum xy}{n} - \bar{x}\bar{y}$.

(2) Cov (X, Y) = Cov (Y, X).
(3) Cov (X, X) = Var (X).
(4) Cov (X, constant) = 0.
(5) Covariance may be negative, positive, zero whereas variance is non-negative.
(6) If a, b, h, k are constants then

$$\text{Cov}(X - a, Y - b) = \text{Cov}(X, Y)$$

$$\text{Cov}\left(\frac{X-a}{h}, \frac{Y-b}{k}\right) = \frac{1}{hk}\text{Cov}(X, Y), \quad h \neq 0, k \neq 0$$

5.6 Karl Pearson's Coefficient of Correlation (Or Product Moment Correlation Coefficient)

If X and Y are correlated, then we get scatter diagrams of the following types. Here we plot the deviations $(x - \bar{x}, y - \bar{y})$.

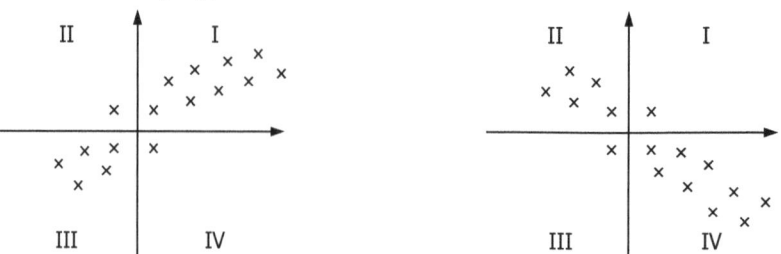

Fig. 5.10 : Positive Correlation   Fig. 5.11 : Negative Correlation

Let us examine the two situations independently. In Fig. 5.10 of positive correlation, observe that both the co-ordinates have same sign, either positive or negative. Thus, $\sum (x - \bar{x})(y - \bar{y}) > 0$. In other words Cov $(x, y) > 0$ for positively correlated variables. On the other hand in Fig. 5.11, one of the co-ordinates is always negative. Hence, $\sum (x - \bar{x})(y - \bar{y}) < 0$. That is Cov $(x, y) < 0$ for negatively correlated variables. Also, covariance measures the extent of joint variation between x and y. Due to these properties of covariance, a relative measure of correlation is defined using covariance. It is discussed below :

Karl Pearson's coefficient of correlation : Karl Pearson's coefficient of correlation is denoted by r and it is defined as follows :

$$r = \frac{\sum (x - \bar{x})(y - \bar{y})}{\sqrt{\sum (x - \bar{x})^2 \times \sum (y - \bar{y})^2}} \quad \ldots (5.1)$$

where $\bar{x}$ and $\bar{y}$ are arithmetic means of x and y respectively. Formula given by (5.1) can be put in simplified way for calculation purpose.

$$r = \frac{\sum xy - n\bar{x}\bar{y}}{\sqrt{(\sum x^2 - n\bar{x}^2)(\sum y^2 - n\bar{y}^2)}} \quad \ldots (5.2)$$

or

$$r = \frac{\frac{1}{n}\sum xy - \bar{x}\bar{y}}{\sigma_x \sigma_y} \quad \ldots (5.3)$$

where, σ_x = standard deviation of x, σ_y = standard deviation of y.

Using covariance, correlation will be

$$r = \frac{\text{Cov}(X, Y)}{\sigma_x \sigma_y} \quad \ldots (5.4)$$

The above (5.1), (5.2), (5.3), (5.4) formulae give one and the same numerical value; however according to convenience and type of data available we choose formula.

In most of the cases where raw or unsummerised data are given we use formula (b).

To study the algebraic properties the formulae (d) or (a) are most suitable.

Properties of correlation coefficient 'r' :

1. Correlation coefficient 'r' lies between -1 and 1 (i.e. $-1 < r < 1$).

Interpretation : If $r > 0$ the correlation is positive and if $r < 0$. The correlation is negative. If $r = 0$ we say the variables are uncorrelated. Larger the numerical value of r more close is the extent of relationship between the variables. In general for $|r| > 0.8$, we consider high correlation. If $|r|$ is between 0.3 to 0.8 we say that correlation is considerable. If $|r| < 0.3$ we say that correlation is negligible. If $r = 1$ we say that there is perfect positive correlation whereas if $r = -1$ we say that there is perfect negative correlation. The above interpretation is general. For more valid interpretation one has to take into account value of n also. Details are beyond the scope of book.

2. Correlation coefficient does not change due to change of origin. In other words if a constant is added or subtracted from each observation, correlation coefficient remains same. Corr $(x \pm a, y \pm b)$ = Corr (x, y).

3. Correlation remains numerically same under the change of scale. In other words if we divide or multiply each observation by constant correlation remains same numerically.

$$\text{Corr (ax, by)} = \text{Corr (x, y)} \quad \text{if a and b have same algebraic signs.}$$
$$= -\text{Corr (x, y)} \quad \text{if a and b have opposite algebraic signs.}$$

4. Correlation coefficient between X and Y is same as that of between Y and X.
i.e. Corr (x, y) = Corr (y, x).

5. Corr $(x, x) = 1$, Corr $(x, -x) = -1$.

5.7 Computational Procedure of Correlation Coefficient

We propose two methods for computing correlation coefficient.
(i) Direct method.
(ii) Deviation method.

(i) Direct method : Following are the steps involved in the calculations of Karl Pearson's correlation coefficients.

Step 1 : Obtain sum of x values i.e. $\sum x$ and hence ($\bar{x}$).

Step 2 : Obtain sum of y values, i.e. $\sum y$ and hence ($\bar{y}$).

Step 3 : Obtain sum of squares of x, i.e. $\sum x^2$.

Step 4 : Obtain sum of squares of y, i.e. $\sum y^2$

Step 5 : Obtain sum of products of x and y, i.e. $\sum xy$.

Step 6 : Find r by applying formula

$$r = \frac{\sum xy - n\bar{x}\bar{y}}{\sqrt{\sum (x^2 - n\bar{x}^2) \times \sum (y^2 - n\bar{y}^2)}}$$

Illustration 2 : *Following are the values of import of raw material and export of finished products in suitable units.*

Export	10	11	14	14	20	22	16	12	15	13
Import	12	14	15	16	21	26	21	15	16	14

Calculate the coefficient of correlation between the import values and export values.

Solution : Let x : Quantity exported, y : Quantity imported.

Preparing table as follows calculations can be made simple. Here we use direct method

x	y	x^2	y^2	xy
10	12	100	144	120
11	14	121	196	154
14	15	196	225	210
14	16	196	256	224
20	21	400	441	420
22	26	484	676	572
16	21	256	441	336
12	15	144	225	180
15	16	225	256	240
13	14	169	196	182
Total = 147	170	2291	3056	2638

Here n = 10, hence $\bar{x} = \dfrac{\Sigma x}{n} = \dfrac{147}{10} = 14.7$ and $\bar{y} = \dfrac{\Sigma y}{n} = \dfrac{170}{10} = 17.$

$$r = \dfrac{\Sigma xy - n\bar{x}\cdot\bar{y}}{\sqrt{(\Sigma x^2 - n\bar{x}^2)\times \Sigma(y^2 - n\bar{y}^2)}}$$

$$= \dfrac{2638 - 10\times 14.7 \times 17}{\sqrt{(2291 - 10\times 14.7^2)(3056 - 10\times 17^2)}}$$

$$= \dfrac{139}{\sqrt{130.1 \times 166}}$$

$$= 0.9458$$

Interpretation : There is a high positive correlation between import of raw material and export of finished product.

(ii) Deviation method : Sometimes original values are large. In order to reduce the bulk of calculation we use deviation method. Here we subtract a convenient number from x observations, similarly we subtract some other number from y observations. Due to the property of correlation coefficient it does not affect the correlation coefficient. Procedural steps involved in this method are as follows :

Step 1 : Obtain deviations $u = x - a$ (a being constant)
Step 2 : Obtain deviations $v = y - b$ (b being constant)
Step 3 : Obtain sum of u and v. i.e. $\sum u$ and $\sum v$.
Step 4 : Obtain sum of squares of u and v. i.e. $\sum u^2$ and $\sum v^2$.
Step 5 : Obtain sum of products of u and v' i.e. $\sum uv$.
Step 6 : Find r by applying the formula.

$$r = \frac{\sum uv - n\bar{u}\bar{v}}{\sqrt{\sum(u^2 - n\bar{u}^2) \times \sum(v^2 - n\bar{v}^2)}}$$

where $\bar{u} = \frac{\sum u}{n}$ and $\bar{v} = \frac{\sum v}{n}$.

Illustration 3 : Compare correlation between the heights of father and son from the following data.

Height of father (in inches) : 65 63 67 64 68 70 68 71
Height of son (in inches) :   68 65 68 65 69 68 71 70

Solution : Let x = Height of father, y = Height of son.

We use deviation method by taking $u = x - 60$ and $v = y - 65$.

x	y	u	v	u²	v²	uv
65	68	5	3	25	9	18
63	65	3	0	9	0	0
67	68	7	3	49	9	21
64	65	4	0	16	0	0
68	69	8	4	64	16	32
70	68	10	3	100	9	30
68	71	8	6	64	36	48
71	70	11	5	121	25	55
Total	–	56	24	448	104	183

$$\bar{u} = \frac{\sum u}{n} = \frac{56}{8} = 7, \quad \bar{v} = \frac{\sum v}{n} = \frac{24}{8} = 3$$

$$r = \frac{\sum uv - n\bar{u}\bar{v}}{\sqrt{\sum(u^2 - n\bar{u}^2) \times (\sum v^2 - n\bar{v}^2)}}$$

$$= \frac{183 - 8 \times 7 \times 3}{\sqrt{(448 - 8 \times 7^2)(104 - 8 \times 3^2)}}$$

$$= \frac{15}{\sqrt{56 \times 32}} = 0.3543$$

Illustration 4 : *Compute correlation coefficient between supply and price of commodity using following data.*

Supply	152	158	169	182	160	166	182
Price	198	178	167	152	180	170	162

Solution : Here we use deviation method to find r.

Let x = supply, $u = x - 150$, y = price, $v = y - 160$.

x	y	u	v	u²	v²	uv
152	198	2	38	4	1444	76
158	178	8	18	64	324	144
169	167	19	7	361	49	133
182	152	32	– 8	1024	64	– 256
160	180	10	20	100	400	200
166	170	16	10	256	100	160
182	162	32	2	1024	4	64
Total	–	87	87	2833	2385	521

Here $n = 7$, $\sum u = 119$, $\sum v = 87$, $\sum u^2 = 2833$, $\sum v^2 = 2385$, $\sum uv = 521$

$\therefore \quad \bar{u} = 17$, $\bar{v} = 12.4286$

$$r = \frac{\sum uv - n\bar{u}\bar{v}}{\sqrt{(\sum u^2 - n\bar{u}^2) \times (\sum v^2 - n\bar{v}^2)}}$$

$$r = \frac{521 - 7 \times 17 \times 12.4286}{\sqrt{(2833 - 7 \times 17^2)(2.385 - 7 \times 12.4286^2)}}$$

$$r = \frac{-958}{\sqrt{810 \times 1303.7142}} = \frac{-958}{1027.6227}$$

$$= -0.9322$$

Interpretation : There is high negative correlation between supply and price.

Illustration 5 : *Find correlation coefficient between X and Y, given that,*

$n = 25$, $\sum x = 75$, $\sum y = 100$, $\sum x^2 = 250$, $\sum y^2 = 500$, $\sum xy = 325$.

Solution : Here $\bar{x} = \frac{75}{25} = 3$, $\bar{y} = \frac{100}{25} = 4$

$\therefore \quad r = \frac{\sum xy - n\bar{x}\bar{y}}{\sqrt{(\sum x^2 - n\bar{x}^2) \times \sum(y^2 - n\bar{y}^2)}}$

$r = \frac{325 - 25 \times 3 \times 4}{\sqrt{(250 - 25 \times 9)(500 - 25 \times 16)}}$

$= \frac{25}{\sqrt{25 \times 100}} = \frac{25}{50} = 0.5$

Illustration 6 : *Compute the product moment coefficient of correlation for the following data :* $n = 100$, $\bar{x} = 62$, $\bar{y} = 53$, $\sigma_x = 10$, $\sigma_y = 12$, $\sum (x - \bar{x})(y - \bar{y}) = 8000$.

Solution :
$$r = \frac{\sum (x - \bar{x})(y - \bar{y})}{\sqrt{\sum (x - \bar{x})^2 \sum (y - \bar{y})^2}}$$

Dividing numerator and denominator by n we get,

$$r = \frac{\sum (x - \bar{x})(y - \bar{y})/n}{\sqrt{\frac{\sum (x - \bar{x})^2}{n} \frac{\sum (y - \bar{y})^2}{n}}} = \frac{\sum (x - \bar{x})(y - \bar{y})/n}{\sigma_x \sigma_y}$$

$$= \frac{8000/100}{10 \times 12} = 0.6667$$

Illustration 7 : *Compute correlation coefficient between X and Y given that :*
$n = 100$, $\sum (x - 35) = 25$, $\sum (y - 19) = 68$, $\sum (x - 35)^2 = 167$,
$\sum (y - 19)^2 = 162$, $\sum (x - 35)(y - 19) = 130$

Solution : Let, $u = x - 35$ and $v = y - 19$

∴ $\bar{u} = 0.25$ $\bar{v} = 0.68$

$$r = \frac{\sum uv - n\bar{u}\bar{v}}{(\sum u^2 - n\bar{u}^2) \times (\sum v^2 - n\bar{v}^2)} = \frac{113}{\sqrt{160.75 \times 115.76}}$$

$$= 0.8283$$

5.8 Merits and Demerits of Karl Pearson's Coefficient of Correlation

Merits :
1. Karl Pearson's coefficient of correlation determines a single value which summarises the extent of linear relationship. It also indicates type of correlation.
2. It depends upon all observations.

Demerits :
1. It cannot be computed for qualitative data such as honesty and intelligence, beauty and intelligence.
2. It is unduly affected by extreme values.
3. It measures only linear relationship.
   For example : Suppose

X :	-2	-1	0	1	2
Y :	4	1	0	1	4

Here $\sum x = 0$, $\sum y = 10$, $\sum xy = 0$. Hence, Cov $(X, Y) = \frac{\sum xy}{n} - \bar{x}\bar{y} = 0$.

Therefore, Corr $(X, Y) = 0$. However $Y = X^2$, which is non-linear. Hence, correlation fails to measure non-linear relationship. Details are beyond the scope of book.

Note : To overcome the demerit (1) Spearman's rank correlation is used which is discussed below.

5.9 Regression As Prediction Model

In earlier discussions we have studied correlation. It gives extent of linear relationship between two variables. If two variables are correlated, we can use this correlation for prediction of variable given the other variable.

Regression : Technique of prediction on the basis of correlation is called as *regression*.

Since correlation measures the linear relation between two variables, we find a linear equation in these variables. In otherwords, we state the relation in terms of equation of straight line. Using scatter diagram we get an idea of correlation. One can obtain a line passing through these points. However, if correlation is not perfect (i.e. $r \neq \pm 1$) then several lines can be drawn through these points. Out of those lines, how to choose the best line is a problem. So a line which minimizes the total of sum of squares of differences between true value and the value given by straight line is chosen. The principle is called as *least square principle*. The equation so obtained is called as *least square regression line*.

Using regression equation one can find relation between advertising expenses and increase in sales, similarly the relation between sales and profit.

Suppose $(x_1, y_1), (x_2, y_2), \ldots, (x_n, y_n)$ are n pairs of observations on variable X and Y. Since there are two variables, there will be two regression lines.

1. Regression line of Y on X : In this case we assume y as dependent variable or *response variable* and x as independent variable or *explanatory variable*. Therefore this line can be used to predict values of y for known values of x. Suppose the equation of such a line is $y = a + bx$. Mainly we need to fix the constants a and b. This can be done by least square of differences between actual value of y and its estimate ($\hat{y}$) ($\hat{y}$ is read as y hat) obtained from equation.

$$\text{Error in estimation} = \text{True value} - \text{Estimate using the line } y = a + bx$$
$$= y - \hat{y} = y - (a + bx) = y - a - bx$$

Sum of squares of errors is denoted by,
$$S = \sum (y - a - bx)^2$$

Using mathematical methods we choose the constants a and b so that S is minimum. These methods gives rise the following two equations in a and b

$$\sum y = na + b \sum x$$
$$\sum xy = a \sum x + b \sum x^2$$

The above equations are called as *normal equations*. Solving the normal equations simultaneously we get, a and b

$$b = \frac{n \sum xy - \sum x \cdot \sum y}{n \sum x^2 - (\sum x)^2} \quad \text{and} \quad a = b \frac{\sum x}{n} - \frac{\sum y}{n}$$

Hence,
$$b = \frac{\frac{\sum xy}{n} - \bar{x}\bar{y}}{\sigma_x^2} \quad \text{and} \quad a = b\bar{x} - \bar{y}$$

$\therefore$
$$b = \frac{\text{Cov}(x, y)}{\sigma_x^2} \quad \text{and} \quad a = b\bar{x} - \bar{y}$$

The constant b involved in the equation is called as *regression coefficient of y on x*. Hence instead of writing it as b, henceforth we write it as b_{yx}.

$$\therefore \quad b_{yx} = \frac{\text{Cov}(x, y)}{\sigma_x^2}$$

Substituting these values of a and b in y = a + bx and simplifying the same we get,

$$y - \bar{y} = b_{yx}(x - \bar{x})$$

as least square regression equation of y on x.

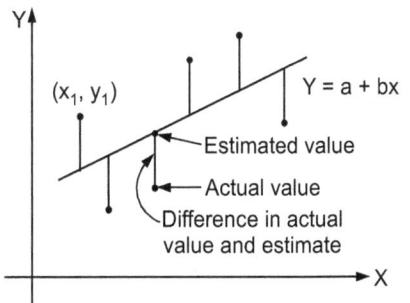
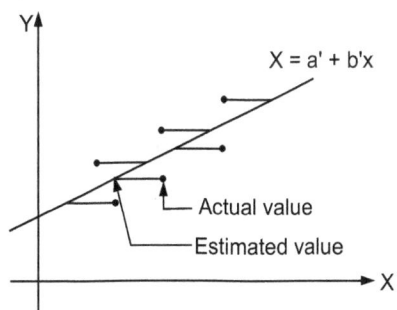

Fig. 5.12   Fig. 5.13

2. Regression line of X on Y : In this case we assume x as dependent variable and y as independent variable. This line is used to predict values of x for known values of y. Its least square equation is obtained using same technique which is used for obtaining regression equation of y on x.

Thus the equation of line will be

$$x - \bar{x} = b_{xy}(y - \bar{y})$$

Coefficient involved in the above equation is known as *regression coefficient of X on Y*.

$$\therefore \quad b_{xy} = \frac{\sum(x - \bar{x})(y - \bar{y})/n}{\sigma_y^2} = \frac{\frac{\sum xy}{n} - \bar{x}\bar{y}}{\sigma_y^2}$$

$$= \frac{\text{Cov}(x, y)}{\sigma^2 x}$$

Illustration 8 : *Following data gives expenditure incurred on advertisement and the sales for 10 years.*

Advertisement expenses in thousand ₹(X)	10	12	15	14	16	20	19	24	26	30
Sales in lakh ₹(Y)	5.0	5.1	5.4	5.5	5.7	5.9	6.0	7.3	7.5	7.8

(i) Find the appropriate line of regression to estimate sales for given advertisement. Also estimate sales if advertisement expenses is ₹ 35,000.

(ii) To achieve sales target of ₹ 10 lakhs how much you need to invest in advertisement.

(iii) If company does not invest any amount in advertisement what will be the sales?

(iv) Find the increase in sales per thousand ₹ advertisement expenses.

Solution : Let X = Advertisement expenses
Y = Sales.

Here to estimate sales we need to find the regression line of Y on X, similarly to estimate expenditure required to achieve the target sales we need the regression line of X on Y.

Procedure :

(1) Prepare the table to find $\sum x, \sum y, \sum x^2, \sum y^2, \sum xy$.

(2) Find $\bar{X}, \bar{Y}, \sigma_x^2, \sigma_y^2$, Cov (X, Y), b_{xy}, b_{yx}.

(3) Determine the regression lines.

X	Y	X²	Y²	XY
10	5.0	100	25.00	50.0
12	5.1	144	26.01	61.2
15	5.4	225	29.16	81.0
14	5.5	196	30.25	77.0
16	5.7	256	32.49	91.2
20	5.9	400	34.81	118.0
19	6.0	361	36.00	114.0
24	7.3	576	53.29	175.2
26	7.5	676	56.25	195.0
30	7.8	900	60.84	234.0
Total = 186	61.2	3834	384.10	1196.6

$n = 10, \bar{X} = \dfrac{\sum x}{n} = \dfrac{186}{10} = 18.6, \bar{Y} = \dfrac{\sum y}{n} = \dfrac{61.2}{10} = 6.12$

$\sigma_x^2 = \dfrac{\sum x^2}{n} - \bar{X}^2 = \dfrac{3834}{10} - 18.6^2 = 383.40 - 345.96 = 37.44$

$\sigma_y^2 = \dfrac{\sum y^2}{n} - \bar{y}^2 = \dfrac{384.10}{10} - 6.12^2 = 38.4100 - 37.4544 = 0.9556$

Cov (x, y) $= \dfrac{\sum xy}{n} - \bar{X}\bar{Y} = \dfrac{1196.6}{10} - 18.5 \times 6.12 = 119.660 - 113.832$

= 5.828

$b_{yx} = \dfrac{\text{Cov (x, y)}}{\sigma_x^2} = \dfrac{5.828}{37.44} = 0.1557$

$b_{xy} = \dfrac{\text{Cov (x, y)}}{\sigma_y^2} = \dfrac{5.828}{0.9556} = 6.0988$

(i) To estimate sales (y) for given advertisement express (x), we use regression line of y on x

$$y - \bar{y} = b_{yx}(x - \bar{x})$$
$$y - 6.12 = 0.1557(x - 18.6)$$
$$y - 6.12 = 0.1557x - 2.89602$$
$$y = 0.1557x + 3.2240$$

Estimate of y for x = 35 we substitute x = 35 in the above equation

$$y = 0.1557 \times 35 + 3.2240 = 8.6735$$

Interpretation : If we spend ₹ 35,000 on advertisement then sales will be approximately ₹ 8.6735 lakhs.

(ii) To estimate advertisement expenses (X) for achieving sales target (Y) we use regression line of X on Y.

$$x - \bar{x} = b_{xy}(y - \bar{y})$$
$$x - 18.6 = 6.0988(y - 6.12)$$
$$x - 18.6 = 6.0988y - 37.3247$$
$$x = 6.0988y - 18.7247$$

To estimate x for y = 10, substitute y = 10 in the above equation

∴ $$x = 6.0988 \times 10 - 18.7247$$
$$= 42.2633 \text{ thousand } ₹$$

To achieve sales target of ₹ 10 lakhs. We have to spend ₹ 42,263.30.

(iii) To find sales when advertisement expenses is zero, we put x = 0 in the regression line of y on x.

$$y = 0.1557(0) + 3.224 = 3.224$$
$$y = 3.224 \text{ lakhs } ₹$$

Interpretation : If y = a + bx is equation of regression line then the intercept a is the value of y for x = 0.

(iv) y = 0.1557x + 3.224 is equation in which slope is 0.1557. Thus for unit increase in x, y increases by 0.1557 lakhs of ₹. Hence if we increase advertisement expenses by ₹ one thousand, sales will approximately increase by 0.1557 lakhs of ₹ or ₹ 15,570.

Geometric Interpretation of Regression line :

We can visualise the line, slope intercept geometrically in the following figure.

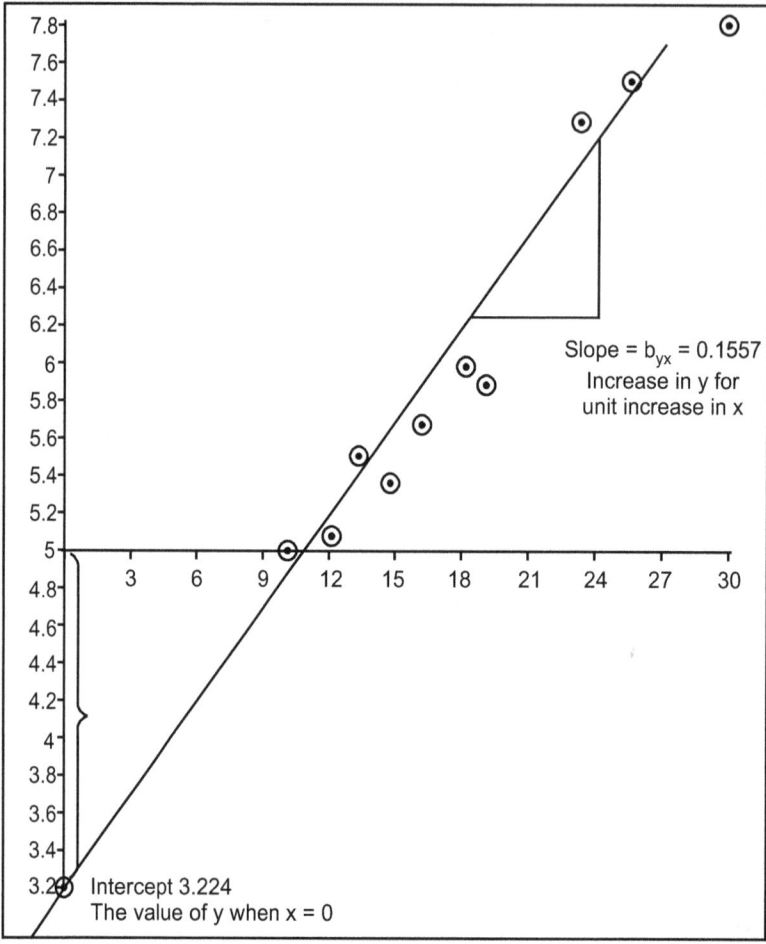

Fig. 5.14

5.10 Interpretation of Regression Coefficient

The regression line of Y on X is $y - \bar{y} = b_{yx}(x - \bar{x})$, we can write it as $Y = b_{yx} X + C$. Clearly, unit change in X will make change of b_{yx} units in Y. If b_{yx} is positive, then increase (or decrease) in X by one unit will be associated with increase (or decrease) in Y by b_{yx} units. On the other hand, if b_{yx} is negative, then increase (or decrease) in X by one unit is going to cause decrease (or increase) in Y by b_{yx} units.

For example, suppose X = supply and Y = price (₹) and the regression line is Y = – 1.2 X + 5. Here we interpret the regression coefficient as follows. If supply (X) increases by one unit, the price is going to decrease by ₹ 1.20, or unit decrease in supply is going to cause increase in price by ₹ 1.20. Thus b_{yx} is the amount of change in Y per unit change in X.

Let X = expenditure on advertisement in ₹ and Y = annual profit in ₹. Suppose Y = 12 X + 19 is the regression line, then we interpret it as follows. For every rupee spent on advertisement, profit is estimated to rise by ₹ 12.

Coefficient of determination :

Definition : If r is the correlation coefficient then r^2 is called as coefficient of determination.

The coefficient of determination measures the **strength** of regression of Y on X. Larger the value of r^2, more powerful is the regression model. In other words, reliability in determining the Y values on the basis of X is more. Hence, it is called as the **coefficient of determination**. Also note that $|r| > r^2$; since $0 < |r| < 1$. Thus correlation coefficient overestimates the actual extent of linear relationship. Hence, in advanced studies, use of r^2 is recommended than that of r. However, a drawback of coefficient of determination is that it is always positive, hence fails to give the idea about the type of relationship between X and Y.

5.11 Applications of Correlation and Regression

There are number of fields where correlation and regression are used as tools in the analysis.

(a) In agricultural experiments, one can use regression line to estimate change in agricultural production due to various factors viz. fertilizers, irrigation facility, fertility of soil etc.

Similarly, one can study the relation between two variables such as germination time (Y) and temperature of soil (X).

Relation between alkalinity of water in a river (or pond) and growth of fungi can be studied using regression and correlation.

(b) In business and trade, correlation and regression helps in planning and forecasting to a great extent.

In portfolio analysis, β (beta) index is used quite often. Suppose Y is return on a security (a share of particular company) and X is the return on all other remaining securities measured in terms of index, then regression coefficient b_{yx} is called as beta index of a security. If $β > 1$, the share is treated as aggressive otherwise defensive.

(c) In medical sciences, we can find the regression line between age of a person (X) and blood pressure (Y). This helps in preparing the scale for blood pressure agewise. Further it may be used in finding abnormalities. Similarly using regression analysis one can find growth chart for a normal baby. It may be about age in months and weight or age and height.

(d) An economist may be interested to know the relationship between age and productivity index. Effect of training or education on change in total turnover can be measured using similar techniques.

(e) In portfolio analysis, risk is measured in terms of variances and covariances. If Y = Return of a security, X = Market return then,

Systematic risk of $Y = b_{yx}^2 \, \sigma_x^2$

Unsystematic risk of $Y = \sigma_y^2 - b_{yx}^2 \, \sigma_x^2$.

Thus the total risk σ_y^2 is partitioned into systematic and unsystematic risks.

An optimal way of investing in two or more portfolios can be obtained using linear combination, which has the least variance.

(f) We see a wonderful application of correlation in the field of physical education and sports.

Several aptitude tests are given for players. There are certain events or activities in the sport with performances correlated to each other.

For example, the performance in athletics events discuss (disc-throw), shot-put (iron ball throw) and javelin (spear throw) are correlated. Among three events correlation between any two is high positive. This indicates that the aptitude required for any of these there is same. Thus one can reduce the number of tests. Performance in one event can be used to estimate the performance in other.

5.12 Linear Regression : Cause and Effect

By means of correlation analysis we get an idea about the type of correlation and the extent of correlation between two variables. However, this does not tell us anything about cause and effect relationship. If X and Y are correlated, then we cannot say X is the cause and Y is the effect or vice versa. Even in case of perfect correlation also, we cannot conclude that one of the variable is the cause and the other is effect. If X is the cause and Y is effect, then X and Y are correlated (or dependent) but not vice-versa. It is possible that some common factors influence both X and Y, due to which they turn out to be correlated. For example, price of a commodity and demand.

Sometimes correlation between two variables is found just due to pure chance. It is called as *'spurious or non-sense correlation'*.

For example, suppose X = Number of literates in a country and Y = Number of criminals in a country. Clearly as X increases, in majority cases Y also increases; thus there is a high positive correlation between X and Y. However, we cannot say that X is cause and Y is effect. In other words, we cannot conclude that literacy is the cause of crime. Both X and Y show similar trend because of third common variable that the population. Increase (or decrease) in population will have effect on X and Y of similar kind. Hence there will be positive correlation between X and Y.

We have seen in the above discussion that the correlated variables cannot be sorted out as cause and effect. However, regression does this job. This demands two separate prediction equations for the two variables. For example, suppose X is the intelligence quotient (I.Q.) and Y is the marks in an examination. Then we can have regression line of Y on X to estimate marks in examination, given the I.Q. Here we assume that I.Q. is the cause and marks is the effect. Similarly using regression line of X on Y, we can estimate I.Q. whenever marks are available, reversing the role of cause and effect.

Suppose X is the total rainfall in a certain period and Y is the agricultural yield. In this case, there is no point in finding regression line of X on Y, as yield cannot be cause to rainfall. Regression line of Y on X makes sense and hence is of much use.

Thus we note the importance of two regression lines for prediction purposes.

Illustration 9 : *Obtain regression lines for following data :*

X	2	3	5	7	8	10	12	15
Y	2	5	8	10	12	14	15	16

Find estimate of :

(i) *Y when X = 6.*

(ii) *X when Y = 20.*

Solution : To find regression lines we require to calculate regression coefficients b_{xy} and b_{yx}. These coefficients depend upon $\sum x, \sum y, \sum x^2, \sum y^2, \sum xy$. So we prepare the following table and simplify the calculations :

	x	y	x²	y²	xy
	2	2	4	4	4
	3	5	9	25	15
	5	8	25	64	40
	7	10	49	100	70
	9	12	81	144	108
	10	14	100	196	140
	12	15	144	225	180
	15	16	225	256	240
Total	63	82	637	1014	797

$$n = \text{number of pairs of observations} = 8$$

$$\bar{x} = \frac{\sum x}{n} = \frac{63}{8} = 7.875$$

$$\sigma^2 x = \frac{\sum x^2}{n} - \bar{x}^2 = \frac{637}{8} - (7.875)^2 = 17.6094$$

$$\bar{y} = \frac{82}{8} = 10.25$$

$$\sigma^2 y = \frac{\sum y^2}{n} - \bar{y}^2 = \frac{1014}{8} - (10.25)^2 = 21.6875$$

$$\text{Cov}(x, y) = \frac{\sum xy}{n} - \bar{x}\bar{y} = \frac{797}{8} - 7.875 \times 10.25 = 18.9063$$

$$b_{yx} = \frac{\text{Cov}(x, y)}{\sigma_y^2} = \frac{18.9063}{17.6094} = 1.0736$$

$$b_{xy} = \frac{\text{Cov}(x, y)}{\sigma_y^2} = \frac{18.9063}{21.6875} = 0.8718$$

Regression line of Y on X :

$$y - \bar{y} = b_{yx}(x - \bar{x})$$
$$y - 10.25 = 1.0736(x - 7.875)$$
$$y = 1.0736x + 1.7954$$

(i) Estimate of y for x = 6, can be obtained by substituting x = 6 in the above regression equation.

$$\therefore \quad y = 1.0736 \times 6 + 1.7954$$
$$y = 8.237$$

Regression line of X on Y :

$$x - \bar{x} = b_{xy}(y - \bar{y})$$
$$x - 7.875 = 0.8718(y - 10.25)$$
$$x - 7.875 = 0.8718y - 8.93595$$
$$x = 0.8718y - 1.06095$$

(ii) Estimate of x can be obtained by substituting y = 20 in the above equation.

$$\therefore \quad x = 16.37505$$

Note : For estimation of x and estimation of y separate equations are to be used.

The above problem using MS-EXCEL is solved as follows :

Enter the data in columns A and B (X and Y respectively). Then use following path to obtain regression lines directly. Click on **Tools** then following Fig. 5.15 appears on screen.

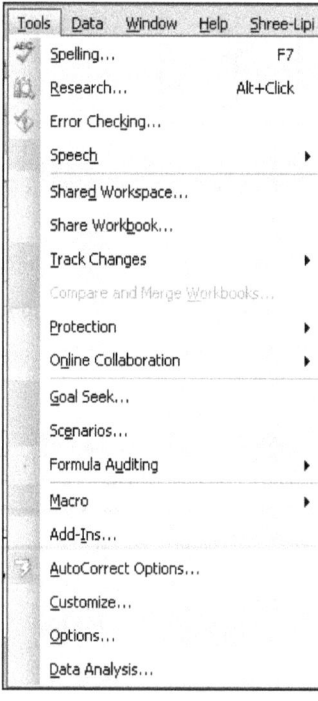

Fig. 5.15

Then click on **Data Analysis**, following window appears.

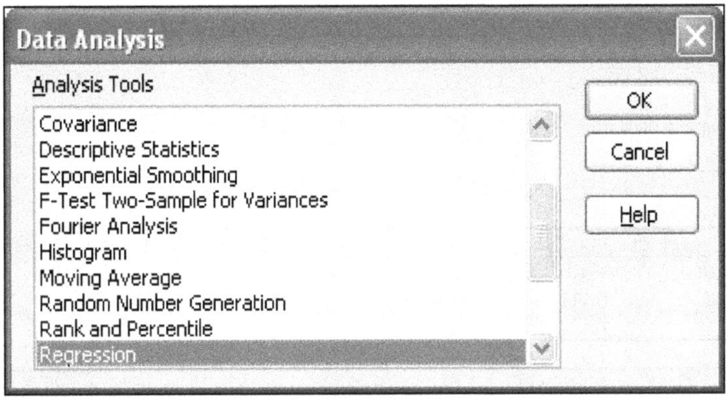

Fig. 5.16

Then click on **Regression** function.

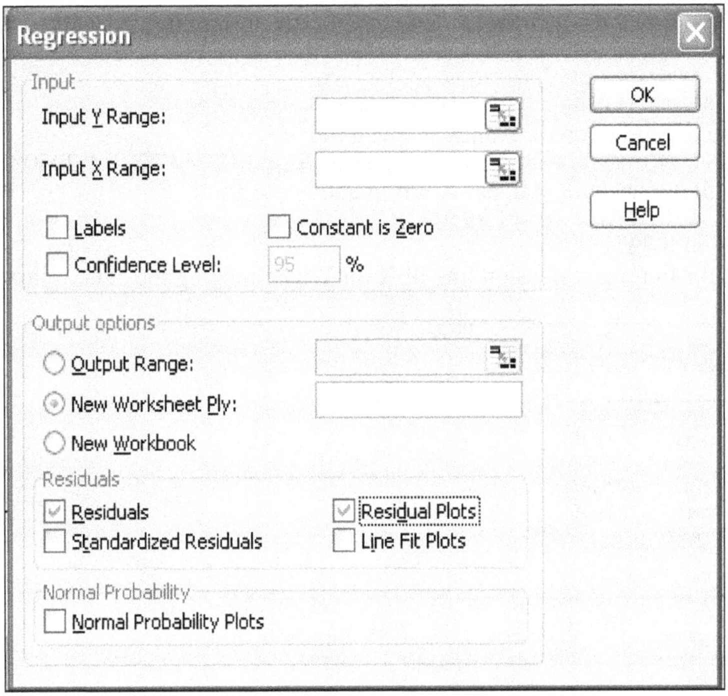

Fig. 5.17

Now, if we want to find regression line of Y on X, then enter the data range of Y in input Y range and X in input X range and click on OK. Then it will create new worksheet having following summary output i.e. dependent variable in Y range and independent variable in input X range.

	A	B	C	D	E	F	G	H	I
1	SUMMARY OUTPUT								
2									
3	Regression Statistics								
4	Multiple R	0.96745							
5	R Square	0.93596							
6	Adjusted R	0.925287							
7	Standard E	1.360816							
8	Observatio	8							
9									
10	ANOVA								
11		df	SS	MS	F	ignificance F			
12	Regression	1	162.3891	162.3891	87.69166	8.41E-05			
13	Residual	6	11.11091	1.851819					
14	Total	7	173.5						
15									
16		Coefficients	andard Err	t Stat	P-value	Lower 95%	Upper 95%	ower 95.0%	pper 95.0%
17	Intercept	1.795031	1.023074	1.754547	0.129871	-0.70834	4.298403	-0.70834	4.298403
18	X Variable	1.073647	0.114652	9.364383	8.41E-05	0.793103	1.354191	0.793103	1.354191
19									

Fig. 5.18

It returns many values but we are interested only in highlighted values. We know that equation of line is given by Y = mX + c,

where, m is slope (i.e. b_{yx}) and intercept (i.e. $\overline{X} - b_{yx} \overline{Y}$)

Hence line of regression of Y on X is given by
Y = (slope) X + intercept i.e. here Y = 1.073647 X + 1.795031
For estimating Y when X = 6, put X = 6 in above equation.
Y = 1.073647 ∗ 6 + 1.795031,
Y = 8.237

Similarly, for finding regression line of X on Y by changing the data in input Y range and input X range.

	A	B	C	D	E	F	G	H	I
1	SUMMARY OUTPUT								
2									
3	Regression Statistics								
4	Multiple R	0.96745							
5	R Square	0.93596							
6	Adjusted R	0.925287							
7	Standard E	1.226215							
8	Observatio	8							
9									
10	ANOVA								
11		df	SS	MS	F	ignificance F			
12	Regression	1	131.8534	131.8534	87.69166	8.41E-05			
13	Residual	6	9.021614	1.503602					
14	Total	7	140.875						
15									
16		Coefficients	andard Err	t Stat	P-value	Lower 95%	Upper 95%	ower 95.0%	pper 95.0%
17	Intercept	-1.06052	1.048071	-1.01188	0.350649	-3.62506	1.504019	-3.62506	1.504019
18	X Variable	0.871758	0.093093	9.364383	8.41E-05	0.643968	1.099548	0.643968	1.099548
19									

Fig. 5.19

Hence line of regression of X on Y is X = 0.871758∗Y − 1.06052 and estimated value of X = 16.37505 for y = 20.

5.13 Properties of Regression Coefficient (B.B.A. Oct. 2014)

1. Correlation coefficient and regression coefficients have same algebraic signs.

Proof : Note that $b_{xy} = \dfrac{\text{Cov}(x, y)}{\sigma_y^2}$, $b_{yx} = \dfrac{\text{Cov}(x, y)}{\sigma_x^2}$

and $r = \dfrac{\text{Cov}(x, y)}{\sigma_x \sigma_y}$

Clearly, numerator of each coefficient is same and denominator of each coefficient is positive. Hence, numerator decides algebraic sign. Thus, all coefficients have same algebraic sign. Hence, if $r > 0$, then $b_{yx} > 0$ and $b_{xy} > 0$. If $r = 0$, $b_{yx} = b_{xy} = 0$. If $r < 0$ then, $b_{xy} < 0$ and $b_{yx} < 0$.

2. Correlation coefficient is a square root of product of regression coefficients. (i.e. $r = \sqrt{b_{yx} \cdot b_{xy}}$) or correlation coefficient is geometric mean of regression coefficients.

Proof : $b_{yx} \cdot b_{xy} = \dfrac{\text{Cov}(x, y)}{\sigma_x^2} \times \dfrac{\text{Cov}(x, y)}{\sigma_y^2} = \left(\dfrac{\text{Cov}(x, y)}{\sigma_x \sigma_y}\right)^2 = r^2$

$\therefore \quad r = \sqrt{b_{yx} b_{xy}}$

Note : Choose positive square root if regression coefficients are positive, otherwise, negative.

3. Both regression coefficients cannot exceed unity simultaneously.

Proof : If possible let us assume $b_{yx} > 1$ and $b_{xy} > 1$.

Hence, $b_{xy} \cdot b_{yx} > 1$

$\therefore \quad r^2 > 1$

which is impossible ($\because r < 1$). Thus our assumption is incorrect.

We state few more properties without proof.

4. Regression coefficient can be expressed in terms of correlation coefficient as follows :

$$b_{yx} = r \cdot \dfrac{\sigma_y}{\sigma_x} \text{ and } b_{xy} = r \cdot \dfrac{\sigma_x}{\sigma_y}$$

5. Correlation coefficient lies between two regression coefficients.

6. Regression coefficients remain unchanged due to change of origin. In otherwords if a constant is substracted or added from each observation, regression coefficients remain same.

7. Regression coefficients are affected by change of scale as follows

If $u = \dfrac{x - a}{h}$ and $v = \dfrac{y - b}{k}$

then $b_{uv} = \dfrac{k}{h} b_{xy}$ and $b_{vu} = \dfrac{h}{k} b_{yx}$

8. If $r = \pm 1$ then, regression coefficients are reciprocals of each other.

9. Regression coefficients are equal if $\sigma_x = \sigma_y$.

5.14 Properties of Regression Lines

(1) Regression lines coincide if $r = \pm 1$. Thus if there exists perfect correlation, points in scatter diagram lie on the same straight line.

(2) Regression lines are perpendicular to each other, if $r = 0$. Thus if the variables are uncorrelated, points on scatter diagram will exhibit maximum spread.

(3) The point of intersection of regression lines is $(\bar{x}, \bar{y})$.

(4) Larger the value of correlation coefficient smaller is the acute angle between regression lines.

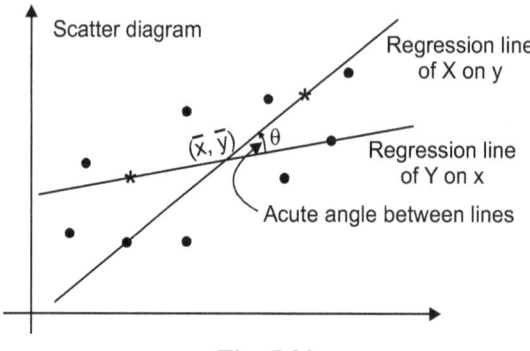

Fig. 5.20

5.15 Standard Error of Regression Estimate

With usual notation r as correlation coefficient σ_x and σ_y as standard deviations of x and y respectively; we state standard error of regression estimate.

(1) Standard error of regression estimate of y on x is $\sigma_y \sqrt{1 - r^2}/\sqrt{n - 2}$.

(2) Standard error of regression estimate of x on y is $\sigma_x \sqrt{1 - r^2}/\sqrt{n - 2}$.

Hence estimates are reliable for larger value of r^2.

Note : The above discussion leads to conclusion that rather than r we should consider r^2 for testing reliability of regression estimates. Therefore, regression analysis claims validity if r^2 is sufficiently large. The quantity r^2 is called as the coefficient of determination.

5.16 Correlation and Regression Analysis

Correlation coefficient gives the extent of linear relationship between two variables. Whereas regression analysis establishes the functional relationship between two correlated variables. Regression analysis helps in estimation, prediction etc. however correlation coefficient is an indicator of linear relationship.

Correlation coefficient is symmetric i.e. Corr (x, y) = Corr (y, x), however regression coefficients are not symmetric i.e. $b_{xy} \neq b_{yx}$.

Correlation coefficient is unitless quantity, however regression coefficients posses units of measurement.

Computation of regression coefficients by deviation method : Note that by one of the property of regression coefficients we can subtract a suitable constant and make computations easy.

Procedure :
(1) Substract a constant 'a' from x values and constant 'b' from y values.
 Denote $u = x - a$ and $v = y - b$.
(2) Prepare table containing columns u, v, u², v² and uv.
(3) Use the following formulae and compute regression coefficients.

$$b_{xy} = b_{uv} = \frac{\frac{\sum uv}{n} - \bar{u}\bar{v}}{\sigma_v^2}$$

and

$$b_{yx} = b_{vu} = \frac{\frac{\sum uv}{n} - \bar{u}\bar{v}}{\sigma_u^2}$$

where,

$$\bar{u} = \frac{\sum u}{n} \qquad \bar{v} = \frac{\sum v}{n}$$

$$\sigma_u^2 = \frac{\sum u^2}{n} - \bar{u}^2 \quad \text{and} \quad \sigma_v^2 = \frac{\sum v^2}{n} - \bar{v}^2$$

Illustration 10 : *The table below gives the respective heights x and y of a sample of 10 fathers and their sons :*
(i) Find regression line of y on x.
(ii) Find regression line of x on y.
(iii) Estimate son's height if father's height is 65 inches.
(iv) Estimate father's height if son's height is 60 inches.
(v) Compute correlation coefficient between x and y.

Height of father x (inches)	65	63	67	64	68	62	70	66	68	67
Height of son y (inches)	68	66	68	65	69	66	68	65	71	67

Solution : Let $u = x - 62$, $v = y - 65$. We prepare the table to simplify the computations.

x	y	u	v	u²	v²	uv
65	68	3	3	9	9	9
63	66	1	1	1	1	1
67	68	5	3	25	9	15
64	65	2	0	4	0	0
68	69	6	4	36	16	24
62	66	0	1	0	1	0
70	68	8	3	64	9	24
66	65	4	0	16	0	0
68	71	6	6	36	36	36
67	67	5	2	25	4	10
Total		40	23	216	85	119

$$n = \text{number of pairs} = 10$$

$$\bar{u} = \frac{40}{10} = 4, \quad \sigma_u^2 = \frac{216}{10} - 4^2 = 5.6$$

$$\bar{v} = \frac{23}{10} = 2.3, \quad \sigma_v^2 = \frac{85}{10} - (2.3)^2 = 3.21$$

$$\text{Cov}(u, v) = \frac{119}{10} - 4 \times 2.3 = 2.7$$

$$\therefore \quad b_{xy} = b_{uv} = \frac{2.7}{3.21} = 0.8411, \text{ and } b_{yx} = b_{vu} = \frac{2.7}{5.6} = 0.4821$$

$$\bar{x} = \bar{u} + 62 = 66, \quad \bar{y} = \bar{v} + 65 = 67.3$$

(i) Regression line of Y on X is $y - \bar{y} = b_{yx}(x - \bar{x})$

$$\therefore \quad y - 67.3 = 0.4821(x - 66)$$

$$\therefore \quad y = 0.4821x + 35.4814$$

(ii) Regression line of X on Y is $x - \bar{x} = b_{xy}(y - \bar{y})$

$$\therefore \quad x - 66 = 0.8411(y - 67.3)$$

$$\therefore \quad x = 0.8411y + 9.3940$$

(iii) Estimate of son's height y for x = 65

$$y = 0.4821 \times 65 + 35.4814 = 66.8179 \text{ inches}$$

(iv) Estimate of father's height x for y = 60

$$x = 0.8411 \times 60 + 9.394 = 59.86 \text{ inches}$$

(v) Correlation coefficient,

$$r = \sqrt{b_{xy} \cdot b_{yx}} = \sqrt{0.8411 \times 0.4821} = 0.63678$$

We choose positive square root because regression coefficients are positive.

Illustration 11 : *Revenue department is trying to estimate the monthly amount of unpaid taxes. Suppose x denote field audit labour hours and y denote unpaid taxes. Using last 10 months data the following summary is obtained.*

$\sum x = 441, \sum y = 272, \sum x^2 = 19461, \sum y^2 = 7428, \sum xy = 12{,}005.$

Determine regression line of y on x. Also obtain standard error of regression estimate.

Solution : Here we require to find b_{yx}.

$$\bar{x} = \frac{441}{10} = 44.1 \quad \bar{y} = \frac{272}{10} = 27.2$$

$$\sigma_x^2 = \frac{19461}{10} - (44.1)^2 = 1.29$$

$$\sigma_y^2 = \frac{7428}{10} - (27.2)^2 = 2.96$$

$$\text{Cov}(x, y) = \frac{12005}{10} - 44.1 \times 27.2 = 0.98$$

$$b_{yx} = \frac{\text{Cov}(x, y)}{\sigma_x^2} = \frac{0.98}{1.29} = 0.7597$$

Regression line of y on x is :

$$y - \bar{y} = b_{yx}(x - \bar{x})$$

$$y - 27.2 = 0.7597(x - 44.1)$$

$$y = 0.7597x - 6.3023$$

S.E. of regression estimate of y on x = $\sigma_y = \sqrt{1 - r^2}/\sqrt{n - 2}$.

Note that :
$$r^2 = \frac{\text{Cov}(x, y)}{\sigma_x^2 \sigma_y^2}$$

$$= \frac{0.98}{1.29 \times 2.96} = 0.256652$$

∴ $$\text{S.E.} = \sqrt{2.96 \times (1 - 0.256652)}/\sqrt{8}$$

$$= \frac{1.4833}{2.8284} = 0.5244$$

Illustration 12 : *Determine regression line for price given the supply, hence estimate price when supply is 180 units, from the following information.*

x = Supply, y = Price in ₹ per unit, n = 7

$\Sigma(x - 150) = 119$, $\qquad \Sigma(y - 160) = 84$

$\Sigma(x - 150)^2 = 2835$, $\qquad \Sigma(y - 160)^2 = 2387$

$\Sigma(x - 150)(y - 160) = 525$.

Also find correlation coefficient between price and supply.

Solution : Let, u = x – 150, v = y – 160

∴ $$\bar{u} = \frac{119}{7} = 17, \quad \bar{v} = \frac{84}{7} = 12$$

$$\sigma_u^2 = \frac{2835}{7} - (17)^2 = 405 - 289 = 116$$

$$\sigma_v^2 = \frac{2387}{7} - (12)^2 = 341 - 144 = 197$$

$$\text{Cov}(x, y) = \text{Cov}(u, v) = \frac{525}{7} - 17 \times 12 = -129$$

$$\bar{x} = 150 + \bar{u} = 167 \quad \text{and} \quad \bar{y} = 160 + \bar{v} = 172$$

$$b_{yx} = b_{vu} = \frac{\text{Cov}(u, v)}{\sigma_u^2} = \frac{-129}{116} = -1.1121$$

Equation of regression line of y on x is,

$$y - \bar{y} = b_{yx}(x - \bar{x})$$
$$y - 172 = -1.1121(x - 167)$$
$$y = -1.1121x + 357.7207$$

Estimate of y for x = 180

$$y = -1.1121 \times 180 + 357.7207$$
$$= 157.54$$

$$r = \text{Corr}(x, y) = \frac{\text{Cov}(u, v)}{\sigma_u \sigma_v}$$

$$= \frac{-129}{\sqrt{116 \times 197}} = -0.8534$$

Illustration 13 : *Compute regression coefficients and hence verify that correlation coefficient lies between them.*

$n = 100$, $\bar{x} = 60$, $\bar{y} = 50$, $\sigma_x = 10$, $\sigma_y = 12$, $\sum(x - \bar{x})(y - \bar{y}) = 8400$.

Solution :
$$\text{Cov}(x, y) = \frac{\sum(x - \bar{x})-(y - \bar{y})}{n}$$

$$= \frac{8400}{100} = 84$$

∴
$$b_{xy} = \frac{\text{Cov}(x, y)}{\sigma_y^2}$$

$$= \frac{84}{144} = 0.5833$$

$$b_{yx} = \frac{\text{Cov}(x, y)}{\sigma_x^2}$$

$$= \frac{84}{100} = 0.84$$

$$r = \frac{\text{Cov}(x, y)}{\sigma_x \sigma_y} = \frac{84}{120} = 0.7$$

Clearly r lies between the two regression coefficients.

Illustration 14 : *A study of wheat prices at Mumbai and Kanpur yield the following data :*

	Mumbai	Kanpur
Arithmetic mean	₹20	₹21
Standard deviation	₹0.326	₹0.207

Correlation coefficient between the prices at Mumbai and Kanpur is 0.774. Estimate the price at Kanpur if the price at Mumbai is ₹25 using the above data.

Solution : Let y : Price of wheat at Kanpur, x : Price of wheat at Mumbai.

We obtain regression line of y on x from estimation of price at Kanpur.

$$y - \bar{y} = r \cdot \frac{\sigma_y}{\sigma_x}(x - \bar{x}) \quad \left(\because b_{yx} = r\frac{\sigma_y}{\sigma_x}\right)$$

$$y - 21 = 0.774 \times \frac{0.207}{0.326}(25 - 20)$$

$$y - 21 = 2.457$$

$$y = 23.46 ₹$$

Therefore price at Kanpur is ₹ 23.46.

Illustration 15 : Given $x - 4y = 5$ and $x - 16y = -64$ are the regression lines, find (i) regression coefficient of x on y, (ii) regression coefficient of y on x, (iii) Corr (x, y), (iv) $\bar{x}, \bar{y}$, (v) σ_y if $\sigma_x = 8$.

Solution : Here by looking at the equations we cannot decide which of the equation is regression equation of x on y and which is of y on x. We arbitrarily decide one of the line as regression line of y on x, and find regression coefficients. Then we verify whether these values are admissible.

Suppose the equation $x - 16y = -64$ represent regression line of x on y. We write it in usual form as

$$x - \bar{x} = b_{xy}(y - \bar{y}) \quad \ldots (1)$$

Therefore the equation can be reformed as

$$x = 16y - 64. \quad \ldots (2)$$

Comparing coefficients of y in equations (1) and (2) we get $b_{xy} = 16$.

On the other hand, $x - 4y = 5$ will be regression line of y on x. Writing it in usual form we get $4y = x - 5$.

$$\therefore \quad y = \frac{1}{4}x - \frac{5}{4} \quad \ldots (3)$$

Theoretically, equation of y on x is

$$y - \bar{y} = b_{yx}(x - \bar{x}) \quad \ldots (4)$$

Comparing coefficients of x in equations (3) and (4) we get, $b_{yx} = \frac{1}{4}$

We know that, $b_{yx} \cdot b_{xy} \leq 1$

However here, $b_{xy} \cdot b_{yx} = 16 \times \frac{1}{4} = 4 < 1$

Hence, our choice of regression lines is incorrect. Exchanging the choice we get $x - 16y = -64$ as regression line of y on x. Writing it in usual manner we get :

$$y = \frac{1}{16}x + 4 \quad \ldots (5)$$

Comparing equations (4) and (5) we get, $b_{yx} = \frac{1}{16}$. Similarly, $x - 4y = 5$ will be the regression line of x on y. Writing it in usual form we get,

$$x = 4y + 5 \qquad \ldots (6)$$

Comparing equations (1) and (6) we get, $b_{xy} = 4$.

∴ Correlation coefficient $= r^2 = b_{yx} \cdot b_{xy} = \frac{1}{16} \times 4 = \frac{1}{4}$

∴ $\quad r = \sqrt{\frac{1}{4}} = \frac{1}{2}$

(We choose positive square root because regression coefficients are positive).

(iv) Note that $(\bar{x}, \bar{y})$ is the point of intersection of regression lines. Thus $(\bar{x}, \bar{y})$ will satisfy both the equations.

Therefore, we get,

$$\bar{x} - 4\bar{y} = 5 \qquad \ldots (7)$$

and $\quad \bar{x} - 16\bar{y} = -64 \qquad \ldots (8)$

Solving equations (7) and (8), we get,

$$\bar{x} = 28, \quad \bar{y} = \frac{23}{4}$$

(v) To find σ_y we use $b_{xy} = r\frac{\sigma_x}{\sigma_y} = 4$.

$$\frac{1}{2} \times \frac{\sigma_x}{\sigma_y} = 4 \qquad \sigma_y = \frac{\sigma_x}{8} = 1$$

Illustrative 16 : *Find correlation coefficient between heights of fathers and their sons from the following data : (heights in inches).*

Height of Fathers	65	66	67	68	69	70	72	67
Height of Sons	67	68	66	68	72	72	69	70

Solution : Let Father's height (X), Son's height (Y). $U = X - 65$, $V = Y - 65$

X	Y	U	V	U²	V²	UV
65	67	0	2	0	4	0
66	68	1	3	1	9	3
67	66	2	1	4	1	2
68	68	3	3	9	9	9
69	72	4	7	16	49	28
70	72	5	7	25	49	35
72	69	7	4	49	16	28
67	70	2	5	4	25	10
Total	–	24	32	108	162	115

$n = 8$, $\bar{U} = \dfrac{\sum U}{n} = \dfrac{24}{8} = 3$, $\bar{V} = \dfrac{\sum V}{n} = \dfrac{32}{8} = 4$

$$\sigma_u = \sqrt{\dfrac{\sum U^2}{n} - \bar{U}^2} = \sqrt{\dfrac{108}{8} - 3^2} = \sqrt{4.5} = 2.1213$$

$$\sigma_v = \sqrt{\dfrac{\sum V^2}{n} - \bar{V}^2} = \sqrt{\dfrac{162}{8} - 4^2} = \sqrt{4.25} = 2.0616$$

$$\text{Corr} = \dfrac{\dfrac{\sum UV}{n} - \bar{U}\bar{V}}{\sigma_u \sigma_v} = \dfrac{\dfrac{115}{8} - 3 \times 4}{2.1213 \times 2.0616} = 0.5431$$

Illustrative 17 : *The correlation coefficient between two variables X and Y is 0.6. If the means of two series are 13 and 27 respectively and standard deviations are 1.5 and 2 respectively, find the regression line of Y on X.*

Solution : Given : $\bar{X} = 13$, $\bar{Y} = 27$, $\sigma_x = 1.5$, $\sigma_y = 2$, $r = 0.6$.

Regression line of Y on X

$$Y - \bar{Y} = b_{yx}(X - \bar{X})$$

$$Y - 27 = 0.6 \times \dfrac{2}{1.5} \times (X - 13)$$

$$Y = 0.8(X - 13) + 27$$

$$Y = 0.8X + 16.6$$

Case Study :

Alto Pharmaceuticals Ltd. is a company in manufacturing various life saving drugs. It has a manufacturing unit in Anand (Gujrat) and India wide distribution network. Many sales executives, sales representatives and medical representatives are working throughout the country.

It has been observed by the company that since last six months sales have gone down and had a adverse effect on the company's profit.

Senior market executives had a meeting to discuss the problem and concluded that a incentive scheme is to be introduced to promote the sale. Company collected the data for last six months regarding actual incentive given the sales representative and the sales. Suggest the appropriate statistical tools to know whether the incentive scheme has a effect on the company's sale.

Points to Remember

1. Correlation coefficient (r) lies between -1 and 1.

2. $r = \dfrac{\frac{1}{n}\Sigma(x-\bar{x})(y-\bar{y})}{\sigma_x \sigma_y} = \dfrac{\frac{1}{n}\Sigma xy - \bar{x}\bar{y}}{\sigma_x \sigma_y}$.

3. Corr $(ax + b, cy + d)$ = Corr (x, y), if a and b have same signs
   $= -$ Corr (x, y), if a and b have opposite signs

4. Regression coefficient of y and x = $b_{yx} = r\dfrac{\sigma_y}{\sigma_x} = \dfrac{\frac{1}{n}\Sigma xy - \bar{x}\bar{y}}{\sigma_x^2}$.

   Regression coefficient of x on y = $b_{xy} = r\dfrac{\sigma_x}{\sigma_y} = \dfrac{\frac{1}{n}\Sigma xy - \bar{x}\bar{y}}{\sigma_y^2}$.

5. $r = \sqrt{b_{xy} \, b_{yx}}$.
6. r, b_{xy}, b_{yx} have same signs.
7. If $r = \pm 1$ regression lines coinside.
8. If $r = \pm 1$ and $\sigma_x = \sigma_y$ then $b_{xy} = b_{yx}$.
9. The two regression lines intersect at $(\bar{x}, \bar{y})$.
10. Regression line of y on x is $y - \bar{y} = b_{yx}(x - \bar{x})$. It is used to predict y.

    Regression line of x on y is $x - \bar{x} = b_{xy}(y - \bar{y})$. It is used to predict x.

Exercise 5.1

A. Theory Questions :

1. Explain the terms : Bivariate data, covariance, correlation, regression.
2. State the different measures of correlation and describe each of the measures in detail.
3. Describe scatter diagram and explain how it is used to measure correlation.
4. State merits and limitations of scatter diagram as a measure of correlation.
5. Define Karl Pearson's coefficient of correlation or product moment correlation coefficient 'r'. State its merits and demerits. How will you interpret the cases (i) $r = +1$, (ii) $r = -1$, (iii) $r = 0$?
6. State the properties of Karl Person's correlation coefficient.
7. State the limitations of Karl Pearson's coefficient of correlation.
8. State the merits and demerits of Karl Pearson's correlation coefficient.
9. Explain the term 'regression analysis'.

10. Write a note on 'correlation'.
11. State the equations for regression lines of (i) y on x, (ii) x on y. Discuss the nature of the regression equations in case of $r = -1$, $r = \pm 1$, $r = 0$.
12. Why there are two regression lines ?
13. State utility of regression lines.
14. Explain the least square principle for obtaining regression lines.
15. Define regression coefficients and state the properties.
16. Distinguish between regression and correlation.
17. Can any two lines be regression lines ? Give reasons in support of your answer.
18. How would you interpret regression coefficients ?
19. State the situations where regression analysis is used.
20. State the properties of regression (i) lines, (ii) coefficients.
21. With usual notation, prove that

    (a) $b_{yx} \cdot b_{xy} = r^2$, (b) b_{yx} and b_{xy} cannot exceed unity simultaneously.
22. Define coefficient of determination and state its utility.
23. Show that r, b_{yx} and b_{xy} have same algebraic sign.

Exercise 5.2

B. Karl Pearson's Coefficient of Correlation from Raw Data :

1. Find the Karl Pearson's correlation coefficient between sales (X) and expenses (Y) from the following data and interpret your results :

Firms	1	2	3	4	5	6	7	8	9	10
Sales (X) (Lakhs ₹)	50	50	56	60	64	65	65	60	60	50
Expenses (Y) (Lakhs ₹)	11	13	14	15	14	15	15	14	16	13

2. Calculate the Karl-Pearson's coefficient of correlation from following data :

Price	22	24	26	28	30	32	34	36	38	40
Demand	60	58	58	50	48	48	48	42	36	32

3. Calculate the Karl-Pearson's coefficient of correlation from the following data :

Demand in Tonnes	9	11	13	15	17	19	21	23
Supply in Tonnes	6	8	10	12	14	16	18	20

4. Compute product moment correlation coefficient between income and expenditure from the following data.

Year	1981	1982	1983	1884	1885	1886	1887	1888
Daily income (₹)	100	110	115	120	125	130	132	140
Average daily expenditure (₹)	85	90	92	100	110	125	125	130

5. From the following data of marks in Mathematics and Statistics, calculate product moment correlation coefficient and interpret the result.

Marks in Statistics	60	70	80	90	10	20	30	40	50
Marks in Mathematics	65	70	80	75	45	40	50	60	55

6. Daily income and savings in ₹ for 10 employees in a certain company are given below :

Income	250	750	820	900	780	360	980	390	650	620
Savings	60	68	62	86	84	51	91	47	53	58

Compute the Karl Pearson's coefficient of correlation between income and savings.

7. Calculate the Karl Pearson's correlation coefficient between advertisement cost and sales from the following data :

Advertisement cost (in thousand ₹)	41	67	65	92	84	77	27	100	38	80
Sales in lakh ₹	46	52	57	85	61	67	59	90	50	83

8. Obtain correlation coefficient between population density (per square miles) and death rate (per thousand persons) from data related to 5 cities.

Population density	200	500	400	700	300
Death rate	12	18	16	21	10

9. The following table gives frequency distribution of 50 clerks in a certain office according to age and pay. Find Karl Pearson's correlation, if any, between age and pay.

Age (in years)	20-30	30-40	40-50	50-60	60-70
Pay (in ₹)	4000	6000	5500	5000	4500

Hint : Take x = the age in years with values as mid-points of class interval.

10. Find the Karl-Pearson's coefficient of correlation between population and pollution.

Population in lakhs (X)	11	12	13	14	15
Pollution in suitable units (Y)	50	52	60	68	80

C. Karl Pearson's Coefficient of Correlation (Summarised Data):

11. Given that : $r = 0.4$, $\sum (x - \bar{x})(y - \bar{y}) = 108$, $\sigma_y = 3$ and $\sum (x - \bar{x})^2 = 900$. Find number of pairs of observations viz. n.

12. Find number of pairs of observations from the following data.
    $r = -0.4$, $\sum x = 100$, $\sum x^2 = 2250$, $\sum y = 100$, $\sum y^2 = 2250$, $\sum xy = 1900$.

13. Find correlation coefficient between x and y given that : $n = 8$,
    $\sum (x - \bar{x})^2 = 36$, $(y - \bar{y})^2 = 44$, $\sum (x - \bar{x})(y - \bar{y}) = 24$.

14. Find coefficient of correlation from the following information.
    $n = 10$, $\sum (x - 30) = 11$, $\sum (y - 25) = 7$, $\sum (x - 30)^2 = 215$, $\sum (y - 25)^2 = 163$,
    $\sum (x - \bar{x})(y - \bar{y}) = 186$.

15. Given : $n = 6$, $\sum (x - 18.5) = -3$, $\sum (y - 50) = 20$, $\sum (x - 18.5)^2 = 19$,
    $\sum (y - 50)^2 = 850$, $\sum (x - 18.5)(y - 50) = -120$. Calculate coefficient of correlation.

16. Calculate coefficient of correlation from the following information.
    $n = 5$, $\sum x = 20$, $\sum x^2 = 90$, $\sum y = 20$, $\sum y^2 = 90$, $\sum xy = 73$.

17. Given :
Number of pairs of X and Y series	= 15
Arithmetic mean of X	= 25
Arithmetic mean of Y	= 18
Standard deviation of X	= 3
Standard deviation of Y	= 3
Sum of products of X and Y ($\sum XY$)	= 6870

    Find correlation coefficient between X and Y.

18. From the following data compute the coefficient of correlation :
Number of pairs of observations	= 10
Sum of X series	= 9
Sum of Y series	= 5
Sum of squares of X series	= 653
Sum of squares of Y series	= 595
Sum of product of X and Y series	= 534

19. From the following data compute the coefficient of correlation between X and Y.
Number of pairs of observations	= 10
Sum of deviations of X series	= –170
Sum of deviations of Y series	= –20
Sum of squares of deviations of X series	= 8000
Sum of squares of deviations of Y series	= 2000
Sum of products of deviations of X and Y series	= 2500

20. Coefficient of correlation between variables X and Y is 0.3 and their covariance is 12. The variance of X is 9, find the standard deviation of Y.

21. If correlation coefficient between X and Y is 0.8 find that between :
    (i) X and – Y
    (ii) 2X and 3Y (B.B.A. April 2015)
    (iii) X – 10 and Y + 15
    (iv) $\dfrac{X}{2}$ and $\dfrac{Y}{5}$
    (v) $\dfrac{X-10}{3}$ and $\dfrac{10-Y}{5}$

D. Spearman's Rank Correlation Coefficient :

22. Obtain 'Rank Correlation Coefficient' for the results of beauty contest :

Ranks by Judge A	1	5	6	7	8	2	4	3
Ranks by Judge B	1	7	6	2	8	4	5	3

23. Eight contestants in a musical contest were ranked by two judges A and B, in the following manner :

Sr. No.	1	2	3	4	5	6	7	8
Ranks by Judge A	7	6	2	4	5	3	1	8
Ranks by Judge B	5	4	6	3	8	2	1	7

Compute rank correlation coefficient between the two judges and comment on it.

24. Ranks obtained by 6 students in Statistics and Accountancy are given below :

Ranks in Statistics	5	6	4	3	2	1
Ranks in Accountancy	6	2	1	4	3	5

Compute Spearman's Rank Correlation Coefficient.

25. Obtain the Rank Correlation Coefficient for the ranks given by two judges in a contest :

Rank by Judge 'A'	3	6	2	4	5	1
Rank by Judge 'B'	4	5	2	3	6	1

26. The following data relates to the ranks given by judges in a contest :

Sr. No. of Candidate	1	2	3	4	5	6	7	8	9	10
Rank by Judge A	1	5	6	1	2	3	4	7	9	8
Rank by Judge B	5	6	9	2	8	7	3	4	10	1

Compute the rank correlation between the ranks given by judge A and that of judge B. Interprete.

27. The scores obtained by 6 candidates in drawing (X) and in music (Y) are given below :

Candidate	1	2	3	4	5	6
X	24	29	19	14	30	19
Y	37	35	16	26	23	27

Allot the ranks to X and Y and compute Spearman's rank correlation coefficient.

E. Regression (Raw Data):

28. Obtain line of regression of y on x for the data given below:

x	06	02	10	04	08
y	09	11	05	08	07

Also estimate y when x = 5.

29. The following data given the sales and expenses of 10 firms.

Firm No.	1	2	3	4	5	6	7	8	9	10
Sales (in '000 ₹)	45	70	65	30	90	40	50	75	85	60
Expenses (in '000 ₹)	35	90	70	40	95	40	60	80	80	50

Obtain the least square regression line of expenses on sales. Estimate expenses if sales are ₹ 75000.

30. A panel of examiners A and B assessed 7 candidates independently and awarded the following marks.

Candidate	1	2	3	4	5	6	7
Marks By A	40	34	28	30	44	38	31
Marks by B	32	39	26	30	38	34	28

Eighth candidate was awarded 36 marks by examiner A. Using appropriate regression line, estimate the marks awarded by the examiner B.

31. The failure of a certain electronic device is suspected to increase linearly with its temperature. Fit a least square regression line through the following data to predict failure rate.

Temperature °F	55	65	75	85	95	105
Failure rate	0	3	7	10	11	11

Also predict the failure rate at 70°C.

32. Samples of soils are collected from various depths below ground level and tested in the laboratory to determine their shear strength. The collected field data are given below:

Depth (m)	2	3	4	5	6	7
Shear strength	14	20	32	39	42	56

Find the Karl Pearson's coefficient of correlation between depth and shear strength. Interpret the result. Also predict shear strength at depth 10 m.

33. A departmental store gives in-service training to its salesmen followed by a test to consider whether it should terminate the services of any of the salesman who does not qualify in the test. The following data give the test scores and sales made by ten salesmen during a certain period.

Test score	14	19	24	21	28	22	15	20	19	20
Sales ('00 ₹)	31	36	48	37	50	45	33	41	39	40

Calculate the coefficient of correlation between the test scores and sales. Does it indicate that the termination of services of the low test scores is justified ? If the firm wants a minimum sales volume of ₹ 3000, what is the minimum test score that will ensure continuation of the services ? Also obtain the standard error of regression estimate.

34. Suppose x is rainfall in suitable units and y is level of rusting of iron material used for construction measured in suitable units ?

x	43	45	59	21	80
y	6	7	8	1	10

Estimate y if x = 30 using regression analysis.

F. Regression (Summarized Data) :

35. Given the regression equations : $3x + 2y - 26 = 0$ and $6x + y - 31 = 0$.
    find : (i) means of x and y. (ii) correlation between x and y.

36. If the regression equation of Y on X is $2X + 3Y = 1$, obtain the regression coefficient of Y on X.

37. Given : $\bar{X} = 80, \bar{Y} = 50, \sigma_x = 15, \sigma_y = 10$ and $r = -0.4$. Find line of regression of X on Y. Also estimate X when Y = 60.

38. The correlation coefficient between two variables X and Y is 0.6. If the means of two series and 13 and 27 respectively and standard deviations are 1.5 and 2 respectively, find the regression line of Y on X.

39. Given the following data : (P.U. 2011)

	Rainfall (in inches)	Yield (in quintals)
Mean	27	40
Standard Deviation	3	6

Correlation coefficient = 0.8. Estimate the yield when rainfall is 29 inches.

40. Following is the information about the bivariate frequency distribution :
    $n = 20, \sum x = 80, \sum y = 40, \sum x^2 = 1680, \sum y^2 = 320, \sum xy = 480$.
    (i) Obtain the regression lines.
    (ii) Estimate y for x = 3 and estimate x for y = 3.

41. You are given the following information about two variables x and y.
    $n = 10, \sum x^2 = 385, \sum y^2 = 192, \bar{x} = 5.5, \bar{y} = 4, \sum xy = 185$.
    Find (i) Regression line of y on x. (ii) regression line of x on y.
    (iii) Standard error of regression estimate of y on x.

42. Compute regression coefficients from the following data :
    $n = 8, \sum(x - 45) = -40, \sum(x - 45)^2 = 4400, \sum(y - 150) = 280$,
    $\sum(y - 150)^2 = 167432, \sum(x - 45)(y - 150) = 21680$.

43. For a bivariate data we have $\bar{X} = 53, \bar{Y} = 28, b_{yx} = -1.5, b_{xy} = -0.2$.
    Find (i) correlation coefficient between X and Y.
    (ii) estimate of y for x = 60.
    (iii) estimate of x for y = 30.

44. The regression equations are $3x - y - 5 = 0$ and $4x - 3y = 0$. Find
    (i) Arithmetic mean of x and y.
    (ii) Coefficient variations of x and y, if $\sigma_x = 2$.
    (iii) Correlation coefficient between x and y.

45. The following results were obtained from records of age (X) and systolic blood pressure (Y), of a group of 10 men :

	X	Y
Mean	53	142
Variance	130	165

$\sum (x - \bar{x})(y - \bar{y}) = 1220$

Find the appropriate regression equation and use it to estimate the blood pressure of a man with age 45 years.

46. The two regression equations of variables x and y are x = 19.13 − 0.87 y and y = 11.64 − 0.5 x. Find $\bar{x}, \bar{y}$ and Corr (x, y).

47. The regression equations are given by 8x − 10y + 66 = 0 and 40x − 18y − 214 = 0. Find $\bar{x}, \bar{y}$, Corr (x, y). Also find σ_y given that $\sigma_x = 3$.

48. Given the following data :

	Marks in Mathematics	Marks in English
Mean	80	50
Standard Deviation	15	10

The correlation coefficient between marks in Mathematics and English is − 0.4. Estimate the marks in Mathematics obtained by student who scored 60 marks in English.

Answers 5.2

1. 0.7647
2. − 0.9673
3. 1
4. 0.9593
5. 0.95
6. 0.7804
7. 0.7784
8. 0.9207
9. 0
10. 0.9747
11. 9
12. 5
13. 0.6030
14. 0.9955
15. − 0.9395
16. − 0.7
17. 0.8888
18. 0.8566
19. 0.6825
20. 13.3333
21. (i) and (iv) − 0.8, (ii), (iii), (iv) 0.8
22. 0.5952
23. 0.5714
24. − 0.2571
25. 0.8857
26. 0.1030
27. 0.1857
28. y = − 0.65x + 11.9, Estimate of y = 8.65
29. y = 1.01289x + 2.2135, Estimated expenses = ₹ 78180
30. 33
31. y = 0.2343x − 11.7423, Estimated failure rate = 4.6571
32. r = 0.9863, y = 8.2286x − 3.0286, Estimated shear strength = 79.2571
33. r = 0.9425, Justified, x = 0.6156 − 4.4241, Estimate of score = 14.04 Standard error of estimate = 0.454.
34. y = 0.1471x − 0.8966, $\hat{y}$ = 3.5167
35. $\bar{x} = 4, \bar{y} = 7, r = −0.5$
36. − 2/3
37. x = − 0.6y + 110, Estimate of x = 74
38. y = 0.8x + 16.6
39. 43.2 quintals
40. (i) 3x = 4y + 4, 17y = 4x + 18, (ii) x = 5.3333, y = 1.7647

41. (i) y = – 0.4242x + 6.3331, (ii) x = – 1.09375y + 9.875, (iii) 0.4630.
42. b_{yx} = 5.4952, b_{xy} = 0.1484.
43. r = – 0.5477, x = 52.6, y = 17.5.
44. (i) $\bar{x}$ = 3, $\bar{y}$ = 4, (ii) C.V. (X) = 66.6667%, C.V. (Y) = 100%, (iii) r = 0.6667.
45. y = 0.833x + 97.851, 135.336.
46. $\bar{x}$ = 15.9335, $\bar{y}$ = 3.6726, r = – 0.6593
47. $\bar{x}$ = 13, $\bar{y}$ = 17, ρ = 0.6, σ_y = 2.
48. 74

Objective Questions

1. If X + Y = constant then state the Corr (X, Y) giving reasons.
2. If X ∝ Y state the Corr (X, Y) giving reasons.
3. If X ∝ $\frac{1}{Y}$ state the Corr (X, Y) giving reasons.
4. If Corr (X, Y) ± 1 state the nature of regression lines.
5. If Corr (X, Y) = 0 state the nature of regression lines.
6. If Corr (X, Y) = 0.8 then find the Corr (2X, 2Y), Corr (X, –Y), Corr (X/2, Y/3).
7. State the Corr (X, X).
8. State the Corr (X, – X).
9. If σ_x = σ_y = 2, Cov (X, Y) = 0.8, find Corr (X, Y).
10. Give examples of : (i) uncorrelated variables (ii) positively correlated variables (iii) negatively correlated variables.
11. If Corr (X, Y) = 0 then find regression coefficients.
12. If Corr (X, Y) = 1, b_{yx} = 2 find b_{xy}.
13. If Corr (X, Y) = 1, σ_x = σ_y then show that b_{yx} = b_{xy}.
14. Explain why regression coefficients have same algebraic signs.
15. State the point of intersection of regression lines.
16. Find the correlation between X and Y if :

X	1	2	3	4	5
Y	1	2	3	4	5

17. Find the correlation if :

X	1	2	3	4	5
Y	5	4	3	2	1

Answers

1. Corr (X, Y) = – 1
2. Cor (X, Y) = ± 1
3. Corr (X, Y) = 0
4. Lines will coincide
5. Lines will be parallel
6. Corr (2X, 2Y) = 0.8, Corr (X, – Y) = – 0.8, Corr (X/2, Y/3) = 0.8
7. Corr (X, X) = 1
8. Corr (X, – X) = – 1
9. Corr (X, Y) = 0.4
10. b_{yx} = b_{xy} = 0
12. b_{xy} = $\frac{1}{2}$
15. ($\bar{X}$, $\bar{Y}$)
16. r = 1
17. r = – 1

Chapter 6...
Time Series (For B.B.A. Only)

Contents ...

6.1 Introduction
6.2 Meaning of Times Series
6.3 Components of Time Series
6.4 Analysis of Time Series
6.5 Utility of Time Series Analysis
6.6 Measurement of Trend
6.7 Measurement of Seasonal Variation

Key Words :

Time series, Secular trend, Seasonal variations, Cyclical variations, Irregular variations, Business cycle, Additive model, Multiplicative model, Moving average, Least square method.

Objectives :

Business forecasting needs different models appropriate to the situations. Variables which are time dependent need different techniques of analysis. Usual techniques used in descriptive statistics are not sufficient. Separation of components in time series and forecasting are two important tasks to be studied in analysis of time series.

6.1 Introduction

In the field of economics, business commerce and management forecasting is often required for several reasons.

Prices of commodities, agricultural production, mineral production, national income, prices of shares, number of passenger travelling from a certain place, revenue collection, population, volume of import and export, volume of foreign exchange, electricity consumption of a city are the examples where the changes take place every now and then. Thus prices, production, consumption are the main areas where the changes are bound to occur with respect to time. In the examples cited, above reliable forecasting needs the knowledge of the reasons behind the changes, the time epochs of changes and the magnitude of changes. The techniques and tools of forecasting are included in this chapter titled *'Time series'*. Earlier, we have studied some forecasting tools such as regression lines, fitting of curves, interpolation etc. However, those tools are useful for longterm, having steady and smooth curve. In reality we rarely see a smooth curve; how to adjust for these temporary fluctuations is studied in this chapter. The examples given above in the field of commerce, economics are called as 'Time series'. The precise definition is discussed subsequently. Number of definitions of time series are available. Some of them are given below.

6.2 Meaning of Time Series

Definition (According to Morris Hamburg) : Time series is a series of statistical observations arranged in chronological order.

The observations in the chronological order means in the order of occurrence, taken at a regular successive intervals or points of time. The time intervals may be years, months, weeks, days, minutes and seconds also in some cases.

Following are some examples of time series.

1. Daily price of gold.
2. Weekly sales of departmental store.
3. Monthly deposits in a certain bank.
4. Yearly production of food grains in a certain country.
5. Daily record of maximum temperature in a city.
6. Hourly bacterial count in certain culture at laboratory.
7. Population of country at census years.

According to Spiegel, mathematically a time series is defined by the values $Y_1, Y_2, ..., Y_n, ...$ of the variable Y at times $t_1, t_2, ..., t_n, ...$ Thus, time series is a function of time i.e. $Y = F(t)$. In other words, in time series time plays the role of an independent variable and $Y(t)$ is dependent variable. We denote time series by $Y(t)$ or Y_t. In the form of function the time series may be written as follows :

$$t : \quad t_1 \quad t_2 \quad ... \quad t_n \quad ......$$
$$Y_t : \quad Y_1 \quad Y_2 \quad ... \quad Y_n \quad ......$$

The time points $t_1, t_2, t_3, ...$ are equidistant. The analysis of time series is important from many aspects. We plot t on X-axis and Y_t on Y-axis. Consider, the example of population of India in census years.

Year (t)	1901	1911	1921	1931	1941	1951	1961	1971	1981	1991	2001	2011
Population (Cores) Y_t	23.84	25.21	25.13	27.9	31.87	36.11	43.92	54.82	63.33	84.39	102.70	121.02

We observe that the population is measured during census years with intervals of ten years. Hence, the figures are arranged chronologically, that is in order of time. If they are not ordered according to time, then they would not be able to provide information about the pattern of variation. If you carefully observe the above time series, you will notice that the population has an increasing trend. Now have a look at the following graph.

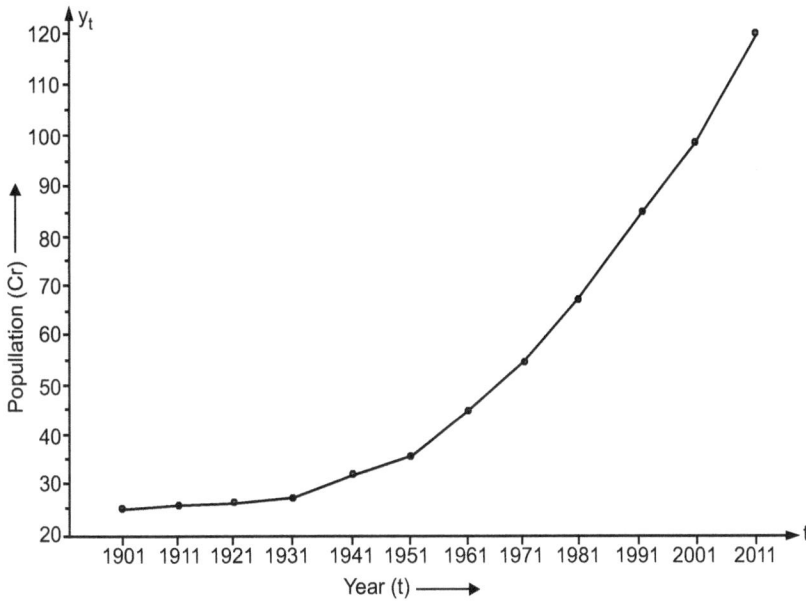

Fig. 6.1

The following things are worth noticing.
(i) India's population is steadily increasing since 1921.
(ii) The rate of population increase accelerates further since 1951, that is, after independence.

Government wants to predict the population of India for future, say for the year 2010; as important policies are to be designed on the basis of such estimates. Time series analysis helps in doing so.

A time series is a summary of past information. Assuming that the 'past' serves a guide to the 'future', time series analysis helps in detecting the underlying patterns and projecting them into future.

Some authors describe the time series data represented graphically as **historigram.**

The nature of time series graph is usually not smooth and not monotonic, it is zig-zag or haphazard. The critical study reveals that these fluctuations are not totally haphazard, however some part is systematic and the only counter part is haphazard in nature.

6.3 Components of Time Series

Time series Y_t is composed of four factors or components viz. (1) Trend, (2) Seasonal variations, (3) Cyclical variations, (4) Irregular variations. These factors cause fluctuations in the values of Y_t. In other words the fluctuations in time series are classified into the above four patterns or categories. A time series may have some or all the components present in it.

1. Trend or Secular Trend (T) : (B.B.A. Oct. 2014)

The trend is the smooth, regular long term movement in time series. It is the general tendency of data. The time series oscillates around trend. The trend may be to go upward to go downword or to remain stagnant.

For example, the yearly population, yearly agricultural production, prices etc. show an upward trend. On the other hand cost of electronic goods, number of illiterates, yearly birth rates etc. show downward trend. Yearly rainfall, daily temperature atmospheric pressure at a certain place, monthly electricity consumption of a family are the examples of constant trend. The trend may be linear or non-linear in nature.

Remarks :

(i) Trend is also called as secular trend. The word secular is derived from the Latin word saeculum which means generation or age.

(ii) Trend is due to the reasons of following nature, changes in population, technological developments, changes in economy, changes in habits and tastes of people.

(iii) Trend is a long period movement however, the period cannot be precisely defined. For example, regarding price of gold, agricultural production the long period cannot be few weeks or 2, 3 years. It may be observed over a period of 10 to 15 years even more than that. Long term period may change from series to series.

(iv) Trend is mostly monotonic although original time series is not.

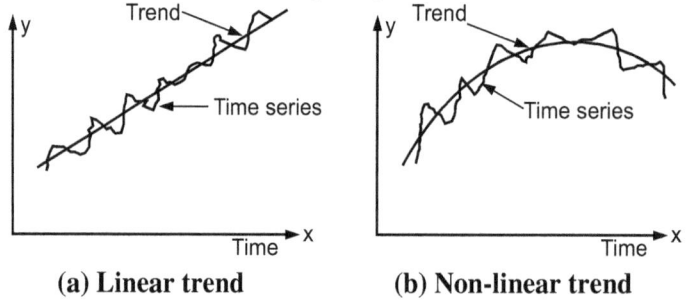

(a) Linear trend   (b) Non-linear trend

Fig. 6.2

In linear trend the values of Y can be approximated by a straight line. This indicates that the rate at 'which the time series values increase or decrease is constant. On the other hand, in non-linear trend, the growth rate is different over different sectors of time. Linear trend is commonly used in business and economics. Non-linear trend is used in the study of population birth rates etc.

(v) Apart from the long-term growth component, there are some short-term periodic rhythmic variations. These variations disturb the smoothness and monotony.

(vi) Trend is useful for two reasons :
   (a) It facilitates the comparison of two time series.
   (b) It helps to extrapolate.

2. Seasonal Variations (s) :   (B.B.A. Oct. 2014)

Seasonal variations are the fluctuations in a time series which repeat regularly every year or some specific period of time.

For example, sales of umbrellas and raincoats is the highest in rainy season; sales of wollen garments attains its peak in winter, sales of luxury items and jewellary is high during festivals. Even the bank deposits and bank clearings are affected by seasonal swings. Here, the 'seasons' may be taken as weeks. Similarly, traffic is maximum during rush hours; so 'seasons' are hours in this case. The "seasons' may be seconds in bacterial population growth.

The seasonal variations may be either due to natural forces such as festivals climatic conditions or due to customs, fashions or habits of the people. These factors operate in a regular and periodic manner where the period of recurrence is generally one year. Following graph shows seasonal variations in the sales of umbrellas (Y) from a store.

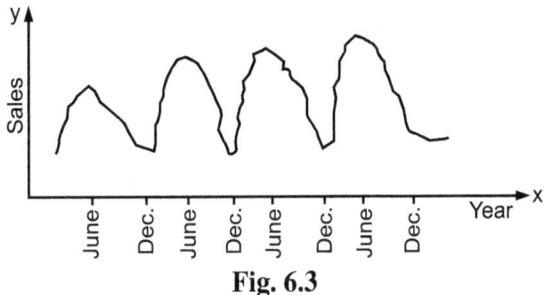

Fig. 6.3

Note that the sales attain maximum in the month of June every year.

Remark : The amplitude may differ from cycle to cycle.

The study of seasonal variations is of prime importance in many time series. Particularly, when the trend is stagnant, seasonal variations become predominant component.

Seasonal variations are extremely useful in marketing and business field in many ways. For example, during summer sales of fans, coolers, refrigerator, cold-drinks, ice-creams increase considerably and reach the peak. Business man has to take care of inventory for seasonal peaks, he has to employ adequate number of salesmen, he has to schedule purchases and sales, he has to arrange for clearance sale, he has to advertise, and give discount on prices for off seasons, he has to arrange for additional finances during seasons. Similarly, bank managers has to arrange for proper cash flow during the beginning of month, festivals.

3. Cyclical variations (c) :

Cyclical variations in a time series are the fluctuations which repeat over a time period of more than one year. The cyclical variations may not be necessarily uniformly periodic. The amplitude of variation also changes from cycle to cycle. That is, the ups and downs may occur at different intervals of time. These fluctuations are typically observed in business. Boom in business is followed by depression and vice-versa. The period of a 'Cycle' is about 7 to 10 years. There are four phases in a cycle. (i) prosperity (boom), (ii) recession, (iii) depression, (iv) recovery. Fig. 6.4 depicts the cyclical variations comprising of these four phases.

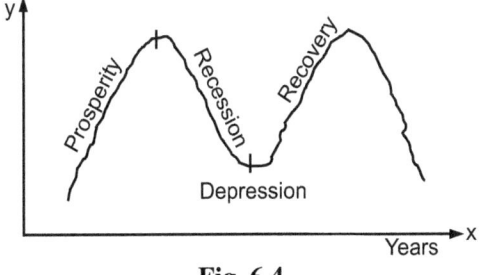

Fig. 6.4

Time series relating to productions, wages bank deposits etc. exhibit cyclical variations in a prominant way.

Business cycle is the main cause behind the cyclical variations. Imbalances in economy, import and export facilities and policies, availability of loans, inflation, over-development, decreasing efficiency of personnel, automation, business competitions are some reasons which result into business cycle.

Difference between 'seasonal variations' and 'cyclical variations' :

(i) **Reason :** Seasonal variations are evident due to seasons, festivals, customs and needs of people. Whereas cyclical variations exist due to business cycle.

(ii) **Period :** Seasonal variations are up and down swings of shorter period less than one year. Cyclical variations are of longer period 5 to 10 years or higher in some series. Seasonal variations occur more or less regularly at a certain time period. Cyclical variations may differ in the period from cycle to cycle. They do not occur at a specific period. Both seasonal variations and cyclical variations do not have successive cycles of uniform amplitude.

(iii) Comparatively intensity of seasonal variations less than that of cyclical variation.

4. Irregular or Erratic Variations (I) :

Irregular variations are unpredictable and are the results of unforeseen forces or abnormal events. These variation therefore do not follow any pattern; neither in their magnitude nor in the time of their occurrence. These variations are generally caused by calamities such as earthquakes, famines floods, epidemics or abnormalities such as war, stikes, lockouts etc. Hence, they are also called as 'episodic fluctuation'.

Irregural variations occur randomly hence they are also called as 'random variations'. These variations are mixed-up with seasonal and cyclical variations. The reasons behind irregular variations are non-recurring hence is difficult to isolate such variations and analyse. Sometimes, the irregular variations are minor in magnitude while in others they are so large due to abnormal reasons, that they produce cyclical variations.

6.4 Analysis of Time Series

Time series analysis, in simple words means, study of time series. The purpose of time series analysis is two fold.

(i) Identifying the above four components which cause variations in the variable, and

(ii) Isolating, studying and measuring each of them independently.

Models for Time Series :

In analysis, it is required to know how the components interact and give the joint effect which is done with the help of models. Generally, two types of models are used to describe a time series Y_t.

1. Additive Model :

Let Y denote the original time series and T, S, C, I the four components. Under additive model,

$$Y = T + S + C + I$$

This model assumes that the original time series is mere sum of the four components. In turn, it assumes that the four components have no interaction and act independently. Whenever, the changes are by a constant amount, additive model is used.

Illustration : Suppose a time series has components Trend (T) = 300, Seasonal variation (S) = 90, Cyclical variation (C) = 20 and Irregular component (I) = – 15 at fixed point t then under additive model

$$Y_t = T + S + C + I = 300 + 90 + 20 - 15 = 395$$

The assumption in the additive model is that the components are non-interactive or independent is non-realistic. In order to overcome these limitations, multiplicative model is popularly used.

2. Multiplicative Model :

Under this model, the original time series Y is assumed to be the effect of the four components working interactively. Hence,

$$Y = T \cdot S \cdot C \cdot I$$

In Economics, wherever the changes are by a constant rate, multiplicative model is used.

Using either of these models, the components are eliminated one by one. This elimination helps in isolating the factors from one another and measuring them independently.

There are other types of models also which involve some components additive and some components multiplicative.

For example, $Y = T \times C + S \times I$, $Y = T \times C \times S + I$.

These are beyond the scope of this book.

Illustration : Suppose a time series with multiplicative model has components Trend (T) = 500, Seasonal variation (S) = 1.3, Cyclical variation (C) = 1.2 and Irregular variation (I) = 0.9 at a certain time point t then

$$Y_t = T \times S \times C \times I = 500 \times 1.3 \times 1.2 \times 0.9 = 702.$$

Note :
1. In additive model the components are expressed in terms of actual absolute (not relative) values and Y_t is the algebraic sum of them. However, in multiplicative model the components except trend are interms of relative values or rates or percentage of trend. The trend is expressed in terms of actual value. Y_t in this case is product of all components.
2. Under the additive model the algebraic sum of seasonal variations in a year is zero per year ($\sum S = 0$, per year), that of cyclical variation per cycle is zero ($\sum C = 0$, per year). In the long run sum of irregular variations ($\sum I = 0$).
3. Multiplicative model can be converted to additive if we take logarithms

$$Y = T \cdot S \cdot C \cdot I$$
$$\log Y = \log T + \log S + \log C + \log I$$

6.5 Utility of Time Series Analysis

Time series analysis is of paramount interest in various disciplines such as economics, business, social sciences. Its uses are discussed below :

(i) **Past behaviour :** It enables to describe the past behaviour of the variables. Time series analysis reveals the forces working behind the series such as technological and economical developments, changes in import and export policies.

(ii) Forecasting : Forecasting is one of the important use of analysis of time series. The forecasting in business plays an important role in planning decision-making, inventory, scheduling of purchases and sales etc.

Isolating and measuring the effects of various components help the investigator to forecast the value of variable in future with fairly good reliability.

(iii) Comparison : Time series analysis facilitates the comparison between the two related time series. For example,

(a) Prices of gold and prices of shares,

(b) National income and cost of living indices.

Comparison between actual and expected performance can be made comparison between two similar time series at two different places.

6.6 Measurement of Trend

Trend can be estimated by several methods of which we consider the following. (1) Graphical Method (2) method of Semi Averages (3) Method of Moving Averages (4) Least Squares Method.

(i) Graphical Method of Free Hand Curve Fitting : This method of estimating trend is also known as "free hand curve fitting" method. It consists of (i) plotting the time series data by taking 'time' on X-axis and the variable of interest on Y-axis and (ii) drawing a smooth free hand curve which would exhibit the long term tendency in the series. [see Fig. 6.5]

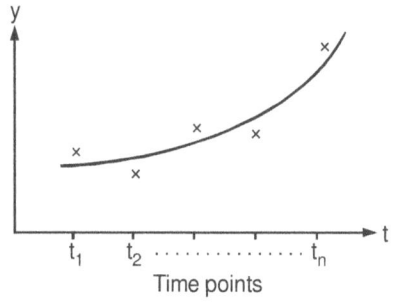

Fig. 6.5

While drawing the curve the following points should be taken care of :

(i) It should be a smooth curve.

(ii) It should pass through as many as points it can.

(iii) Almost equal number of points should lie on either side of the curve. So that the curve is as close as possible to the points.

(iv) The sum of vertical deviations from the curve should be approximately zero.

(v) Almost equal number of cycles should be on the either side of the curve.

(vi) If the curve bisects the cycles then the area between cycles and curve on both sides should approximately same.

(vii) Fluctuations of smaller magnitude be ignored.

Merits of Graphical Method :
  (i) It is the simplest and crudest method of estimating trend.
  (ii) It saves time and does not need any mathematical calculations.

Demerits of Graphical Method :
  (i) It is rather subjective method. Different persons can get different curves for the same time series.
  (ii) Due to this subjectivity, it is dangerous to use this method for forecasting purposes.

(2) Method of Semi Averages : In this method data is divided into two equal parts with respect to time. If there are n even number of data points we can make two equal parts each containing n/2 data points. In case n is odd (n = 2m + 1) then we omit the middle value and make two parts. Each will have m data points.

We compute average of $\bar{y}_t$ for each of the part. We plot the graph of y_t and against t. The average of each part is plotted against the centre of the respective period. Suppose the mid-point of first period is t' and the respective average is $\bar{y}'$ and the mid-point of second part is t" with the average $\bar{y}''$. Thus we get two points (t', $\bar{y}'$) and (t", $\bar{y}''$). The line joining these points is considered as trend line. The line can be extended as per requirement for future as well as for past.

Illustration 1 : Fit the trend to the following data using the method of semi-averages.

Year	2001	2002	2003	2004	2005	2006	2007	2008	2009	2010
Profit (in lakhs)	202	226	228	238	256	261	265	285	289	315

Solution : We divide data into two parts or groups. The first group of the years is 2001 to 2005. The centre is 2003. The second group of the years is 2006 to 2010. The centre is 2008. Following table gives the original values and trend.

	Year	Observations y_t	Trend $\bar{y}_t$ by semi-average
Group I	2001	202	
	2002	226	
	2003 t'	228	230 = $\bar{y}'$
	2004	238	
	2005	256	
Group II	2206	261	
	2007	265	
	2008 t"	285	283 = $\bar{y}''$
	2009	289	
	2010	315	

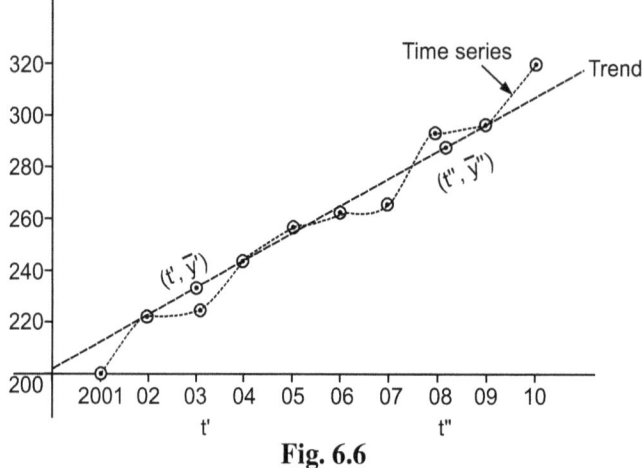

Fig. 6.6

Merits :
(1) The method is objective as compared to graphical method.
(2) The method is simple to use.

Demerits :
The method assumes the time series is linear. It may not be true in many cases.

(3) Method of Moving Averages : Measurement of trend is possible only when fluctuations arising due to other three components of time series (viz. seasonal, cyclical and irregular) are smoothened out. This is nicely achieved in the method of moving averages. It consists of obtaining arithmetic means of successive overlapping values. The method proceeds as follows.

Suppose the following is a time series.

$$\begin{array}{ccccc} \text{Time} & t_1 & t_2 & \ldots & t_n \\ Y & Y_1 & Y_2 & \ldots & Y_n \end{array}$$

Suppose, we want to find moving averages of period 'm' say. This 'm' called period of moving average is generally taken equal to the time interval for which two successive maxima of y are seen.

The series of moving averages is calculated as follows.

$$\text{First M.A.} = \frac{Y_1 + Y_2 + \ldots\ldots + Y_m}{m}$$

$$\text{Second M.A.} = \frac{Y_2 + Y_3 + \ldots\ldots + Y_{m+1}}{m}$$

$$\text{Third M.A.} = \frac{Y_3 + Y_4 + \ldots\ldots + Y_{m+2}}{m} \quad \text{and so on.}$$

Two cases arise.

(i) m odd : In this situation moving average is placed against the mid value of the time interval it covers. For example, if m = 5, the moving average will be placed in front of the third value in the group.

(ii) m even : When m is even, the mid value does not coincide with the original time series, in order to make it coincide with the time series, moving averages of order two are again taken. This process is called centering.

Illustrative Examples

Example 6.1 : The following data give the sales (in '000 ₹) of a company for the years 1985-1994.

Year (t)	1985	1986	1987	1988	1989	1990	1991	1992	1993	1994
Sales (y)	50	82	65	86	70	52	90	65	87	43

Calculate :
(i) 3 yearly moving averages.
(ii) 5 yearly moving averages.
(iii) Plot the original time series alongwith the 3 yearly and 5 yearly moving averages.

Solution :

t	y	3 yearly total	3 yearly m.a.	5 yearly total	5 yearly m.a.
1985	50	–	–	–	–
1986	82	197	65.67	–	–
1987	65	233	77.67	353	70.6
1988	86	221	73.67	355	71.0
1989	70	208	69.33	363	72.6
1990	52	212	70.67	363	72.6
1991	90	207	60.00	264	72.8
1992	65	242	80.67	337	67.4
1993	87	195	65.00	–	–
1994	43	–	–	–	–

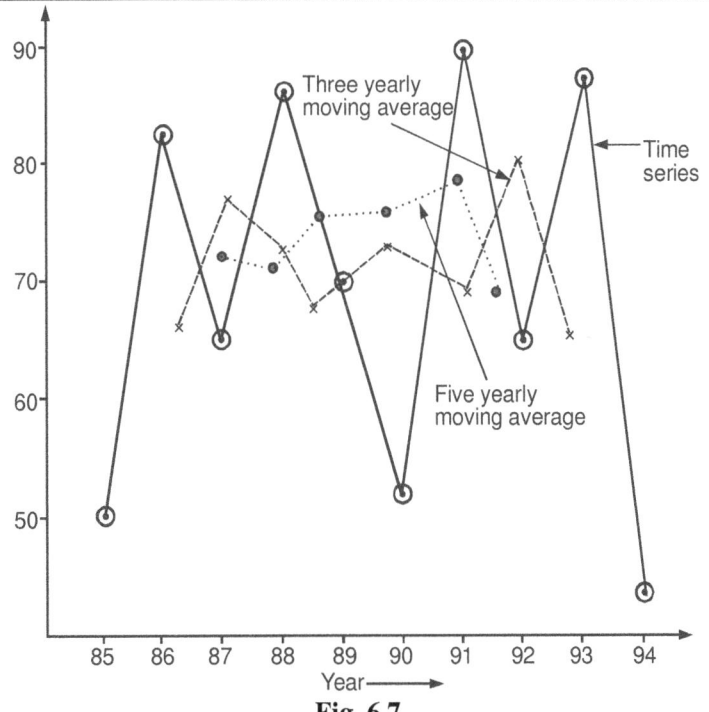

Fig. 6.7

Obtaining Moving Averages using MS-EXCEL

We exhibit how to compute moving averages using MS-EXCEL for the data in example.

Procedural Steps :

1. Enter 'years' in column A (Fig. 6.8)
2. Enter 'sales' in column B.
3. Click Tools at menu bar. It gives the following window Fig. 6.9.

	A	B	C	D
1				
2				
3	Year	Sales	3-Yearly M.A.	5-Yearly M.A.
4				
5	1985	50		
6	1986	82	65.6667	
7	1987	65	77.66667	70.6
8	1988	86	73.66667	71
9	1989	70	69.33333	72.6
10	1990	52	70.66667	72.6
11	1991	90	69	72.8
12	1992	65	80.66667	67.4
13	1993	87	65	
14	1994	43		

Fig. 6.8

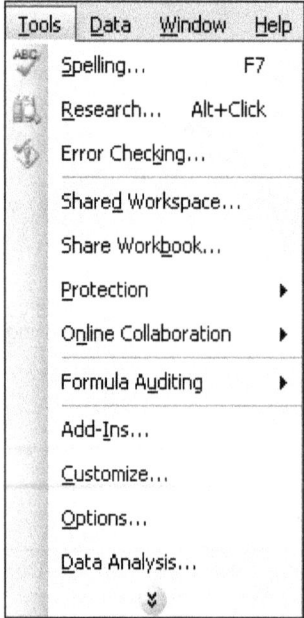

Fig. 6.9

4. Select Data Analysis , which gives Fig. 6.10.

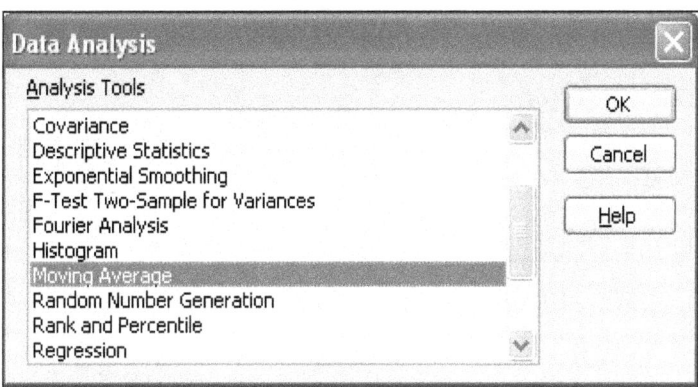

Fig. 6.10

5. Select Moving average , which gives dialogue box Fig. 6.11.

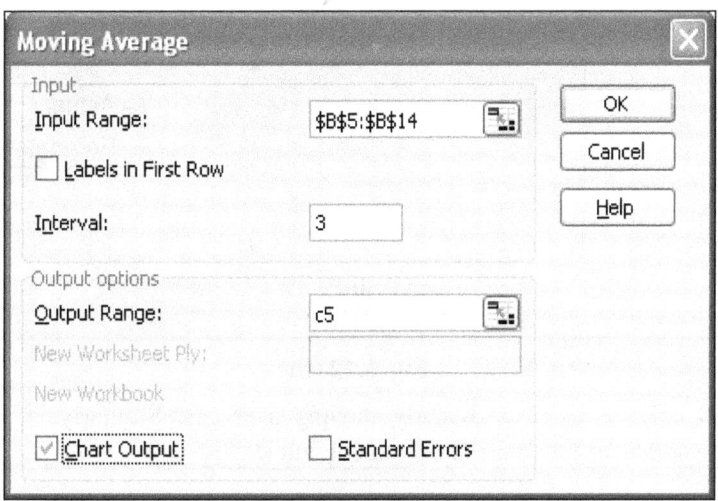

Fig. 6.11

Select input range   B5 : B14

Interval   3   (Period of moving average)

Output range   C5

Select   √   chart output.

It gives graph of original data, moving averages. Fig. 6.12 and 6.13.

3 Yearly moving average

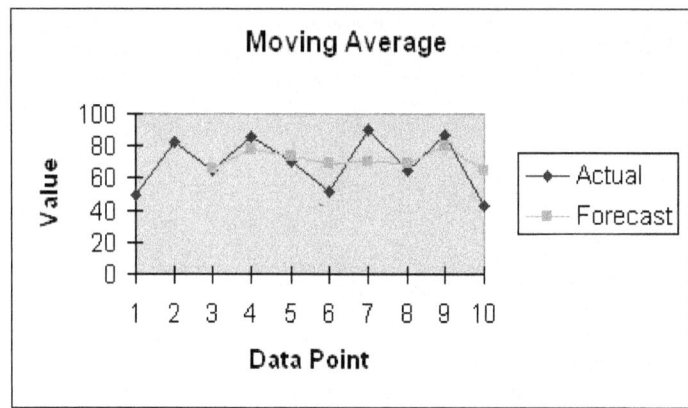

Fig. 6.12 (a)

5 Yearly moving average

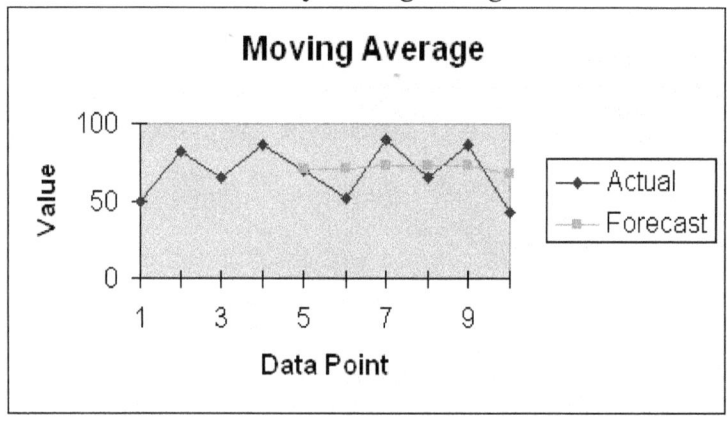

Fig. 6.12 (b)

In Fig. 6.8 column C gives 3-yearly moving averages. Similarly, 5 yearly moving averages can be obtained. Those are shown in column D.

Note : To get moving averages of even order centreing is not done automatically in MS-EXCEL, however we need to take two point moving average.

Example 6.2 : Following data relate to the average retail price ₹ per kg of ground nut during four quarters of 5 years 1998-2002.

Year	Quarters			
	I	II	III	IV
1998	40	35	38	40
1999	42	37	39	38
2000	41	35	38	42
2001	45	36	36	41
2002	44	38	38	42

Obtain 4 point moving average.

Solution : The period of moving average is even, hence it needs to be centred. Thus in the beginning we find 4 point moving average and then 2 point average of these averages. It will ensure centering.

Calculation of moving averages

Year	Quarter	Price Y_t	4-point moving total	4-point moving average	2-point moving total	Centred moving average
1998	I	40				
	II	35				
	III	38	153	38.25	77	38.50
	IV	40	155	38.75	78	39.00
1999	I	42	157	39.25	78.75	39.38
	II	37	158	39.50	78.50	39.25
	III	39	156	39.00	77.75	38.88
	IV	38	155	38.75	77	38.50
2000	I	41	153	38.25	76.25	38.13
	II	35	152	38.00	77	38.50
	III	38	156	39.00	79	39.50
	IV	42	160	40.00	80.25	40.13
2001	I	45	161	40.25	80	40.00
	II	36	159	39.75	79.25	39.63
	III	36	158	39.50	78.75	39.38
	IV	41	157	39.25	79	39.50
2002	I	44	159	39.75	80	40
	II	38	161	40.25	80.75	40.38
	III	38	162	40.50		
	IV	42				

Remark : The 4 point centred moving average is equivalent to a weighted moving average of period 5 with weight 1, 2, 2, 2, 1.

The first centred moving average = 38.50. The five point weighted moving average with weights 1, 2, 2, 2, 1 is

$$\frac{40 + (2 \times 35) + (2 \times 38) + (2 \times 40) + 42}{8} = 38.5$$

$$\text{Note that first M.A.} = \frac{Y_1 + Y_2 + Y_3 + Y_4}{4} = \bar{Y}_1$$

$$\text{Second M.A.} = \frac{Y_2 + Y_3 + Y_4 + Y_5}{4} = \bar{Y}_2$$

$$\text{Centred total} = \bar{Y}_1 + \bar{Y}_2$$

$$\text{Centred M.A.} = \frac{\bar{Y}_1 + \bar{Y}_2}{2} = \frac{1}{2}\left[\frac{Y_1 + Y_2 + Y_3 + Y_4}{4} + \frac{Y_2 + Y_3 + Y_4 + Y_5}{4}\right]$$

$$= \frac{1}{8}[Y_1 + 2Y_2 + 2Y_3 + 2Y_4 + Y_5]$$

= Weighted average of Y_1, Y_2, Y_3, Y_4, Y_5 with weights 1, 2, 2, 2, 1 respectively.

Merits and Demerits of Moving Average Method :

Merits :
- (i) The method is simple and easy to work with.
- (ii) The method is not subjective.
- (iii) A proper choice of period can remove seasonal, cyclical fluctuations completely and irregular fluctuations to some extent.
- (iv) The method is flexible in the sense that if few more observations are added to the series, the moving averages obtained earlier remain the same.

Demerits :
- (i) The method can not provide trend values for some initial and last points of time.
- (ii) It can not be used for forecasting purposes.
- (iii) The moving average method estimates the trend fairly well only if the trend is linear, and the ups and downs in the time series are periodic.

(4) Least Squares Method : The method of least square is an analytical method used to estimate the trend values. The relationship between the variable 'Y' and time 't' is assumed according to a mathematical function.

For example,
- (i) $Y = a + bt$ (Linear trend)
- (ii) $Y = a + bt + ct^2$ (Parabolic trend)
- (iii) $Y = ab^t$ (Exponential trend)
- or $\log Y = \log a + t \log b$ (Log-linear trend)
- (iv) $Y = a_0 + a_1 t + a_2 t^2 + \ldots + a_n t^n$ (n^{th} degree polynomial trend)
- (v) $Y = a + bc^t$ (Modified exponential trend)
- (vi) $Y = a \cdot b^{c^t}$ (Gompertz curve)
- (vii) $Y = \dfrac{k}{1 + e^{a + bt}}$ (Logistic curve)

How to choose proper type of trend equation ?

The guidelines to choose proper type or trend equation are as follows :

One can use graphical method to get an idea about the nature of curve whether it is straight line or second degree of growth curves such as exponential Gompertz, Logistic curves.

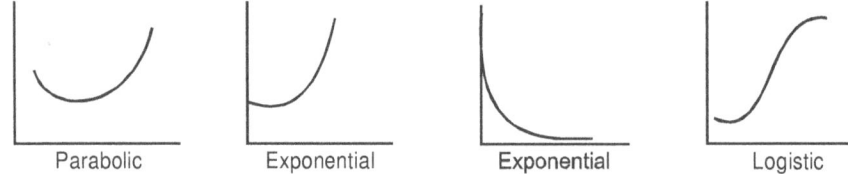

| Parabolic | Exponential | Exponential | Logistic |

Fig. 6.13

Once, the curve to be fitted is decided, one can use least square method to fit the curve and estimate constants involved in the equation. The least square method takes care to reduce the sum of squares of errors, where error is the difference between actual value and estimate given by the equation. The method ensures that the points in the data are as close as possible to the curve.

Note : Modified exponential, Gompertz curve and Logistic curves are called as growth curves. These give best fit for population data or biomass production data.

(B) Using software : Residual sum of squares : One can fit the curves by trial and error method. The measure of goodness of fit is the residual error sum of squares (S.S.E.). Smaller the R.S.S. is the fit. Software gives :

$$R^2 = 1 - \frac{\text{Residual Sum of Squares (S.S.E.)}}{\text{Total Sum of Squares (S.S.T.)}}$$

Thus large the R^2 better is the fit. The value of R^2 is readily available by just clicking the menu in MS-EXCEL. There is a separate software package called as 'curve fit'. One can make it's best use in fitting of most approximate curve.

This problem can be looked upon as the problem in regression, where Y is the dependent variable and t, the time, as independent variable. Hence, the methods of fitting a straight line, is same as finding regression line of Y only.

Fitting of Linear Trend :

Consider, the model $Y = a + bt$, where a and b are the constants to be estimated. The least squares method obtains the values of a and b such that the sum $\sum (Y - a - bt)^2$ is minimum, where the sum is taken over all pointing the time series. If we change the origin for the variable t and consider $t' = t - \bar{t}$ then the straight line can be written as,

$$Y = a + at'$$

Then the solutions are,

$$\hat{b} = \frac{\sum t' Y}{\sum t'^2}$$

$$\hat{a} = \frac{\sum Y}{n} = \bar{Y}$$

Where,

$$t' = t - \bar{t} \; ; \; \bar{t} = \frac{\sum t_i}{n}$$

Example 6.3 : Fit a trend line to the following time series by the least squares method.

Year (t)	1998	1999	2000	2001	2002
Production (Y) : (in lakh tons)	12	20	28	32	50

Obtain the trend value of production for 2005 and 2007.

Solution : Let the trend line be $Y = a + bt$. Since, $\bar{t} = 2000$, $t' = t - 1998$.

t	y	t'	y'	t'²
1998	12	−2	−24	4
1999	20	−1	−20	1
2000	28	0	00	0
2001	32	1	32	1
2002	50	2	100	4
Total	142	0	88	10

∴ $\hat{b} = \frac{\sum t'y}{\sum t'^2} = \frac{88}{10} = 8.8$

$\hat{b} = \bar{y} = \frac{142}{5} = 28.4$

Hence, the trend line is

$Y = 28.4 + 8.8 (t - 2000) = 8.8t - 17571.6$.

Using this, we estimate y for (i) 2005 and (ii) 2007.

(i) $t = 2005$

then, $y = 28.4 + 8.8 (5) = 72.4$ lakh tons.

(ii) $t = 2007$

$y = 28.4 + 8.8 (7) = 90$ lakh tons

Note : 1. The above trend equation $Y = a + bt$ is yearly trend equation. However, sometimes we require seasonal trend estimates. If seasons are months then monthly trend equation is $Y = \frac{a}{12} + \frac{b}{144} t$; t : month and corresponding value of Y is monthly trend estimate. In the above example,

Yearly equation is $y = 28.4 + 8.8 t'$ t' : 1st year, origin : 2000

Monthly equation is $y = \frac{28.4}{12} + \frac{8.8}{144} t'$ t': 1st month, origin : 1st July 2000.

2. Similarly, quarterly trend equation is given by $Y = \frac{a}{4} + \frac{b}{48} t$.

t = quarter, Y = quarterly trend estimate.

Merits of Least Squares Method :

(i) The method is very objective and hence, it is the most popular and widely used method.

(ii) The method gives trend values for all time periods.

(iii) The method can very well be used for forecasting purposes.

(iv) The method can be used to estimate the values of the variable for intermediate time points also.

(v) If $Y = a + bt$, linear trend is fitted to the data, then value of b provides the rate of change in the variable Y. In fact, it is the regression coefficients of Y on t.

Demerits of least Squares Method :

(i) Choice of fit viz linear, parabolic or exponential is difficult. It needs to plot the time series. The predictions are based on the type of model fitted. If the choice is wrong, the estimates are not reliable.

(ii) The method requites heavy calculations and is not easy to understand.

(iii) If some more data points are added to the original time series, then entire calculations are to be done again to obtain the trend line. Thus, it is less flexible.

6.7 Measurement of Seasonal Variations

In time series, seasonal variations are those periodic fluctuations which occurs regularly within a period of one year. For instance, demand for cold-drinks in goes up in summer and goes down in winter. During Diwali holidays, there may be increasing demand for sweets and clothes. A business executive has to study the nature of such type of variations in order to take policy decisions regarding inventory, purchase and sale schedule etc.

The important reasons for measurement of seasonal variations are as follows :
(i) To separate the seasonal variation, assuming that those are superimposed on time series. It gives the amount of changes due to seasonal factors in original time series.
(ii) To eliminate the effects of seasonal factors from time series. So that the values in the time series free from seasonal factors can be computed.

The following are different methods of estimating seasonal component of a time series.
(a) Method of simple averages.
(b) Ratio to moving averages method.
(c) Ratio to trend method.
(d) Method of link relatives.

Note : Methods (a) and (b) are to be covered in theory and (c), (d) are to be covered in practicals.

6.7.1 Method of Simple Averages

It is the simplest method of estimating seasonal variations. The stepwise procedure is as follows :

(i) Arrange the data seasonwise (quarters, months, days) for all the years.

(ii) Compute the totals for each season.

(iii) Compute the arithmetic mean for each season. If there are k seasons then $\bar{X}_1, \bar{X}_2, ..., \bar{X}_k$ are means of k seasons.

(iv) Compute the mean $\bar{X}$ of seasonal means $\bar{X} = \dfrac{\bar{X}_1 + \bar{X}_2 + ... + \bar{X}_k}{k}$.

In particular, for monthly indices $\bar{X} = \dfrac{\bar{X}_1 + \bar{X}_2 + ... + \bar{X}_{12}}{12}$

Similarly, for quarterly indices $\bar{X} = \dfrac{\bar{X}_1 + \bar{X}_2 + \bar{X}_3 + \bar{X}_4}{4}$

(v) The seasonal index for i^{th} season = $S_i = \dfrac{\bar{X}_i}{\bar{X}} \times 100$ $i = 1, 2, ..., k$.

Thus we get $S_1, S_2, ..., S_k$ the seasonal indices for k seasons. The seasonal index is a expressed as percentage of $\bar{X}$.

Remarks : (1) The number of indices is equal to the number of seasons. Thus number of monthly, quarterly and daily indices will be 12, 4, 7 respectively.

(2) The sum of indices is $\sum S_i = 100\,k$. In particular, sum of monthly indices = 1200, sum of quarterly indices = 400.

(3) The indices obtained in this method give rough estimate of seasonal variation due to the reason that the trend is not eliminated. If trend is constant and cycles are absent then the seasonal indices obtained by simple averages will be proper.

Merits :

(1) It is the easiest method.

(2) It is simple to compute seasonal indices by simple averages.

Demerits :

(1) Trend and cyclical variations are not eliminated in this method, assuming that those are insignificant. The assumption is non-realistic.

(2) The seasonal indices by this method gives only rough estimates.

Example 7 : Obtain the monthly indices for the following data on production of a commodity by method of simple averages.

Month	Production in lakhs of tonnes in years		
	2010	2011	2012
January	16	19	20
February	15	18	19
March	14	17	18
April	18	20	20
May	19	20	19
June	19	19	21
July	20	21	20
August	17	16	17
September	15	17	14
October	14	16	14
November	16	17	15
December	19	18	19

Solution : We find monthly total for every month.

Let T_i : Total of values for i^{th} month; $i = 1, 2, \ldots 12$

and $\bar{T} = \dfrac{\sum T_i}{12}$ = Average of monthly totals.

The table given below shows that in this example $\bar{T} = 53$.

Hence, seasonal index for i^{th} month $= \dfrac{T_i}{\bar{T}} \times 100$; $i = 1, 2, \ldots 12$.

Simple averages method for computation of seasonal indices.

Month	Production in lakhs of tonnes			Monthly Total (T_i)	Seasonal index $T_i = \dfrac{T_i}{\bar{T}} \times 100$
	2010	2011	2012		
(1)	(2)	(3)	(4)	(5)	
January	16	19	20	55	103.7736
February	15	18	19	52	98.1132
March	14	17	18	49	92.4528
April	18	20	20	58	109.4340
May	19	20	19	58	109.4340
June	19	19	21	59	111.3207
July	20	21	20	61	115.0943
August	17	16	17	50	94.3396
September	15	17	14	46	86.7925
October	14	16	14	44	83.0189
November	16	17	15	48	90.5660
December	19	18	19	56	105.6604
Total	–	–	–	636	1200.000
Average	–	–	–	$\bar{T} = \dfrac{636}{12} = 53$	100

Example 8 : The following are the quarterly sales in thousands of rupees for different years. Compute seasonal indices for these data using method of simple averages.

Quarter	Year					
	2002	2003	2004	2005	2006	2007
I	36	36	36	41	42	43
II	40	42	40	47	45	47
III	35	38	38	39	43	44
IV	37	49	41	46	46	48

Solution : Computation of seasonal indices.

Year	Quarters				Total
	I	II	III	IV	
2002	36	40	35	37	–
2003	36	42	38	39	–
2004	36	40	38	41	–
2005	41	47	39	46	–
2006	42	45	43	46	–
2007	43	47	44	48	–
Total (T_i)	234	261	237	267	999
Average ($\bar{X}_i$)	39	43.5	39.5	44.5	166.5
Seasonal index = $\dfrac{X_i}{\bar{X}} \times 100$	$\dfrac{39}{41.625} \times 100$ = 93.6937	$\dfrac{43.5}{41.625} \times 100$ = 104.5045	$\dfrac{39.5}{41.625} \times 100$ = 94.8949	$\dfrac{44.5}{41.625} \times 100$ = 106.9069	400

$\bar{X} = \dfrac{166.5}{4} = 41.625$

6.7.2 Ratio to Moving Average Method

The method of simple averages has a drawback that it does not eliminate the trend component. The drawback is removed in 'ratio to moving average method'.

In this method trend is first estimated using moving average of the period equal to the number of seasons. Under the multiplicative model trend is eliminated by taking ratio of Y_t to T (trend estimate) on the other hand under additive model trend is removed just by subtracting trend estimate from Y_t. The residuals are used for determining the seasonal variations.

We describe the stepwise procedure of finding seasonal indices by ratio to moving average method.

(i) Calculate moving average of period k (where k is number of seasons). If k is even obtain centred moving average.

(ii) Eliminate trend by expressing data as percentage of moving average (to be centred if essential). In other words compute

$$\frac{\text{Original value } (Y_t)}{\text{Moving average}} \times 100$$

(Here we assume that the model is multiplicative). Due to moving averages cyclical variations are removed. Thus we are left with

$$\frac{Y}{T \cdot C} \times 100 = \frac{T \cdot S \cdot C \cdot I}{T \cdot C} \times 100 = S \cdot I \times 100$$

(iii) Arrange these percentage seasonwise (monthwise or quarterwise as the case may be) for all the years and find the average (either arithmetic mean or median) for each season. Let us denote the seasonwise averages by $S_1, S_2, ..., S_k$. This S_i is preliminary seasonal index for the ith season. The process of averaging eliminates irregular variations. Thus only seasonal variations are left.

(iv) Compute $\sum S_i$, if $\sum S_i \neq 100\ k$, determine adjustment factor $C = \dfrac{100\ k}{\sum S_i}$. Find adjusted seasonal indices as $C\ S_i$.

It will ensure that the sum of adjusted indices is 100 k.

In particular for monthly indices, $C = \dfrac{1200}{\sum S_i}$, for quarterly indices, $C = \dfrac{400}{\sum S_i}$.

Note :

(1) To obtain S_i median may be used as average, since it is least affected by extreme values.

(2) If the model is additive the procedure is slightly different it is as follows :

 (i) Eliminate trend by subtracting moving average from Y_t.

 (ii) Average these differences seasonwise for all years and find average. Let the averages be $S_1, S_2, \ldots, S_k$. S_i is the preliminary seasonal index for i^{th} season.

 (iii) Compute $\sum S_i$. If $\sum S_i \neq 0$, determine adjustment factor $C = \dfrac{\sum S_i}{k}$. Finally, the adjusted seasonal index $= S_i - C$. This will ensure that sum of adjusted seasonal indices is zero (for additive model). Some seasonal indices will be positive and other will be zero or negative.

Merits :

(1) Among all the methods of obtaining seasonal indices ratio to moving average is considered to be the best and most satisfactory. Because the indices obtained by this methods generally do not fluctuate much as compared to other methods.

(2) Due to moving averages cyclical variations are also smoothened.

(3) The method is flexible.

(4) As compared to the method of simple averages the procedure of obtaining seasonal indices by this method is more logical.

Demerits :

(1) The drawback of moving average is that we do not get trend estimate for first k/2 seasons and last k/2 seasons. Thus, the method does not use the data completely.

(2) Cyclical variations are not regular in periodicity and amplitude, hence those are not totally wiped out.

Example 10 : Compute seasonal indices using the ratio to moving average method for the data given below :

Year \ Quarter	I	II	III	IV
1998	680	620	610	630
1999	650	580	660	610
2000	680	630	630	670

Solution :

Table : Computations of ratio to moving average

Year and quarter	Original values	4 quarterly moving totals	2 point moving total of col. (3)	Centred 12 quarterly M.A. $(5) = \dfrac{\text{col. (4)}}{8}$	Ratio of M.A. $\left[\dfrac{\text{col (2)}}{\text{col (5)}} \times 100\right]$ = col. (6)
(1)	(2)	(3)	(4)	(5)	(6)
1998 Ist	680	–	–	–	–
IInd	620	2540	–	–	–
IIIrd	610	2510	5050	631.25	96.63366
IVth	630	2470	4980	622.50	101.20481
1999 Ist	650	2520	4990	623.75	104.20841
IInd	580	2500	5020	627.50	92.43027
IIIrd	660	2530	5030	628.75	104.97017
IVth	610	2580	5110	638.75	95.49902
2000 Ist	680	2550	5130	641.25	106.04288
IInd	630	2610	5160	645.00	97.67441
IIIrd	630	–	–	–	–
IVth	670	–	–	–	–

Table : Computation of seasonal indices

Quarter No.	Ratio to M.A. for years			Preliminary seasonal indices (A.M.)	Adjusted seasonal indices (S_i) = [col (5)] [C] C = [1.0017]
	1998	1999	2000	(5)	(6)
(1)	(2)	(3)	(4)		
I	–	104.21	106.04	105.13	105.31
II	–	92.43	97.67	95.05	95.21
III	96.63	104.97	–	100.80	100.97
IV	101.20	95.50	–	98.35	98.52
Total	–	–		399.33	400

Correction factor = $\dfrac{400}{\text{Sum of preliminary quarterly indices (sum of col. 5)}} = \dfrac{400}{399.33} = 1.0017$

6.7.3 Ratio to Trend

In this method trend is first estimated using method of least squares. Under the multiplicate model trend is eliminated by taking ratio of Y_t to T (trend estimate) on the other hand under additive model trend is removed just by subtracting trend estimate from Y_t. The residuals are used for determining the seasonal variations.

We describe the stepwise procedure of finding seasonal indices by ratio to trend method.

(i) Estimate yearly trend using method least square. Obtain trend for each season (month, quarter etc.)

(ii) Eliminate trend by expressing data as percentage of trend. In other words compute

$$\frac{\text{Original value } (Y_t)}{\text{Estimate of T}} \times 100$$

(Here we assume that the model is multiplicative).

$$\frac{Y}{T \cdot C} \times 100 = \frac{T \cdot S \cdot C \cdot I}{T \cdot C} \times 100 = S \cdot I \times 100$$

(iii) Arrange these percentage seasonwise (monthwise or quarterwise as the case may be) for all the years and find the average (either arithmetic mean or median) for each season. Let us denote the seasonwise averages by $S_1, S_2, ..., S_k$. This S_i is preliminary seasonal index for the ith season. The process of averaging eliminates irregular and cyclical variations. Thus only seasonal variations are left.

(iv) Compute $\sum S_i$, if $\sum S_i \neq 100 \ k$, determine adjustment factor $C = \frac{100 \ k}{\sum S_i}$. Find adjusted seasonal indices as $C \ S_i$.

It will ensure that the sum of adjusted indices is 100 k.

In particular for monthly indices, $C = \frac{1200}{\sum S_i}$, for quarterly indices, $C = \frac{400}{\sum S_i}$.

Note :

(1) To obtain S_i median may be used as average, since it is least affected by extreme values.

(2) If the model is additive the procedure is slightly different it is as follows :

   (i) Eliminate trend by subtracting moving average from Y_t.

   (ii) Average these differences seasonwise for all years and find average. Let the averages be $S_1, S_2, ..., S_k$. S_i is the preliminary seasonal index for i^{th} season.

   (iii) Compute $\sum S_i$. If $\sum S_i \neq 0$, determine adjustment factor $C = \frac{\sum S_i}{k}$. Finally, the adjusted seasonal index = $S_i - C$. This will ensure that sum of adjusted seasonal indices is zero (for additive model). Some seasonal indices will be positive and other will be zero or negative.

Merits :

There is no loss of data unlike method of moving averages.

Demerits :

The cyclical variations are totally wiped out. Hence, the method is effective if cyclical variations are small in magnitude.

Example 12 : Calculate seasonal variation for the following data on sales, using the ratio to trend method. Estimate the trend using straight line.

Year	First quarter	Second quarter	Third quarter	Fourth quarter
2003	60	80	72	68
2004	68	104	100	88
2005	80	116	108	96
2006	108	152	136	124
2007	160	184	172	164

Solution : First of all we find yearly totals and fit linear trend by method of least square to yearly averages.

Year X	Yearly total scale	Yearly average scale Y	U-X-2005	UY	U²	Trend estimate
(1)	(2)	(3)	(4)	(5)	(6)	(7)
2003	280	70	−2	−140	4	64
2004	360	90	−1	−90	1	88
2005	400	100	0	0	0	112
2006	520	130	1	130	1	136
2007	680	170	2	340	4	160
Total	2240	560	0	240	10	−

Let $Y = a + bX = a' + b'U$, where $U = X - 2005$ the normal equations to fit the line are

$$\sum Y = na' + b'\sum U \text{ gives } 560 = 5a' + b' \times 0, \therefore a' = 112$$

$$\sum UY = a'\sum U + b'\sum U^2 \text{ gives } 240 = a' \times 0 + b' \times 10, \therefore b' = 24$$

∴ The yearly trend equation is

$$Y = 112 + 24\,U.$$

Column (7) can be filled using the trend equation

Yearly increment $= b = 24$

Quarterly independent $= \dfrac{b}{4} = 6$

Trend for the year 2003 is 64. It gives value at the middle of year or at the end of 2nd quarter and at the beginning of 3rd quarter. Since quarterly increment is 6, half quarterly increment is 3. Therefore, at the middle of second quarter the trend is 64 − 3 = 61 and at the middle of third quarter it is 64 + 3 = 67. Shifting trend 6 for every quarter we get quarterly trend. It is given in the following table.

Year 2003

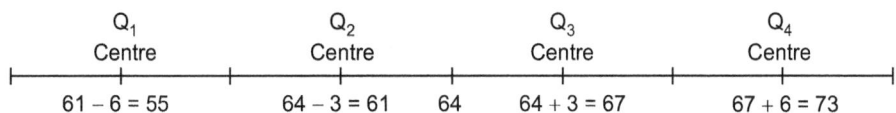

Year and quarter t		Quarterly sales Y	Quarterly trend estimate $\hat{T}$	Ratio to trend $\frac{Y}{\hat{T}} \times 100$
2003	Q_1	60	55	$60/55 \times 100 = 109.09$
	Q_2	80	61	131.15
	Q_3	72	67	107.46
	Q_4	68	73	93.15
2004	Q_1	68	79	86.08
	Q_2	104	85	122.35
	Q_3	100	94	109.89
	Q_4	88	97	90.72
2005	Q_1	80	103	77.67
	Q_2	116	109	106.42
	Q_3	108	115	93.51
	Q_4	96	121	79.34
2006	Q_1	108	127	85.04
	Q_2	152	133	114.29
	Q_3	136	139	97.84
	Q_4	124	145	85.52
2007	Q_1	160	151	105.96
	Q_2	184	157	117.20
	Q_3	172	163	105.52
	Q_4	164	169	97.94

We arrange the above determined ratio trend values seasonwise in the following table.

	1st quarter	2nd quarter	3rd quarter	4th quarter	
	109.09	131.15	107.46	93.15	
	86.08	122.35	109.85	90.72	
	77.67	106.42	93.91	79.34	
	85.04	114.29	97.84	85.52	
	105.96	117.20	105.52	97.04	
Total	463.84	591.41	514.63	445.77	Total
Arithmetic mean ($\bar{X}_i$)	92.77	118.28	102.93	89.15	**403.13**
Adjusted seasonal indices $(S_i) = C \cdot \bar{X}_i$	92.77×0.99224 $= 92.05$	118.28×0.99224 $= 117.36$	102.93×0.99224 $= 102.13$	89.15×0.99224 $= 88.46$	

Total of arithmetic means of 4 seasons is expected to be 400. Hence seasonwise arithmetic means are treated as seasonal indices (unadjusted). The sum of those arithmetic means is 403.13. To get adjusted seasonal indices we multiply each index by adjustment factor $C = \dfrac{400}{403.13} = 0.99224$.

6.7.4 Method of Link Relatives

This is an altogether different method. It is also called as Pearson's method. In stead of taking the usual (absolute) values, method of link relative considers the relative change in Y_t with respect to preceding value. The average of relative changes give seasonal indices. These relative changes are called as link relatives.

$$\text{Link relative (L.R.)} = \frac{\text{Current value } Y_t}{\text{Preceeding value } Y_{t-1}} \times 100$$

Thus, link relative gives current value as percentage of preceding value.

In particular,

$$\text{Link relative for June 2003} = \frac{\text{Value in June 2003}}{\text{Value in May 2003}} \times 100$$

$$\text{Link relative for third quarter of 2002} = \frac{\text{Value of third quarter of 2002}}{\text{Value of second quarter of 2002}} \times 100$$

Procedure of seasonal indices by link relative method :

1. Convert the original values to link relatives. Except the first value, for which link relative is not obtained.
2. Arrange the link relatives seasonwise for all the years.
3. Compute average (mean or median) of link relatives for every season.

Note : If data pertains to n years, for first season we get n – 1 link relatives hence the average for first season is of n – 1 values, however for second and subsequent (remaining) seasons the average is of n values.

4. The seasonwise k averages of link relatives obtained earlier are to be converted into chain relatives (C.R.) as follows. Chain relative for first season = 100.

$$\text{Chain relative for } i^{th} \text{ season (C.R.)} = \frac{\left(\begin{array}{c}\text{Average link}\\\text{relative for } i^{th}\\\text{season}\end{array}\right) \times \left(\begin{array}{c}\text{Chain relative}\\\text{for } (i-1)^{th} \text{ season}\end{array}\right)}{100} \; ; \; i = 1, 2, ..., k$$

In particular, for monthly indices C.R. for January = 100.

$$\text{C.R. for Feb.} = \frac{(\text{Average link relatives for Feb.}) \times (\text{Chain relative for January})}{100}$$

5. We compute new C.R. for first season based on last season C.R.

$$= \frac{(\text{Average L.R. of } 1^{st} \text{ season}) \times (\text{C.R. of } k^{th} \text{ season})}{100}$$

For example, C.R. of January $= \dfrac{(\text{Average L.R. of January}) \times (\text{C.R. of December})}{100}$

We expect that the new C.R. would be 100. Generally, it is not 100, due to presence of trend. Hence we need to adjust the chain relatives accordingly applying correction factor.

Correction factor, $d = \dfrac{\text{New C.R. for 1}^{st}\text{ season} - 100}{k}$

For monthly indices, $d = \dfrac{\text{New C.R. for Jan.} - 100}{12}$

For quarterly indices, $d = \dfrac{\text{New C.R. for 1}^{st}\text{ quarter} - 100}{4}$

6. Assuming the trend to be linear we obtain corrected C.R. by subtracting d, 2d, 3d, …, (k–1) d from 2nd season C.R., 3rd season. R … and kth season C.R. respectively. In particular for monthly indices subtract d from C.R. of Feb., 2d from C.R. of March and so on 11d from C.R. of Dec. In case of quarterly indices subtract d, 2d, 3d from C.R. of, 2nd, 3rd, 4th season respectively.

Thus the adjusted seasonal C.R. are preliminary seasonal indices.

7. Compute the sum of corrected seasonal C.R., if it is not 100 k, determine adjustment factor, $C = \dfrac{100\,k}{\text{Sum of corrected C.R.}}$

Thus, finally seasonal index for ith season S_i = C (Corrected C.R. of ith season).

In particular, for monthly indices $C = \dfrac{1200}{\text{Sum of corrected C.R.}}$.

Merits :

1. As compared to the method of ratio to moving averages, this method utilises almost entire data. There is a loss of only one link relative.
2. The method is effective if a linear trend is present.

Demerits :

1. The method is not simple as compared to other two methods.
2. The method is not useful when non-linear trend is present. Since, such trend is not removed.
3. Cyclical variations are not removed whereas those are reduced in the method of ratio to moving averages.

Example 11 : The data given below give average quarterly prices of a certain type of wheat (in ₹) for different years. Compute seasonal indices by the link relative method for these data :

Quarter \ Year	I	II	III	IV
1997	15.0	13.0	11.0	15.5
1998	17.5	14.0	11.0	18.0
1999	15.5	14.5	14.0	16.0
2000	15.5	15.5	12.5	17.5
2001	17.0	18.0	13.0	16.5

Solution : Computation of seasonal indices by link relatives method.

Year	Link Relatives				Total
	Ist quarter	IInd quarter	IIIrd quarter	IVth quarter	
1997	–	86.67	84.61	140.91	
1998	112.90	80.00	78.57	163.64	
1999	86.11	93.55	96.55	114.28	–
2000	96.87	100.00	80.65	140.00	
2001	97.14	105.88	72.22	126.92	
A.M. of link relatives	$\frac{393.02}{4} =$ 98.255	$\frac{466.1}{5} = 93.22$	$\frac{412.5}{5} = 82.52$	$\frac{685.75}{5} =$ 137.15	–
Chain relatives	100	$\frac{100 \times 93.22}{100}$ $= 93.22$	$\frac{93.22 \times 82.52}{100}$ $= 76.9251$	105.5027	–
Corrected chain relatives	100	93.22 – d $= 92.304575$	76.9251 – 2d $= 75.09425$	105.5027 – 3d $= 102.75643$	370.15525
Adjusted seasonal indices	108.06276	99.746871	81.148919	111.04143	400

$$\text{Link relative of a quarter} = \frac{\text{Value of current quarter}}{\text{Value of preceding quarter}} \times 100$$

Thus L.R. for quarter II of 1997 $= \frac{13}{15} \times 100 = 86.67$

$$\text{New, C.R. of quarter I} = \frac{(\text{L.R. of quarter I}) \times (\text{C.R. of quarter IV})}{100}$$

$$= \frac{98.255 \times 105.5027}{100} = 103.6617$$

$$\text{Correction factor} = d = \frac{\text{New C.R. for quarter I} - 100}{4}$$

$$= \frac{103.6617 - 100}{4} = 0.915425$$

Total of corrected C.R. = 370.15525

$$C = \frac{400}{\text{Sum of corrected C.R.}} = \frac{400}{370.15525}$$

$$= 1.08063$$

Adjusted quarterly seasonal index = Corrected C.R. × C

Choice of Method :

Among all the methods the ratio to moving averages is the best. It eliminates trend and cyclical variations. Comparing the merits the method is preferred to other methods.

Method of simple averages is the simplest one gives better results only when trend is constant and cyclical variations are negligible.

Method of link relative gives good results when the trend is linear and cyclical variation are insignificant.

Thus taking into account the nature of data, objectives of study the suitable method can be chosen.

Example 13 : Deseasonalise the data using multiplicative model.

Quarter :	Jan. – Mar.	Apr. – Jun.	Jul. – Sept.	Oct. – Dec.
Sales (in thousand ₹.)	660	529.2	418.2	374.4
Seasonal index	132	108	82	78

Solution :

Quarter	Sales Y_t	Seasonal index S_i	Deseasonalised data $\left(\dfrac{Y_t}{S_i} \times 100\right)$
1	660.0	132	$\dfrac{660}{132} \times 100 = 500$
2	529.2	108	$\dfrac{529.2}{108} \times 100 = 490$
3	418.2	82	$\dfrac{418.2}{82} \times 100 = 510$
4	374.4	78	$\dfrac{374.4}{78} \times 100 = 480$

Example 14 : The total sales of a company is expected to be ₹ 60 lakhs during the year, find expected sales in each month given the monthly indices of sales as follows :

Month	Jan.	Feb.	Mar.	April	May	June	July	Aug.	Sept.	Oct.	Nov.	Dec.
Seasonal index	110	105	102	101	99	97	92	90	95	100	101	108

Solution : Yearly sales = ₹ 60 lacks.

$$\text{Average monthly sales} = \frac{60}{12} = ₹ 5 \text{ lacks}$$

$$\text{Monthly estimated sales} = \frac{\text{Average monthly sales} \times \text{Seasonal index}}{100}$$

Month (1)	Seasonal index (2)	Estimated sales = $\frac{5 \times \text{col. 2}}{100}$ ₹ in lacks
Jan.	110	5.50
Feb.	105	5.25
Mar.	102	5.10
April	101	5.05
May	99	4.95
June	97	4.85
July	92	4.60
Aug.	90	4.50
Sept.	95	4.75
Oct.	100	5.00
Nov.	101	4.05
Dec.	108	5.40
Total	1200	60.00

Exercise 6.1

A. **Theory Questions :**
1. What is a time series ? Give four illustrations of time series in different fields.
2. Define 'time series' and give illustrations of time series from various fields.
3. Discuss the importance and utility of time series analysis in various fields.
4. Discuss the four components of time series.
5. Illustrate with examples the following terms :
   (i) Secular trend.
   (ii) Seasonal variations.
   (iii) Cyclical variations.
   (iv) Irregular variations.
6. Explain in detail the meaning of 'time series analysis'.
7. Discuss long-term and short-term fluctuations in analysis of time series.
8. How would you distinguish the cyclical fluctuations from the trend and the seasonal fluctuations ? Give suitable illustrations.
9. Are all 'periodical movements' necessarily seasonal ? Justify your answer with appropriate illustrations.
10. Explain the different components of a time series with illustrations.
11. What do you mean by 'Secular trend' ? Give two illustrations.
12. Distinguish between seasonal variations and cyclical variations.

13. Explain the concepts of additive and multiplicative models in the analysis of time series. Compare their utility.
14. How do the additive and multiplicative models of the time series differ from each other ? Why is the multiplicative model the most commonly used in time series analysis ?
15. Write a note on irregular variations.
16. Mention the component which is predominant in the following time series. Give explanation of your answer :
    (i)   Daily attendance of students in a study hall.
    (ii) Hourly record of the number of customers visiting a restaurant.
    (iii) Prices of shares of a prospering concern.
    (iv) The sales of a departmental store in ₹ over a period of one year.
    (v)   Price of residential constructions.
    (vi) Fall in number of deaths as a result of advances in medical science.
    (vii) Reduced production in a factory due to strike.
    (viii) Sales of ice-cream over a period of one year.
17. Describe the term 'Business cycle'. What are the four phases of business cycle ? What are the subjects of studying business cycles ?
18. Write a note on 'Business Forecasting'.
19. Describe the (i) moving average method and (ii) least square method (iii) method of exponential smoothing used for the estimation of trend.
20. Explain how to fit (i) Straight line trend, (ii) parabolic trend, (iii) exponential trend, (iv) autoregressive models by the method of least square.
21. Explain the following methods of estimating the trend values in a time series.
    (i)   method of moving averages.
    (ii) method of least squares.
    (iii) graphical method.
22. Make a comparison between moving average and exponential smoothing.
23. Explain the difference between the method of moving averages and method of least squares.
24. Explain when the least square method of estimation of trend is suitable as compared to moving average method.
25. Explain how the smoothing constant α is chosen in the method of exponential smoothing.
26. Write notes on (i) business cycle, (ii) seasons in time series.

27. A power meter went out of order in the month of December, 1979. If the Electric Supply Company has a practice of preparing monthly bills, how should it estimate the power consumption for that month ? The data of power consumption per month are available for the last ten years.

28. State whether each of the following statements is true or false. Justify your answer :

    (i) A monthly or quarterly trend equation can not be converted into an yearly trend equation.

    (ii) A logical reasoning for the ratio to trend method can be given under additive model.

    (iii) Cyclical fluctuations are caused by strikes and lockouts only.

    (iv) An overall tendency of rise or fall in a time series is called as secular trend.

    (v) If the trend is absent in a time series then seasonal indices are obtained by the method of ratio to trend by moving averages.

    (vi) A seasonal index of 140 for the month of March means that because of seasonal factors the March value will be 40 per cent above the monthly average for the year.

    (vii) A need for increased wheat production due to constant increase in population is due to seasonal variations.

29. Write a note on selection of proper method of obtaining (i) trend, (ii) seasonal indices.

30. State the uses of estimation of trend.

31. Explain how to estimate monthly sales given the total yearly sales and seasonal indices for months.

32. Explain when centered moving averages are required to be calculated and why ?

B. Numerical Problems:

1. Estimate trend by using (i) 5 yearly moving average, (ii) 4 yearly centered moving average for the following time series.

Year	Gross Capital Assets (in crores ₹)	Year	Gross Capital Assets (in crores ₹)
1976	19.3	1985	19.3
1977	20.9	1986	18.1
1978	17.8	1987	19.5
1979	16.1	1988	19.2
1980	17.6	1989	22.2
1981	17.8	1990	20.9
1982	18.3	1991	21.5
1983	17.3	1992	21.9
1984	21.4		

2. Estimate trend using 4 yearly centered moving average.

Year	1998	1989	1990	1991	1992	1993	1994	1995	1996	1997
Production (in tonnes)	78	73	71	73	75	78	73	77	70	69

3. Compute 5 yearly moving average and estimate trend.

Year	1	2	3	4	5	6	7	8	9	10	11	12
National Income (in crores)	260	270	275	300	310	315	300	290	310	320	335	380

4. Compute (i) 4 yearly centred moving average (ii) 5 yearly moving average for the following data :

Year	1977	1978	1979	1980	1981	1982	1983	1984
Annual Sales (in lakhs)	3.6	4.3	4.3	3.4	4.4	5.4	3.4	2.4

5. Estimate the trend by using 3 yearly moving averages for the following data :

Year	2000	2001	2002	2003	2004	2005	2006	2007	2008	2009
Sales in '000	242	238	252	257	250	273	270	268	288	284

6. Compute 4 yearly centered moving averages for the following data :

Year	1997	1998	1999	2000	2001	2002	2003	2004
Annual Sale (laks of ₹)	36	43	43	34	44	54	34	24

7. Compute 5 yearly moving average for the following data :

Year	2003	2004	2005	2006	2007	2008	2009	2010	2011	2012
Yield of Wheat per acre in quintals	10	11	9	9	10	8	11	11	10	12

8. Calculate trend by 4 yearly centred moving average

Year	2001	2002	2003	2004	2005	2006	2007	2008	2009	2010
Production	464	515	518	467	502	540	557	571	586	612

9. Estimate trend by 4 yearly centered moving average method for the following data :

Year	1991	1992	1993	1994	1995	1996	1997	1998	1999
Electricity generated in million kW	201	207	213	221	236	248	257	269	281

10. Compute 4 yearly centered moving averages for the following data :

Year	1998	1999	2000	2001	2002	2003	2004	2005
Production (in '000 tonnes)	150	165	140	160	158	155	165	170

11. Fit a trend line to the following times series by the least squares method.

Year	2001	2002	2003	2004	2005
Production (in lakh tons)	12	20	28	32	50

12. Fit a straight line trend by the method of least squares to the following data :

Year	1991	1992	1993	1994	1995
Production (in tonnes)	14	11	13	15	16

13. Estimate trend by fitting straight line equation for the following time series.

Year	1993	1994	1995	1996	1997
Sales in 10,000 ₹	35	56	79	80	40

14. Fit a straight line trend to the following data. Also fit AR (1) model.

Year	1989	1990	1991	1992	1993	1994	1995	1996
Profit in, 000 ₹	90	100	102	93	104	109	102	114

15. Estimate trend using parabolic trend to the following data.

Year	1992	1993	1994	1995	1996
Sales in , 000 ₹	20	22	23	20	18

16. Fit $y = ab^x$ and estimate trend to the following time series. Also fit AR (1) model.

Year	1	2	3	4	5	6	7
Expenditure	177.2	185	224.9	254	304.9	359.9	438.8

17. The following are the annual profits in thousand ₹ in a certain firm :

Year	1996	1997	1998	1999	2000	2001	2002
Profit	60	72	75	65	80	85	95

By the method of least squares, fit a straight line trend to the above data. Estimate the profit for 2004.

18. Let the trend equation of annual sales of a certain company be $y_x = 45 + 4.8x$ with 2000 as the origin (x unit = 1 year; y unit = annual sales in one lakh rupees). Write down the monthly trend and quarterly trend equations. Estimate the value of annual sales for 2005.

19. The trend equation for yearly total sales (in '000' ₹) for a commodity with the year 2001 as the origin is $Y = 81.6 + 28.8 X$. Determine the trend equation to give the monthly trend values and calculate the trend value for March 2002.

20. Find seasonal indices using method of simple averages for the following time series relating to consumption of monthly electric power in million of KW hours in Maharastra.

Month \ Years	1998	1999	2000	2001	2002
Jan.	40.0	45.0	47.0	50.0	52.5
Feb.	38.0	41.0	43.5	46.0	47.5
March	37.5	39.5	42.5	43.5	50.0
April	34.0	37.0	39.8	41.0	43.5
May	33.0	35.0	37.0	38.0	42.0
June	31.5	33.5	35.0	37.5	39.0
July	32.5	34.0	35.0	38.5	41.5
Aug.	35.0	35.8	38.0	41.0	43.5
Sep.	37.0	38.9	40.0	42.0	46.0
Oct.	40.0	42.0	45.0	46.0	45.0
Nov.	42.0	44.5	47.0	49.0	46.5
Dec.	44.5	46.0	49.0	51.0	49.0

21. Obtain the seasonal indices for the quarters by simple averages method assuming that trend is absent.

Year	Quarters No.			
	I	II	III	IV
1999	37	41	33	35
2000	37	39	36	36
2001	40	41	33	31
2002	33	44	40	40

22. The following data give the sales of a company (in lakhs of ₹) during 1998–2002. Compute seasonal indices by the method of simple averages.

Year	Jan.	Feb.	Mar.	April	May	June	July	Aug.	Sep.	Oct.	Nov.	Dec.
1998	30	40	90	100	80	60	50	60	70	110	100	140
1999	50	60	70	100	100	60	80	70	80	100	110	150
2000	40	70	80	120	90	80	100	60	90	120	110	170
2001	70	50	80	130	110	70	80	80	70	110	110	170
2002	110	130	130	150	170	130	140	80	90	160	220	270

23. Assume that trend is absent, determine the seasonal indices for various quarters given the following data using the simple averages method.

Quarter \ Year	1995	1996	1997	1998
Ist	52	57	62	35
IInd	57	48	65	50
IIIrd	54	57	53	54
IVth	58	56	48	52

24. Compute seasonal indices by ratio to moving average method using following data :

Year	Cement production (in lakhs of tonnes)			
	1st quarter	IInd quarter	IIIrd quarter	IVth quarter
1998	8.3	8.1	9.8	11.4
1999	12.4	11.3	11.5	15.2
2000	16.3	16.2	16.8	17.5
2001	19.1	18.0	18.4	16.7

25. Obtain the seasonal indices from the following table by (i) ratio to moving average method, (ii) ratio to trend method.

Quarter \ Year	1998	1999	2000	2001	2002
I	400	420	410	450	440
II	350	370	350	360	380
III	380	390	380	360	380
IV	430	310	420	410	420

26. Compute the seasonal indices by (i) ratio to moving average method (ii) ratio to trend method from the following data :

Year and	1995				1996				1997				1998			
Quarter	I	II	III	IV	I	II	III	IV	I	II	III	IV	I	II	III	IV
Value	75	60	54	59	86	65	63	80	90	72	66	85	10	78	72	93

27. Obtain seasonal indices by the method of link relatives for the data given below :

Year	Quarter			
	Jan. - Mar.	April - June	July - Sept.	Oct. – Dec.
1999	750	600	540	590
2000	860	650	630	800
2001	900	720	660	820
2002	1000	780	720	930

28. Obtain the seasonal indices using method of link relatives for the following data relating to average quarterly price of a commodity.

Quarter	Years				
	1999	2000	2001	2002	2003
I	60	70	62	62	68
II	52	56	58	62	72
III	44	44	56	50	52
IV	62	72	64	70	66

29. Apply the method of link relatives to compute seasonal indices for following data :

Year	Months											
	Jan.	Feb.	Mar.	April	May	June	July	Aug.	Sept.	Oct.	Nov.	Dec.
2000	120	115	110	100	90	80	90	100	110	120	130	140
2001	150	140	130	120	110	100	110	120	130	140	150	160
2002	170	160	150	140	130	120	130	140	150	160	170	170

30. Deseasonalise the following data given bimonthly seasonal indices :

Season	Cash balance in lakhs ₹	Seasonal index
Jan. – Feb.	72	120
March – April	80	80
May – June	110	110
July – Aug.	72	85
Sept. – Oct.	70	75
Nov. – Dec.	110	100

31. The seasonal indices of sales of garments of a particular type in a departmental store are as follows :

Quarter	I	II	III	IV
Seasonal index	95	87	80	138

If sales in the year is ₹ 20 lakhs estimate quarterly sales.

Objective Type Questions

A. Answer in Brief :

1. What do you call as the long-term movement in the time series ?
2. State the additive model used in time series.
3. State the multiplicative model used in time series.
4. Name the long-term variations present in the time series.
5. Name the short-term variations present in the time series.

6. State the model to be used when the components of time series are independent.
7. State the model to be used when the components of time series are interdependent.
8. Which is tool used to smooth out the fluctuations in the time series ?
9. What is the independent variable in time series Y_t ?
10. State the four components in time series.
11. State the components of time series which fluctuate for short period ?
12. State the unpredictable component in time series.
13. State the normal equations to fit a straight line trend.
14. State the normal equations to fit a parabolic trend.
15. State the normal equations to fit a exponential trend.
16. State the normal equations to fit a curve $Y_t = at^b$.
17. State uses of time series analysis.
18. In a time series of traffic density of vehicles on road state the seasons.
19. In a time series of daily sales of books, state the seasons.
20. In a time series of cold drink sales, state the seasons.
21. Which components in time series are periodic in nature ?
22. What is achieved by moving averages in time series ?
23. State the stages of business cycle.
24. Business cycle constitutes which component of time series ?
25. Which moving averages are required to be centered ? Why ?
26. Identify the predominant components in the following time series :
    (a) Decrease in sales due to strike.
    (b) Decrease in sales due to slack season.
    (c) Decrease in sales due to decreasing demand because of out dated use of the commodity.
    (d) Decreasing demand due to famine.
    (e) Increased sales due to Diwali festival.
    (f) Decline in the use of cotton clothes.
    (g) Decreasing prices of electronic goods.

B. Simple Numerical Problems :

27. In a time series assuming multiplicative model the components are T = 500%, S = 90%, C = 80%, I = 120% find the value of time series Y_t.
28. In time series with additive model Y_t = 600, T = 430, S = 90, C = 40, find the irregular component.
29. If the annual trend equation is Y = 198 + 144t, find :
    (a) monthly trend equation
    (b) quarterly trend equation.
30. If Y = a + bt is trend equation and a = $\bar{Y}$ then find b.

C. Multiple Choice Questions :

• **Choose the correct alternative :**

31. Secular trend in time series is of nature
    (a) increasing   (b) decreasing   (c) stagnant   (d) all of these

32. Linear trend means
    (a) no change   (b) constant change   (c) changes are in geometric progression
    (d) none of these

33. Moving averages remove the cyclical variation if
    (a) the period is even.
    (b) the period is odd.
    (c) the average is weighted.
    (d) the period is same as that of cycle.

34. Moving average method is not suitable for
    (a) removing rhythmic variations.
    (b) projections.
    (c) estimating seasonal variations.
    (d) none of the above.

35. Moving average methods suffers from the drawback.
    (a) It is a subjective method.
    (b) It does not estimate trend for all the time points.
    (c) both (a) and (b) are true.
    (d) neither (a) nor (b) is true.

36. Least square method
    (a) reduces the calculations.
    (b) does not give estimate for future.
    (c) reduces the sum of squares of errors.
    (d) is subjective.

37. Time series data are arranged in .... order.
    (a) random   (b) increasing   (c) decreasing   (d) chronological

Answers 6.1

1.

Year	76	77	78	79	80	81	82	83	84
(i)	–	–	18.34	18.04	17.52	17.42	18.48	18.82	18.88
(ii)	–	–	18.3125	17.7125	17.3875	17.6	18.225	18.8875	19.05

1.

Year	85	86	87	88	89	90	91	92
(i)	19.12	19.5	19.66	19.98	20.66	21.14	–	–
(ii)	19.3	19.3	19.3875	20.1	20.7	21.2875	–	–

2.

Year	90	91	92	93	94
(i)	73.375	73.625	74.5	75.125	73.375

3.

Year	2	3	4	5	6	7	8	9	10	11	12
MA	–	283	294	300	303	305	307	311	327	–	–

4.

Year	77	78	79	80	81	82	83	84
(i)	–	–	4	4.2375	4.2675	4.025	–	–
(ii)	–	–	4	4.36	4.18	3.8	–	–

5.

Year	2000	01	02	03	04	05	06	07	08	09
	–	244	249	253	260	264.3333	270.333	275.333	280	–

6.

Year	1997	98	99	00	01	02	03	04
	–	–	40	42.375	46.625	40.25	–	–

7.

Year	03	04	05	06	07	08	09	10	11	12
	–	–	9.8	9.4	9.4	9.8	10	10.4	–	–

8.

Year	2001	02	03	04	05	06	07	08	09	10
	–	–	495.75	503.625	511.625	553	572.5	–	–	–

9.

Year	1991	92	93	94	95	96	97	98	99
	–	–	214.875	224.375	235	246.5	258.125	–	–

10.

Year	1998	99	00	01	02	03	04	05
	–	–	154.75	154.5	156.375	160.75	–	–

11. $Y = 8.8x - 17598$

12. $Y = 0.8x - 1580.6$

13. $y = 58 + 3.4 (t - 1995)$

14. $y = 101.75 + 1.25 \left(\dfrac{t - 1992.5}{0.5} \right)$

AR (1) equation $Y_{t+1} = 0.1575\, Y_t + 87.6805$

15. y = 22.314 − 0.6 (t − 1994) − 0.857 (t − 1994)^2

16. y = 264.3 × (1.168)$^{(t−4)}$, Y_{t+1} = 1.3067 Y_t − 33.366, since coefficient of Y_t, 1.3067 is greater than 1, series is not stationary.

17. y = 76 + 4.8571 (t − 1999), $\hat{y}_{2004}$ = 100.2857.

18. Monthly equation : y = a/12 + b/144 x = 3.75 + 0.0333 x x : 1 month, origin : 1st July 2000.

    Quarterly equation : $y = \frac{a}{4} + \frac{b}{48}$ x = 11.25 + 0.1 x.

    x : one quarter origin : 1st July 2000. $\hat{y}_{2005}$ = ₹ 69 lakh.

19. Monthly equation : Y = 6.75 + 0.2x. x : 1 month, origin : 1st July 2001.

    $\hat{y}_{Mar\ 2002}$ = ₹ 8350.

20. Seasonal indices : 113.2, 104.2, 102.8, 94.3, 89.3, 85.2, 87.6, 93.3, 98.4, 105.2, 110.6, 115.6.

21. Quarterly indices : 98.7, 110.8, 95.3, 95.3.

22. Monthly indices : 60, 70, 90, 120, 110, 80, 90, 70, 80, 120, 130, 180.

23. Quarterly indices : 94.6, 103.04, 102.10, 100.2.

24. Quarterly indices : 106, 96, 94.5, 103.5.

25. Seasonal indices :

    (i) by ratio to moving average : 109.55, 92.77, 98.98, 98.69.

    (ii) by ratio to trend : 110.6404, 94.1709, 98.0562, 97.1325.

26. Seasonal indices :

    (i) By ratio to moving average : 122.366, 92.429, 84.694, 100.511.

    (ii) By ratio to trend : 121.8127, 92.9702, 83.9948, 101.2223.

27. Quarterly indices : 124.2, 93.47, 82.49, 99.87.

28. Seasonal indices : 108.2, 99.75, 81.23, 111.0.

29. Monthly seasonal index : 121.13, 113.02, 105.27, 95.46, 86.00, 76.32, 83.34, 90.61, 97.64, 102.60, 111.81, 116.78

30. 60, 100, 100, 90, 93.3333, 110 in lakh ₹

31. 4.75, 4.35, 4.00, 6.90 lakhs ₹

Objective Type Questions

B. 27. 432
28. 50
29. (i) Y = 16.5 + x (ii) Y = 49.5 + 3x
30. b = 0

C. (31) d   (32) b   (33) d   (34) b   (35) b
(36) c   (37) d

Chapter 7...

Index Numbers (For B.B.A. Only)

Contents ...

7.1   Introduction

7.2   Definition and Notation of Index Number

7.3   Types of Index Numbers

7.4   Construction of Index Numbers

7.5   Commonly used Index Numbers in India

Key Words :

Prices, Quantities, Current Year, Base Year, Price Relatives, Index Numbers, Weight, Laspeyre's Index Number, Paasche's Index Number, Fisher's Index Number, Cost of Living Index Numbers, Family Budget Method, Aggregate Expenditure Method, Inflation, Cost Inflation Index.

Objectives :

To built-up a tool to measure the average changes in prices and to use it for various financial and economic activities. Index numbers are often called as economic barometer.

7.1 Introduction   (B.B.A. April 2015)

Index number is a tool used to measure the changes in prices of commodities, industrial and mineral production, sales, imports, exports etc. It was first developed by an Italian economist Mr. Carli, in 1764, for comparison of prices of commodities. Index number serves the purpose of economic indicators. The fields in which index numbers are used are economics, trade, stock market, Government organisations etc. The popularly used index numbers are

(i)   Bombay Stock Exchange (BSE) SENSEX index number.

(ii) National Stock Exchange (NSE) index numbers.

(iii) All India wholesale price index number.

(iv) Consumer price index numbers.

(v)   Index number of Industrial Production (1993-94 as base year).

(vi) Index numbers of agricultural production.

(vii) Cost inflation index (for capital assets).

Index Number - An Economic Barometer :

Economic phenomena are dynamic, we observe that the prices of commodities change from time to time, place to place, wages of workers, prices of shares, exhibit up and down movements, industrial production also undergoes changes. Index numbers measure such changes, infact they measure pulse of economy like inflationary or deflationary tendencies. The apparatus barometer reflects the changes in atmospheric pressure likewise, index numbers reflects the changes in economic activities; hence index numbers are rightly called as **'economic barometers'**.

For the determination of index numbers, we need to consider several commodities. We know that a series of observations can be reduced to a single observation or two series can be compared with the help of averages. Thus, it is essential to find the average change in prices or quantities to find index numbers. But to calculate an average, we require the observations measured in same units. However, the prices and quantities differ in their units.

For example, prices of sugar, rice are expressed in ₹ per kg. whereas prices of milk, petrol etc. are in ₹ per litre, price of cloth is ₹ per metre. Thus, average of prices of such quantities is meaningless and it no longer remains useful. In order to overcome this difficulty, changes are measured in ratios, which are unitless numbers and then average change is calculated. The average so obtained is an index number. Thus, index number is an elegant application of measures of central tendency.

7.2 Definition and Notation of Index Numbers

Definition : Index number is a number designated to measure the average change in the values of a **group of related variables** over two different **situations**.

The group of variables may be prices of specified commodities, quantities of industrial production, volume of imports, exports etc. Two different situations may be two different times or places.

Problems or considerations in the Construction of Index Numbers

The various problems involved in the construction of index numbers are discussed below :

1. Purpose of Index Number : The purpose for which the index number is constructed should be clearly and unambiguously mentioned. Similarly, the scope of index number should also be defined clearly. *For example*, if we want to construct a consumer's price index numbers, accordingly appropriate commodities are to be selected. Similarly, a class of people for which the index number is to be constructed should be clearly stated. Thus, defining the purpose clearly, helps in selection of commodities, base period, weights etc.

2. Selection of Commodities : Selection of commodities is an important factor in the construction of index numbers. There are no rigid rules regarding selection of commodities. Number of commodities should not be too large or too small. Inclusion of large number of commodities results into greater expenses, more time, more volume of work. If number of commodities is too small, the associated index number will not remain proper representative. Thus, a reasonable number of commodities should be included. Moreover, commodities selected should be relevant to the purpose of index number. These should be representative of tastes, customs and necessities of group of population for which index number is constructed.

For example, if we want to find the cost of living index number for poor families, then we should not include luxury goods like cars, washing machines, refrigerators, cell phones etc. Stable commodities are to be selected.

3. Collection of Data : Data may be price quotations or quantity consumed or quantity produced or quantity imported etc. depending upon the purpose of index numbers. The data should be collected from reliable agencies, standard trade journals, periodical reports, official publications etc. The data collected should be accurate and proper representative. For consumer's price index numbers, price quotations should be collected from trusted agencies. Prices vary from place to place, shop to shop and quality to quality. Therefore, prices should be collected with utmost care. As per requirement, retail or wholesale prices should be collected. Sometimes price may be quoted as number of ₹ per unit quantity.

For example, ₹ 10 per kg. On the other hand, price may be quoted as quantity per ₹ *For example*, 100 gm per Re. Price quotations should be of the same type.

4. Choice of Base Period : Index number uses two time periods. In this situation, a period for which index number is determined is called as **current period** and the period of comparison or with respect to which index number is determined is called as **base period.** The base period should be a period for which reliable figures are available. A period of economic importance may be preferably chosen. Following are the guidelines for the selection of base period :

(i) **The base period should be a normal period.** It means that there should not be incidents like war, floods, famine, earthquakes, labour strikes etc. It can be noticed that for the years with above stated abnormal conditions, economic instability will be observed, hence proper price quotations or quantity consumed, production figures may not be available.

(ii) **The base period should not be too distant.** The customs, habits, tastes of people change gradually. Hence, for proper comparison, base period should not be too distant. Sometimes in the meanwhile some old commodities get out of use and new commodities get introduced.

(iii) **The base period should not be too small or too large.** If base period is too short (for example, a single day), the prices are highly unstable. On the other hand, if the period is too large (for example, five years) then prices undergo many variations. Therefore, to get reliable price quotations, period should be of adequate length.

(iv) Sometimes base year is taken as average of many years. For example, Index number of agricultural production is with a triannual average of years 1979-82 as base year determined by Government of Maharashtra.

5. Selection of Type of Average : It is stated above that the index number is a average change in the prices or quantities. In order to combine the data, we need to use appropriate measure of central tendency. Arithmetic mean is suitable in most of the situations since it is a simple and good average. Sometimes geometric mean or median is also used.

6. Selection of Weights : Weighted average is more appropriate than simple average. Weight is a device of giving due or proper importance to the commodity. If weights are not attached, all commodities are regarded equally important. Since changes in prices of different commodities will have different influence on average, weights are essential.

For example, increase in price of salt, and that of wheat will have different influence on index number. Weight plays the role of frequency, however weights can be fractional in nature. Thus, to get true reflection of changes, weighted average is used.

    (i) Quantity weights (q) : Amount of commodity consumed or produced or exported etc. is taken as weight.

    (ii) Value weights (V) : It is a product of price and quantity used or produced.

Note : If $x_1, x_2, \ldots, x_n$ are the observations with weights $w_1, w_2, \ldots w_n$ respectively then weighted arithmetic mean is given by

$$\bar{X}_w = \frac{w_1 x_1 + w_2 x_2 + \ldots + w_n x_n}{w_1 + w_2 + \ldots + w_n} = \frac{\sum w \cdot x}{\sum w}$$

7.3 Types of Index Numbers

Mainly there are three types of index numbers in use viz. price index numbers, quality index numbers and value index numbers.

Price Index Numbers : Price index numbers are computed to measure the relative changes in prices of group of commodities or a single commodity. Government of India regularly computes two series of price index numbers (i) wholesale price index numbers, (ii) consumer price index numbers. Bombay stock exchange (BSE) SENSEX and NSE are two important price index numbers used in stock market to measure the changes in prices of shares.

Quantity Index Numbers : Quantity index numbers are constructed to measure the changes in volume of industrial production, agricultural production, mineral production, import, export etc.

Value Index Number :

Value index number is designed to measure the per cent change in aggregate expenditure for a given period. Thus, it is given by

$$V_{o1} = \frac{\text{Aggregate expenditure in current year}}{\text{Aggregate expenditure in base year}} \times 100$$

$$V_{o1} = \frac{\sum p_1 q_1}{\sum p_0 q_0} \times 100$$

Construction of Index Numbers

Base year is denoted by 0 and current year by 1, price and quantities are denoted by p and q respectively. Hence, value $v = p \cdot q$. Weights are represented by w. Price index number, quantity index number and value index number are denoted by P, Q and V respectively.

Thus,

    p_0 : Price of a commodity in the base year.

    p_1 : Price of a commodity in the current year.

    q_0 : Quantity of a commodity in the base year.

    q_1 : Quantity of a commodity in the current year.

    P_{01} : Price index number for the current period 1 with base period 0.

    Q_{01} : Quantity index number for the current period 1 with base period 0.

There are two types of index numbers (1) Aggregative type (2) Average of price relative type. Further each of these type are classified into two categories (a) Simple and (b) Weighted, thus it gives rise to four types of index numbers :

(i) Simple (unweighted) aggregative index number.
(ii) Weighted aggregative index number.
(iii) Simple average of price relatives
(iv) Weighted average of price relatives.

The following tree diagram summarizes the types of index numbers.

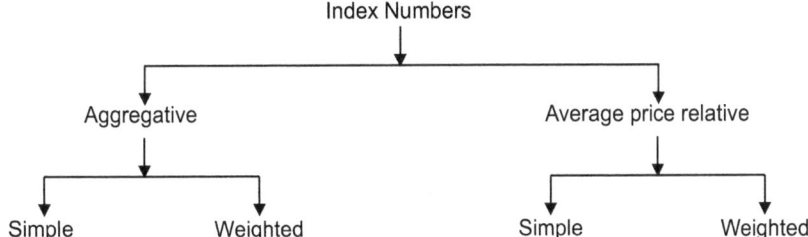

In this book, we discuss only the first two types of aggregative index numbers.

(A) Unweighted or simple aggregative type index numbers :

This type of price index number is given by

$$P_{01} = \frac{\text{Sum of prices in current year}}{\text{Sum of prices in base year}} \times 100 = \frac{\sum p_1}{\sum p_0} \times 100$$

Similarly, quantity index number is

$$Q_{01} = \frac{\sum q_1}{\sum q_0} \times 100$$

Limitations :

1. The main limitation of unweighted index numbers is, that all the commodities are given equal importance which is not the reality.
2. In aggregative type index number, $\sum p_1$ or $\sum p_0$ cannot be computed meaningfully if the units are not same. For example, some price quotations may be ₹ per kg, same may be ₹ per litre or ₹ per metre etc. Sum of such prices is not meaningful.

(B) Weighted aggregative type index numbers :

If w is the weight attached with commodity, then this type of price index number is given by,

$$P_{01} = \frac{\sum p_1 w}{\sum p_0 w} \times 100$$

and quantity index number is given by

$$Q_{01} = \frac{\sum q_1 w}{\sum q_0 w} \times 100$$

Note : In aggregative type price index numbers, quantities consumed are taken as weights and in quantity index numbers, prices are taken as weights.

Example 7.1 : *Compute price index for 2007 with 2008 as base year using simple aggregate method, for the data given below :*

Commodities	A	B	C	D	E
Price in 2006	40	60	20	50	80
Price in 2007	50	60	30	64	104

Solution :

Commodity	Price in 2006 p_0	Price in 2007 p_1
A	40	50
B	60	60
C	20	30
D	50	64
E	80	104
Total	$250 = \sum p_0$	$308 = \sum p_1$

Simple aggregate of price index number

$$P_{01} = \frac{\sum p_1}{\sum p_0} \times 100 = \frac{308}{250} \times 100 = 123.20$$

Interpretation : P_{01} = 123.2 means there is on an average the rise of 23.2% in prices in the year 2007 as compared to those in the year 2006.

7.4 Construction of Index Numbers (B.B.A. Oct. 2014)

According to different weighing systems, different index numbers are obtained. We study some important index numbers below.

Some Specific Index Numbers

(A) Laspeyre's Index Number : It is a weighted aggregative type index number defined by French economist Laspeyre in the year 1871. For price index number, we take quantities of base year (q_0) as weights. Hence, Laspeyre's price index number is

$$P_{01}^L = \frac{\sum p_1 q_0}{\sum p_0 q_0} \times 100$$

Application : Cost of living index number is a Laspeyre's price index number.

(B) Paasche's Index Number : It is a price index number by German Statistician Paasche which was defined in the year 1874, we take current year quantities (q_1) as weights, thus we get

$$P_{01}^P = \frac{\sum p_1 q_1}{\sum p_0 q_1} \times 100$$

Application : To find real gross domestic product (GDP) of a country, the effect of inflation is removed by GDP deflator. GDP deflator is given by Paasche's price index number. GDP is used to compute national income.

Comparison between Laspeyre's and Paasche's Index Numbers :
1. The main drawback of Laspeyre's index number is that it suffers from upward bias. In other words, index number overestimates the value.
   On the other hand, Paasche's index number suffers from a downward bias. It underestimates the index number.

2. Paasche's index number requires more data to be collected as compared to Laspeyre's index number.

   Paasche's index number uses current year quantity as weights. Therefore, data for current year have to be collected. If we want to construct index number for 10 different years with the same base year, then we require to collect quantities for each of these 10 years. Thus, data collection work increases. Whereas Laspeyre's formula uses base year quantities, hence one set of quantities is enough for those 10 years.
3. Paasche's index number requires more calculations. If Paasche's formula is used to calculate index number for 10 different years, we need to compute denominator $\sum p_0 q_1$ for each year separately, whereas in Laspeyre's formula the denominator $\sum p_0 q_0$ calculated once will be sufficient for remaining years.

(C) Irving Fisher's Ideal Index Number : It is defined as positive square root of product of Laspeyre's and Paasche's index numbers. Thus, Fisher's price index number defined in the year 1920 is given by,

$$P_{01}^F = \sqrt{P_{01}^L \times P_{01}^P} = \sqrt{\frac{\sum p_1 q_0}{\sum p_0 q_0} \times \frac{\sum p_1 q_1}{\sum p_0 q_1}} \times 100$$

Remarks :
1. Fisher's index number uses quantities in both the years, current year as well as base year, therefore, it is superior to Laspeyre's and Paasche's index numbers.
2. Fisher's index number satisfies the tests of index numbers, which is a good index number is supposed to satisfy. Hence, it is called as ideal index number.
3. Fisher's index number is difficult to calculate as compared to Laspeyre's and Paasche's index numbers.
4. Fisher's index number lies between Laspeyre's and Paasche's index numbers. Since it is a geometric mean of Laspeyre's and Paasche's index numbers.

Example 7.2 : *Calculate price index numbers for the following data for the year 2007 taking 2006 as base year using the following formulae.*

(i) Laspeyre's, (ii) Paasche's, (iii) Fisher's.

Commodity	Year 2006		Year 2007	
	Price	Quantity	Price	Quantity
A	20	8	40	6
B	50	10	60	5
C	40	15	50	10
D	20	20	20	15

Solution :

Commodity	p_0	q_0	p_1	q_1	$p_0 q_0$	$p_1 q_1$	$p_0 q_1$	$p_1 q_0$
A	20	8	40	6	160	240	120	320
B	50	10	60	5	500	300	250	600
C	40	15	50	10	600	500	400	750
D	20	20	20	15	400	300	300	400
Total	–	–	–	–	1660	1340	1070	2070

(i) Laspeyre's price index number

$$P_{01}^L = \frac{\sum p_1 q_0}{\sum p_0 q_0} \times 100 = \frac{2070}{1660} \times 100 = 124.6988$$

(ii) Paasche's price index number

$$P_{01}^P = \frac{\sum p_1 q_1}{\sum p_0 q_1} \times 100 = \frac{1340}{1070} \times 100 = 125.2336$$

(iii) Fisher's price index number

$$P_{01}^F = \sqrt{P_{01}^L \times P_{01}^P} = 124.9659$$

Remark : It can be noticed that the different formulae of index number give different values for the same data, however, they do not vary to large extent numerically. Ideally, every formulae should give the same value.

Interpretation : The above illustration computes price index number for 2007 with a base year 2006. Here Laspeyre's price index number is 124.6988. It can be interpreted as that the average of prices in the year 2007 is 124.6988 when it was assumed to be 100 in the year 2006. Thus, the prices have increased on an average by 24.6988%.

Uses of Index Numbers : (B.B.A. April 2015)

1. **Index Number as a Economic Barometer :** Index numbers are useful in measuring the changes in prices, production, import, export, stock market etc. Cost of inflation index number helps us to know the appreciation of assets.
   With the help of index numbers, the changes can be quantitatively determined to a considerable accuracy. R.G.D. Allen rightly pointed out that the range of index number is quite large and they can indicate the changes in various variables such as shipping, freights, commodity prices, security prices, volume of output, profit, sales etc.
2. **Index Number helps in Comparison :** Index number helps in comparing the economic, and business activities for two different locations or periods or countries.
3. **Index Number helps in Planning and Policy Making :** Index numbers give the basis for planning it helps in policy making. For example, investments in stock market.
4. **Index Number** helps in finding Real Income or Purchasing power of money.
5. **Dearness Allowances :** Index numbers are used to fix dearness allowances of employees for adjusting the inflations.
6. Real capital gain in the sales of assets such as land, house, gold, jewellery, machinery, shares etc. can be determined using the cost inflation index numbers.
7. Index number gives the progress of industry, trends in stock markets.
8. Index number helps in finding real GDP or net national product, which is the main component in national income.
9. **Measure of inflation :** Using index number, rate of inflation can be obtained.

$$\text{Inflation} = \frac{\text{Current price index number} - \text{Previous price index number}}{\text{Previous year index number}} \times 100$$

Limitations of Index Numbers : (B.B.A. Oct. 2014)
1. **Sampling Error :** The data used to construct an index number is obtained by method of sampling. Therefore, index numbers are subject to sampling errors.
2. **Disregard to Change in Quantity :** Consumption pattern depends upon the habits and tastes of people which change gradually. *For example*, if people tend towards the use of superior quality of commodity, prices of concerned commodity will be higher and gives higher price index. The increase is not due to increase in price but due to changes in habits. Therefore, index number becomes less reliable.
3. **Subjectivity in Base Year :** Index number requires base to be a normal period. But a person may choose a base period which is suitable for him. Thus, there may be a subjectivity in selection of base period.
4. **Limited Scope :** Scope of index number is limited to its purpose. For example, consumer price index number for urban area cannot be used for rural area.
5. Index number suffers from the drawbacks of the average that is used in construction.
6. Drawback of the formula used for the construction of index number affects its value.
7. If value index number shows an increase, then whether it is due to increase in prices or increase in production or both cannot be ascertained.

Example 7.3 : *Suppose in Dec. 1995 land was purchased at cost ₹50,000. It was sold at cost ₹1,50,000 in Feb. 2002. Find the real capital gain if the cost of inflation index in 1995-96 is 281 and that in 2001-02 is 426.*

Solution : Suppose the rise in cost is proportional to index

$$\therefore \frac{\text{Cost in 2001-02}}{\text{Cost inflation index number in 2001-02}} = \frac{\text{Cost in 1995-96}}{\text{Cost inflation index number in 1995-96}}$$

$$\therefore \text{Indexed cost in 2001-02} = \text{Cost in 1995-96} \times \frac{\text{Index number in 2001-02}}{\text{Index number in 1995-96}}$$

$$= 50,000 \times \frac{426}{281} = 75,800.71 \text{ ₹}$$

$$\therefore \text{Capital gain} = \text{Sale price} - \text{Indexed cost}$$
$$= 1,50,000 - 75800.71 = 74,199.29 \text{ ₹}$$
$$\text{Apparent gain} = \text{Sale price} - \text{Purchase price}$$
$$= 1,50,000 - 50,000 = 1,00,000 \text{ ₹}$$

Thus the apparent gain is ₹ 1,00,000 however, taking into account inflation the gain in real sense is ₹ 74,199.29. For tax calculations, real capital gain is used.

Example 7.4 : Obtain value index number from the following data :

Commodity	Base Year		Current Year	
	Price	Quantity	Price	Quantity
A	8	50	10	60
B	10	40	12	50
C	5	100	8	120
D	6	300	9	250

Solution :

Commodity	A	B	C	D	Total
$p_0 q_0$	400	400	500	1800	3100
$p_1 q_1$	600	600	960	2250	4410

$$\therefore \text{ Value index number} = V_{01} = \frac{\Sigma p_1 q_1}{\Sigma p_0 q_0} \times 100 = \frac{4410}{3100} \times 100 = 142.2581$$

Example 7.5 : *Calculate cost of living index number from the following data :*

Group	Index Number	Weight
Food	350	50
Fuel and lighting	200	10
Clothing	240	10
House rent	160	10
Miscellaneous	250	20

Solution :

Group	Index Number (I)	Weight (w)	I × w
Food	350	50	17500
Fuel and lighting	200	10	2000
Clothing	240	10	2400
House rent	160	10	1600
Miscellaneous	250	20	5000
Total	–	$100 = \Sigma w$	$28500 = \Sigma I w$

$$\text{Cost of living index number} = \frac{\Sigma I w}{\Sigma w} = \frac{28500}{100} = 285$$

Example 7.6 : *Cost of living index number of the following data is known to be 126.2, obtain the missing weight.*

Commodity	A	B	C	D	E
Index number	130	120	125	115	120
Weight	60	20	*	6	4

Solution : Suppose missing weight = x. We calculate cost of index number as usual and equate it with given value 126.2.

Commodity	Index Number I	Weight w	I × w
A	130	60	7800
B	120	20	2400
C	125	x	125 x
D	115	6	690
E	120	4	480
Total	–	90 + x	11370 + 125 x

Cost of living I. No. $= \dfrac{\Sigma Iw}{\Sigma w}$

$126.2 = \dfrac{11370 + 125 x}{90 + x}$

$126.2 (90 + x) = 11370 + 125 x$

$(126.2 - 125) x = 11370 - 11358$

$1.2 x = 12$

$x = 10$

Example 7.7 : *An index number is obtained as weighted arithmetic mean of group index numbers. If price index number of food articles is increased by 20% and index numbers of other groups are same, then the index number of all groups taken together shows 8% increase. Obtain the weight assigned to group of food articles.*

Solution : Let weight of group of food articles be x% and the total weight be 100%.

Group	Index number I	Weight w%	Iw
Food	120	x	120 x
Other	100	100 – x	100 (100 – x)
Total	–	100	10000 + 20x

$I = \dfrac{\Sigma Iw}{\Sigma w}$

$108 = \dfrac{10000 + 20x}{100}$

∴ $x = 40$

Example 7.8 : *Calculate price index number using : (i) Laspeyre's, (ii) Paasche's (iii) Fishers Method for the following data :* **(B.B.A. April 2015) (April 2010)**

Commodiites \ Years	1980		1985	
	Price	Quantity	Price	Quantity
Rice	3	5	4.5	6
Cocount Oil	24	2	18	3
Tea	20	1	35	2
Washing Powder	10	4	16	4
Sugar	3.5	4	6	5

Solution :

Commodites	p_0	q_0	p_1	q_1	$p_0 q_0$	$p_0 q_1$	$p_1 q_0$	$p_1 q_1$
Rice	3	5	4.5	6	15	18	22.5	27
Coconut oil	24	2	18	3	48	72	36	54
Tea	20	1	35	2	20	40	35	70
Washing powder	10	4	16	4	40	40	64	64
Sugar	3.5	4	6	5	14	17.5	24	30
Total	–	–	–	–	137	187.5	181.5	245

(i) Laspeyre's price I. No. $= \dfrac{\sum p_1 q_0}{\sum p_0 q_0} \times 100 = \dfrac{181.5}{137} \times 100 = 132.48$

(ii) Paasche's price I. No. $= \dfrac{\sum p_1 q_1}{p_0 q_1} \times 100 = \dfrac{245}{187.5} \times 100 = 130.67$

(iii) Fisher's price I. No. $= \sqrt{\text{Laspeyre's I. NO.} \times \text{Paasche's I. No.}}$

$= \sqrt{132.67 \times 130.67} = 131.57$

7.5 Commonly Used Index Numbers in India

1. Index Number of Industrial Production in India (IIP) : The index number of industrial production (IIP) serves the purpose of measure of industrial growth in country. It is published by Central Statistical Organisation (CSO) for all India as a monthly series, yearly series. The base year is 1993-94.

Year	1996-97	97-98	98-99	99-2000	00-01	01-02	02-03	03-04	04-05	05-06	06-07
IIP	130.8	139.5	145.2	154.9	162.5	164.9	176.6	189.0	204.2	221.5	247.1

IIP is a weighted index number with three major groups.

Group	Mining	Manufacturing	Electricity	Total
Weight	10.47	79.36	10.17	100

Manufacturing is subdivided into 17 subgroups. Those are listed with weights in brackets used to compute IIP.

(1) Food (9.08), (2) Beverages (2.38), (3) Cotton textile (5.52), (4) Wool, silk textiles (2.26), (5) Jute textile (0.59), (6) Textile product (2.54), (7) Wood, Agriculture (2.70), (8) Paper and printing (2.65), (9) Leather (1.14), (10) Chemical (14), (11) Rubber, plastic petroleum, coal (5.73), (12) Non-metallic minerals (4.4), (13) Basic metal and alloys (7.45), (14) Metal products (2.81), (15) Machinery and equipment (9.57), (16) Transport equipments (3.98), (17) Other manufacturing industries (2.56).

Monthly index of industrial production is a weighted average of quantity relatives. Weights are proportional to the value-added in the base year. Monthly indices for sugar, tea and salt are adjusted for seasonality. Seasonal indices are determined using the method moving averages. Simple average of monthly indices is the annual index.

2. All India Wholesale Price Index Number : The Wholesale Price Index Number (WPI) is the most widely used index in business, industry and Government. The office of Economic Advisor to Govt. of India publishes WPI. The annual rate of change in WPI is interpreted as the annual rate of inflation. It is taken to be an important indicator of micro-economic stability in the economy. It is a weighted index number with base year 1993-94. There was a sharp increase in WPI in the year 2000-01 as much as 7.13%. It was due to rise in petroleum, LPG gas, Kerosene etc. in September 2000. There are 3 major subgroups.

(i) Subgroup of primary articles, contains items, food (rice, wheat etc.); cotton, jute, minerals (such as iron, mangenese). In all 80 articles are covered.

(ii) Subgroup of fuel, power, light, lubricant. It is includes 10 items.

(iii) Subgroup of manufactured articles has 270 items in it.

The group-wise weights are given below :

Subgroup	Primary articles	Fuel, power light, lubricants	Manufactured products	Total
Weight	22.025	14.226	63.749	100

WPI for years 1994-95 to 2001-02 are given below :

Year	1994-95	95-96	96-97	97-98	98-99	99-00	00-01	01-02
WPI	112.6	121.6	127.2	132.8	140.7	145.3	155.7	161.3
Year	02-03	03-04	04-05	05-06	06-07	07-08		
WPI	166.8	175.9	187.3	175.6	206.2	214.3		

3. Consumer Price Index Numbers (CPI) : Consumer Price Index (CPI) numbers are intended to measure the movements in retail prices of essential commodities for different sections of the consumers. For example,

(i) CPI for industrial workers on all India basis (also as statewise and citiwise) with a base year 1982.

(ii) CPI for urban non-mannual employees is released by CSO in monthly series on all India basis as well as regionwise and for 59 cities in country.

(iii) CPI for agricultural labours with base year 1986-87.

(iv) CPI for ubran labourers with base year 1982.

(v) CPI for rural labourers with base year with base year 1982.

All India CPI for industrial workers for 1990-91 to 2001-02 are given below :

Year	90-91	91-92	92-93	93-94	94-95	95-96	96-97	97-98	98-99	99-00	00-01	01-02
CPI	193	219	240	258	284	313	342	366	414	428	444	463

Year	02-03	03-04	04-05	05-06
CPI	482	500	519	542

Weights for various CP indices are as follows :

Subgroup	All India CPI for Industrial Workers	CPI for Urban Maharashtra	CPI for Rural Maharashtra
Food	57.00	54.12	61.66
Pan, Supari, Tobacco etc.	3.15	2.02	–
Fuel, power and light etc.	6.28	6.67	7.92
Clothing and bedding etc.	8.54	5.95	7.78
Housing	8.67	–	–
Miscellaneous	16.36	31.24	22.64
Total	100.00	100.00	100.00

4. Index Numbers of Agricultural Production : Index number of agricultural production for Maharashtra is calculated with triannual average base 1979-82. It is a weighted index number based five main groups (i) cereals, (ii) pulses, (iii) oil seeds, (iv) fibers and (v) miscallaneous.

Comparing index number of agricultural production for Maharashtra and all India we realise that the rate of growth in Maharashtra is less than that of in all India level. The fluctuations indicate that the agricultural production in Maharashtra is highly uncertain. In the year 2000-01 the index number is reduced by 38.5 as compared to 1999-2000 which is a substantial reduction.

Groupwise weights are as follows :

Groups	Cereals	Pulses	Oilseeds	Fibres	Miscellaneous	Total
Weights	42.22	10.44	9.16	9.93	28.25	100

The series on index number is as follows :

Year	Index No.	Year	Index No.
1982-83	97.4	1999-00	157.2
1986-87	79.7	2000-01	127.4
1990-91	136.5	2001-02	135.2
1991-92	101.4	2002-03	130.4
1992-93	134.2	2003-04	112.7
1993-94	140.3	2004-05	111.0
1994-95	136.1	2005-06	135.4
1995-96	145.7	2006-07	178.7
1996-97	160.7		
1997-98	114.5		
1998-99	156.8		

Index number of agricultural production is an important measure of economy. It has significant contribution to GDP of country. It is directly and indirectly linked with industrial sector. Fluctuations in mansoon are mainly responsible for the erratic behaviour of growth in agricultural production.

5. Security Price Indices : The Reserve Bank of India (RBI) is computing series of index numbers for security prices with base year 1980-81. Price indices are compiled weekly and the average of weeks for months or years is computed. It is presented on all India basis. For this purpose, there are 5 regions of India, viz. Mumbai, Kolkatta, Chennai, Ahmedabad, Delhi. It considers 338 actively traded shares with regional distribution as follows : Mumbai 32%, Kolkata 26%, Chennai 17%, Ahmedabad 10%, Delhi 15%. The weights are proportional to the average market value of share. A sample of securities is taken then the daily closing prices are taken into account the arithmetic mean of prices is used to compute price relatives with base year prices. The price relative of subgroup is obtained as a unweighted geometric mean of price relatives of Scrips (securities) in subgroup. Finally group indices are compiled using weighted average with weight of subgroup proportional to the number of shares outstanding in the scrip.

BSE Sensitive Index : The Bombay Stock Exchange (BSE) computes prices index since 1986, with a base year 1978-79. It is recognised as BSE sensex. It has 30 Scrips which are actively traded, many of which are in Group A (Specified group) and few are in Group B (non-specified group). These indices are available daily, monthly and yearly in leading newspapers.

BSE National Index : Bombay stock exchange also computes a series of index numbers on all India basis. It includes in all 100 Scrips out of which 22 a quoted in Mumbai only, 72 from BSE and 6 from other stock exchanges. The base year 1983-84 is chosen due to price stability and relative proximity. There are several series of security price indices. NSE is compiling since 1995 with base year 1995. It uses 50 Scrips (called as NIFTY) out of 550 listed Scrips and 1500 trades Scrips.

All these indices are security market indicators.

6. Cost Inflation Index : In order to determine the real capital gain due to the sale of assets, Government of India computes index number of cost of inflation with a base year 1981-82. It is 75% of the rise in consumer price index number for urban non-manual employees. It is used for calculation of income tax for income generated due to sales of capital assets such as land, house, gold, shares etc.

Apparently, profit = Sale price – Purchase price. However one has to take into account the effect of inflation. Price inflation is considered to be proportional to the cost inflation index, accordingly the indexed cost of assets is determined for the year of transaction, then

Real capital gain = Sale price – Indexed cost.

To determine indexed cost we use the following relation.

$$\frac{\text{Purchase price}}{\text{Cost of inflation index in the purchase year}} = \frac{\text{Indexed cost}}{\text{Cost of inflation index in the year of transaction}}$$

$$\therefore \text{Indexed cost} = \text{Purchase cost} \times \frac{\text{Cost inflation index in the year of transaction}}{\text{Cost inflation index in the year of purchase}}$$

The series of index of cost inflation is as follows :

Year	81-82	95-96	96-97	97-98	98-99	99-00	00-01	01-02	02-03
Cost inflation index	100	281	305	331	351	389	406	426	447
Year	03-04	04-05	05-06	06-07					
Cost inflation index	463	480	497	519					

Case Study :

An industrial visits, ABC firm of Charted Accountants. He would like to file his income tax return. He sold his land property at ₹ 5 crores in year 2007-08, it was purchased in 1991-92 at ₹ 1.5 crores. He sold shares of company at ₹ 1 crores in 2007-08, which were obtained from public issue in the year 1995-96 at ₹ 30 lacs. Chartered accountant decided to use cost inflation index number to find the real gain. Apparently his profit is ₹ 3.5 crores on land and ₹ 70 lacks from shares.

Points to Remember

1. Laspeyre's price index number = $P_{01}^L = \dfrac{\sum p_1 q_0}{\sum p_0 q_0} \times 100$

   Paasche's price index number = $P_{01}^P = \dfrac{\sum p_1 q_1}{\sum p_1 q_1} \times 100$

   Fisher's price index number = $P_{01}^F = \sqrt{P_{01}^L \times P_{01}^P}$

2. Fisher's index number numerically lies between Laspeyre's and Pasche's index number.

3. Cost of living index number by aggregate expenditure method $= \dfrac{\sum p_1 q_0}{\sum p_0 q_0} \times 100$.

4. Cost of living index number by family budget method $= \dfrac{\sum Iw}{\sum w}$.

Exercise 7.1

A. Theory Questions :

1. What is meant by Index Numbers ?
2. State the uses of Index Numbers.
3. Explain how index numbers are constructed.
4. Define price relative and discuss how it is used in construction of index numbers.
5. Explain the terms : base year, current year, weight.
6. Discuss the various problems involved in the construction of index numbers.
7. Explain why index numbers are called as economic barometers.
8. Explain what precautions you will take for the selection of base period.
9. Explain the importance of weights in construction of index numbers.
10. State the limitations of index number by the method of simple aggregative.
11. Discuss the problems of :
    (i) selection of commodities (ii) selection of average (iii) selection of weights (iv) collection of data (v) choise of base year in the construction of index numbers.
12. Define (i) Laspeyre's (ii) Paasche's and (iii) Fisher's index numbers.
13. Make a critical comparison between Laspeyre's and Paasche's index numbers.
14. Explain the drawbacks of each of the following index numbers :
    (i) Laspeyre's Index Number. (ii) Paasche's Index Number. (iii) Fisher's Index Number.
15. Mention the limitations of index numbers.
16. What is the cost of living index number ? How does it differ from usual price index numbers ? How cost of index number is constructed ?
17. Discuss the main problems those arise in the construction of cost of living index number.
18. Explain the following methods of cost of living index number (i) family budget method, (ii) aggregate expenditure method.
19. Explain the uses of cost of living index numbers.
20. How cost of living index number is interpreted ?
21. Write a note on : (i) SENSEX, (ii) NIFTY.

Exercise 7.2

B. Index Number using Raw Data :

1. Calculate price index number using :
   (i) Laspeyr'es method.
   (ii) Paasche's method.
   (iii) Fisher's method from the information given below :

Item	Base Year		Current Year	
	Price	Quantity	Price	Quantity
Cheese	18	2	24	1.5
Bread	12	30	15	15
Eggs	20	15	30	15
Milk	10	30	19	25

2. Calculate price index number using :
   (i) Laspeyre's
   (ii) Paasches
   (iii) Fishers method for the following data :

Years Commodities	Base Year		Current Year	
	Price ₹	Quantity	Price ₹	Quantity
Rice	25	5	30	6
Coconut oil	60	2	100	3
Tea	100	1	120	2
Washing powder	100	4	120	4
Sugar	30	4	40	5

3. Compute Fisher's price index number for the following data :

Commodity	Base Year		Current Year	
	Quantity	Expenses	Quantity	Expenses
A	50	300	56	560
B	100	200	120	240
C	60	240	60	360
D	30	300	24	288
E	40	320	36	432

4. Compute Laspeyre's price index number for 1995 from the following data :

Commodity	Price in		Quantity in 1990
	1990	1995	
Wheat	5	7	100
Rice	10	18	60
Jowar	5	8	30
Gram	10	16	10

5. Find Laspeyre's, Paasche's and Fisher's index numbers for the following data.

Commodity	p_0	q_0	p_1	q_1
A	4	5	12	3
B	4	4	6	4
C	2	3	3	5

6. Compute Laspeyre's, Paasche's, Fisher's, price index numbers for the following data :

Commodity	Base Year		Current Year	
	Price	Quantity	Price	Quantity
A	4	6	5	4
B	5	4	6	2
C	6	2	8	1

Interpret the results.

7. Find Laspeyre's, Paasche's and Fisher's price index numbers for the following data :

Commodity	A	B	C	D
p_0	9	8	4	1
q_0	5	10	6	4
p_1	15	12	5	2
q_1	5	11	6	8

8. From the data given below, construct Laspeyre's, Paasche's and Fisher's price index numbers, also verify that Fisher's index number lies between that of Laspeyre's and Paasche's index numbers.

Commodity	2011		2012	
	Price	Quantity	Price	Quantity
A	6	50	10	56
B	2	100	2	120
C	4	60	6	60
D	10	30	12	24
E	8	20	12	36

9. Compute Laspeyre's and Paasche's price index numbers for the following data :

Commodity	p_0	q_0	p_1	q_1
A	5	8	3	4
B	2	6	6	2
C	1	5	2	3

10. Calculate Fisher's price index numbers for the following data :

Commodities	2011		2012	
	Price (₹)	Quantity (kg.)	Price (₹)	Quantity (kg.)
A	20	8	40	6
B	50	10	60	5
C	40	15	50	10
D	20	20	20	15

C. Index Number Summerised Data :

11. Given : $\Sigma p_1q_0 = 1900$, $\Sigma p_0q_0 = 1360$, $\Sigma p_1q_1 = 1880$, $\Sigma p_0q_1 = 1344$.
    Find Laspeyre's, Paasche's and Fisher's Price Index Number.
12. Given : $\Sigma p_1q_0 = 175$, $\Sigma p_0q_0 = 91$, $\Sigma p_1q_1 = 190$, $\Sigma p_0q_1 = 100$.
    Find Laspeyre's, Paasche's and Fisher's price index number.
13. If $\Sigma p_0q_0 = 6000$, $\Sigma p_0q_1 = 8000$, $\Sigma p_1q_0 = 9000$, $\Sigma p_1q_1 = 10{,}000$.
    Find Laspeyre's, Paasche's and Fisher's price index number.

D. Missing Value Problem :

14. Find value of X if for the following data if Laspeyre's price index number is 114.4 :

Commodity	Price		Base Year Quantity
	Base Year	Current Year	
A	36	40	100
B	80	90	12
C	45	41	X
D	5	6	1100

15. Find the missing price if ratio of Laspeyre's price index to Paasche's price index is 28 : 27 for the following data :

Commodity	p_0	q_0	p_1	q_1
A	1	10	2	5
B	1	5	*	2

16. Find the value of x if Laspeyre's and Paasche's price index numbers are equal.

Commodity	p_0	q_0	p_1	q_1
A	20	80	22	x
B	14	64	18	80

E. Cost of Living Index Numbers :

17. Calculate cost of living index number for 2000 with base year as 1990 from the following data :

Commodity	A	B	C	D	E	F
Price in 1990	9	10	5	18	60	2
Price in 2000	12	15	6	20	70	3
Quantity in 1990	100	25	10	20	60	30

18. Find the cost of living index number for the following data :

Items	Price in base year	Price in current year	Expenditure in percentages
Food	90	100	30
House rent	20	30	15
Clothing	60	70	20
Fuel	15	20	10
Others	55	60	25

19. A family enquiry of middle class families in a certain city gave the following data :

Items	Price in 2004	Price in 2005	Expenditure in percentages
Food	250	274	35
House rent	150	160	15
Clothing	100	125	20
Fuel	120	125	10
Others	160	190	20

What changes in the cost of living index number of 2005 have taken place as compared to 2004 ?

20. Compute cost of living index number for 1989 from the following data :

Commodity	A	B	C	D
Price in 1988	10	8	25	16
Price in 1989	12	9	30	28
Quantity in 1988	30	20	25	25

21. Compute cost of living index number given the following data and interprete.

Group	Food	Clothing	Fuel and lighting	Rent	Miscellaneous
Index	300	200	250	150	250
Weight	60	5	10	10	15

22. Compute cost of living index from the following index number.

Group	Index number	Weight
Food	125	50
Clothing	200	15
Fuel and lighting	175	10
House rent	110	15
Miscellaneous	137	10

23. The data below shows the percentage increase in price of a few selected food items and weights associated to each of them. Calculate the index number for the group of food articles.

Food items	Weight	Percentage increase in price
Rice	40	120
Wheat	8	50
Dal	10	100
Oil	7	120
Ghee	5	130
Milk	15	80
Vegetables	10	120
Refreshment	5	200

24. Compute the cost of living index number of group of food articles from the following data :

Food items	Index number	Weight
Rice	220	40
Wheat	150	8
Dal	200	10
Oil	220	7
Ghee	230	5
Milk	180	15
Vegetables	220	10
Refreshment	300	5

25. Construct the index number of industrial production of a certain industry using weighted arithmetic mean from the following data :

Shift	Index number of production	Percentage of total production
Day	150	60
Evening	120	23
Night	115	17

26. Construct index number of business activity of a certain state from the following data.

Item	Weight	Index
Industrial production	28	250
Agricultural production	30	175
Mineral production	4	130
Internal trade	15	200
Financial activity	18	225
Imports and exports	5	200

27. Find the index number of business activity from the following data :

Group	Weight	Quantity Index
Industrial production	35	200
Mineral production	5	130
Internal trade	25	210
Financial activity	20	140
Exports and imports	10	300
Shipping activity	5	250

28. Following table gives the group index numbers and weights of different groups. If index number of all the groups taken together is 199.9, find the missing index number.

Group	Food	Clothing	Fuel & lighting	Rent	Miscellaneous
Index No.	215	*	175	197	155
Weight	40	16	20	12	23

29. If the index number of combined group is 155.2, find the missing group index number.

Group	Food	Clothing	Fuel	House rent	Other
Index No.	170	190	120	*	100
Weight	60	4	6	14	16

30. The consumer price index number for 1985 was 125. The price index number of food items was 120 and index number of other items was 135. Obtain the percentage of total weight assigned to group of food items.

31. Compute missing weight if the combined group index number is 456.9.

Group	Weight	Index Number
Food	60	510
Clothing	5	465
Fuel	8	330
House rent	x	225
Miscellaneous	18	450

32. Obtain index number of clothing from the given data if the cost of living index number is 267.

Group	Food	Clothing	Fuel and Lighting	House Rent	Other
Index No.	300	*	250	150	250
Weight	62	4	6	12	16

33. A family budget enquiry revealed the information that, weights used were : Food 30, Clothing 5, Rent 8, Fuel 5, Miscellaneous 2. Calculate the cost of living index number if average increase in the price of groups over base period were 35, 60, 50, 80, 60 respectively.

If a person from such a group was earning ₹ 12000 in base year, what should be his earnings in current period in order to maintain same standard of living at that of in base year ?

34. The index number for the textile workers in Ahmedabad a particular month is given as 307.1. Using the following data find out the amount that he spent on house rent.

Group	Index Number	Weight
Food	560	180
Clothing	168	150
House rent	*	100
Fuel and lighting	224	110
Miscellaneous	252	80

Answers 7.2

1. 152.41, 151, 151.70
2. 128.32, 129.63, 128.98
3. 188.73
4. 161.48
5. 221.43, 197.37, 205.05
6. 125, 125, 125

7. 152.29, 153.33, 152.81
8. 138.33, 139.88, 139.10
9. 122.8, 111.11
10. 124.97
11. 139.71, 139.88, 139.80
12. 192.31, 190.00, 191.15
13. 150, 125, 136.93
14. 16.35
15. 4
16. 100
17. 123.54
18. 119.77
19. Cost of living index number = 113.53. It is increased by 13.53%
20. 134.01
21. 267.5
22. 140.2
23. 210.9   24. 210.9   25. 137.15
26. 208.2   27. 199.5   28. 260
29. 160   30. 66.67%   31. 9
32. 200   33. 145.4, ₹ 17448   34. 196.02

Objective Questions

1. State the index number of base year.
2. If Laspeyre's and Paasche's price indices are 121 and 100 find Fisher's index number.
3. If Laspeyre's and Paasche's index numbers are same and the common value is 120, then find the Fisher's index number.
4. Comment : The weight can be negative numbers.
5. Comment : The sum of weights is always 100.
6. Comment : Cost of living index number gives the inflation level.
7. State the reason why Fisher's index number lies between Paasche's and Laspeyre's index numbers.

Answers

1. 100   2. 110   3. 120.

Chapter 8...

Linear Programming Problems
(For Two Variables Only) (For B.B.M. Only)

Contents ...
8.1 Introduction
8.2 Meaning of L.P.P.
8.3 Mathematical formulation of L.P.P.
8.4 Solution of L.P.P. by graphical method

Key Words :

Objective function, constraints, convex set of region, solution, feasible region, initial solution, feasible solution, optimal solution, unbounded solution, degenerate solution, alternative solution.

Objectives :

To formulate the problem as L.P.P. To obtain the best solution using graphical method.

8.1 Introduction

In business management there are many activities such as production, inventory, marketing, maintenance etc. Many times the situations are complex. The variables involved behave adversely and they have conflicting effects. In this situation one has to find a golden mean or a break-even point. A set of several techniques to achieve such a solution is developed around 1940, it is now referred as **'Operations Research'**.

Churchman, Ackoff and Arnoff defined operations research as the application of scientific methods, techniques and tools, to problems involving the operations of system so as to provide those in control of the system with optimum solutions to the problem.

The techniques in operations research has its applications in wide areas. It helps decision-making by giving a solution to problem which optimises resources. The various techniques are given by the following tree diagram.

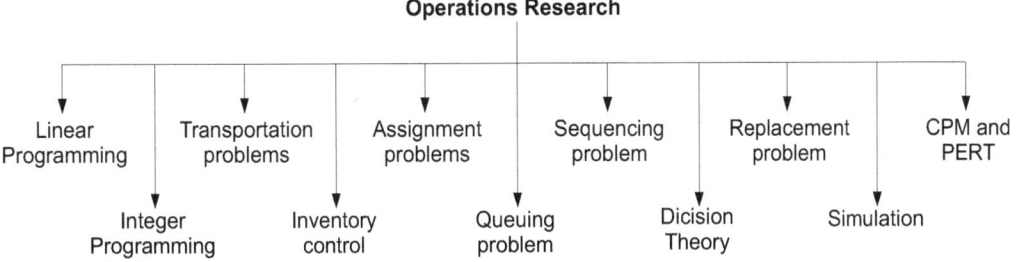

In order to solve the problems using methods in operations research, we need to go through the following steps :

1. Decide the model to be used to solve the problem.
2. Formulation of the problem.
3. Use of appropriate technique to get the best or optimal solution.

In general the resources such as money, raw material, man hours, machine hours, electric supply etc. are limited. These resources are the **decision variables**. The limitations are represented in the form of equations or inequalities using the **decision variables**. These equations are called as **constraints**. The whole exercise is to use the resources to give best results. By best results we mean in most economic way or which minimises the cost of production or minimise the total time required to complete the task or to maximise the profit or to maximise the efficiency. Such criterion is called as an **objective function**. The objective function is also written in terms of mathematical expression. This function is to be maximised or minimised we call it as to be **optimised**.

Thus in short the problem reduces to the three ingredients (i) the decision variables, (ii) constraints, (iii) objective function or optimising function.

There may be many solutions to the problem. We are interested in those solutions which are confined to the constraints. Such solutions are called as **feasible solutions**. Among all feasible solutions we search for the optimum solution, which maximises (or minimises as the case may be) the objective function.

8.2 Meaning of Linear Programming Problem (L.P.P.)   (April 2015)

The meaning of word programme is the plan of action. Particularly a linear programming is a problem of minimising or maximising the objective function, which is linear in nature, subject to the constraints which are also linear in nature.

The general L.P.P., after formulation, with x and y as decision variable is of the type :

Maximize/Minimize $Z = c_1 x + c_2 y$ **Objective function**

Subject to $a_{11} x + a_{12} y\ (\leq, =, \geq)\ b_1$

$a_{21} x + a_{22} y\ (\leq, =, \geq)\ b_2$ **Constraints**

....

....

$a_{m1} x + a_{m2} y\ (\leq, =, \geq)\ b_m$

$x, y \geq 0$ (or unrestricted)   **Non-negativity Restrictions**

x, y

The decision variables x and y may be non-negative or unrestricted. The linear constraints may be equations, less than type inequality or greater than type inequality. The linear objective function involves the coefficients c_1 and c_2 may be costs or profits or time required or efficiencies etc. with respect to the variables x and y respectively.

Illustration :

Maximise $\quad z = 5x + 4y$

Subject to $\quad 2x + 3y \leq 100$

$\qquad\qquad 4x - 5y \geq 30$

$\qquad\qquad 3x + y = 75$

$\qquad\qquad x \geq 0, \ y \geq 0$

8.3 Mathematical Formulation of L.P.P.

Decision variables (B.B.A. Oct. 2010) : In the formulation of L.P.P. or any model in operations research one has to decide the unknowns to be found out. These unknowns are called as decision variables. The decision variables may take non-negative values or they are unrestricted in sign.

Constraints : The conditions, limitations in the given problem are expressed in terms of equations or inequalities in terms of decision variables are called as **constraints.** In L.P.P. the cosntraints are linear in nature.

Objective function : The goal or objective to be achieved in the model is called as objective function. It is to be maximised or minimised (optimised). In L.P.P. the objective function is linear in nature.

Thus in the formulation of L.P.P. one has to :

(i) identify the decision variables

(ii) identify the constraints

(iii) identify the objective function.

Illustrative Examples

Example 8.1 : *Product Mix Problem : A company has to produce A and B the two types of products. Each product has to be processed by three machines (i) moulding (M_1), (ii) grinding (M_2), (iii) finishing (M_3). Suppose machine M_1 can be operated for total time of 2700 minutes. It takes 12 minutes for an item of type A and 5 minutes for an item of type B.*

Machine M_2 is available for 2000 minutes and it takes 5 minutes for processing an item of type A and 10 minutes for an item of type B.

Machine M_3 is available for 450 minutes and it takes 2 minutes for processing an item of type A and 2 minutes for an item of type B.

The profit per item of type A is ₹ 10 and that of per item of type B is ₹ 15. Find the number of items of type A and B to be produced so as maximise the profit. Formulate the L.P.P.

Solution : There are two types of items to be manufactured. Thus, there will be two **decision variables,**

Let x = The number of items of type A
     y = The number of items of type B

The **objective function (z)** is a total profit if x items of type A and y items of type B are manufactured hence z = 10x + 15y. We need to maximise the profit, hence objective is to

Maximize z = 10x + 15y

The constraints will be time required to process x items of A and y items of B on machine M_1, which can run for maximum 2700 minutes.

$$\begin{pmatrix} \text{Sum of time required} \\ \text{for x items of A and} \\ \text{y items of B} \end{pmatrix} \leq 2700$$

∴ 12x + 5y ≤ 2700 ... (1)

Similarly for machine M_2 we get the constraint

5x + 10y ≤ 2000 ... (2)

and for M_3 we get

2x + 2y ≤ 450 ... (3)

Thus the L.P.P. is

Maximise z = 10x + 5y   (Objective function)

Subject to 12x + 5y ≤ 2700
            5x + 10y ≤ 2000   (Constraints)
            2x + 2y ≤ 450

            x ≥ 0, y ≥ 0   (Non-negativity restrictions)

Example 8.2 : *Budget Allocation problem : Two different kinds of foods A and B are being considered to form a weekly diet. The minimum weekly requirements of fats, Carbohydrates and Proteins are 18, 24 and 24 units respectively. One kg of food A contains 4, 16 and 8 units of fats, carbohydrates and proteins respectively. One kg. of food B contains 12, 4 and 6 units of fats, carbohydrates and proteins respectively. The prices of food A is ₹4 per kg. and that of B is ₹3 per kg. Find the quantity food A and B to be purchased so that the total cost is minimum and the requirement is fulfilled.*

Formulate the problem as L.P.P.

Solution : Let x : No. of kg. of food A to be purchased
                   y : No. of kg. of food B to be purchased

Then we require to find x and y such that

Minimize   z = 4x + 3y   (Objective function)
Subject to 4x + 12y ≥ 18   (Fats constraint)
            16x + 4y ≥ 24   (Carbohydrates constraints)
            8x + 6y ≥ 24   (Proteins constraints)
            x, y, ≥ 0   (Non-negativity constraint)

8.4 Solution of L.P.P. by Graphical Method

We need to solve the formulated L.P.P. It involves to find the values of decision variable which will satisfy the constraints and optimize the value of objective function.

Some definitions :

(a) **Solution :** A set of values of decision variables which satisfy the constraints of L.P.P. is called as a solution to corresponding L.P.P.

(b) **Feasible solution :** A solution which satisfies the non-negativity restrictions of L.P.P. is called as feasible solution to corresponding L.P.P.

(c) **Optimal solution (B.B.A. April 2010, Oct. 2010) :** A feasible solution of L.P.P. which optimizes (minimises or maximises as the case may be) the objective function is called as a optimal solution of the corresponding L.P.P.

(d) **Convex set :** A region in X-Y plane is called as a convex region or convex set if the line segment joining any two points in the set lies completely within the region. The following are convex sets, since the line segment AB completely lies in the set.

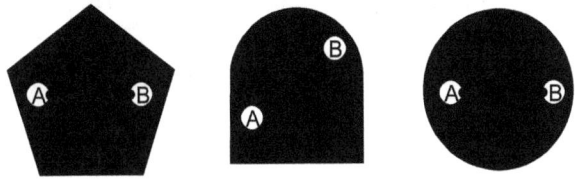

Fig. 8.1

The following are not convex sets.

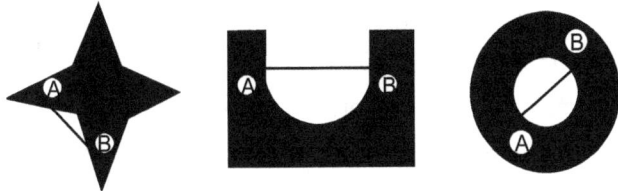

Fig. 8.2

The line segment AB having points A and B within the set does not lie completely in the set, hence those are non-convex sets.

Result (1) : The region formed by the constraints of L.P.P. is a convex set.

Result (2) : Every point in the convex set formed by the constraints of L.P.P. is a feasible solution. Such a region is also called as feasible region.

Result (3) : The extreme points (maxima or minima) of objective function, if exist, are found at the vertices (or boundary) of the convex region.

Hence in order to find the optimal solution, we should plot the linear inequations given by the constraints and find the region common to all the constraints. To find the optimal solution we evaluate the objective function at the vertices of convex set. We find the maximum (or minimum) value of the objective function. We read the co-ordinates of vertex at which optimal solution is found. The co-ordinates are values of decision variable which give optimal solution to L.P.P.

Note that the line ax + by = c divides the x-y plane in two parts. One of the side of the line we observe ax + by < c, the other side gives ax + by > c and for the points on line we get ax + by = c. Thus, the constraints in the form of linear inequalities define the region in X-Y plane.

Example 8.3 : *Plot the inequality $12x + 5y \leq 2700$.*

Solution : To plot the line $12x + 5y = 2700$ we take the intercepts on the axes (or any two points on the line).

If $x = 0$, $5y = 2700$, $y = \dfrac{2700}{5} = 540$ hence A(0, 540) is a point in the line. If $y = 0$, $12x = 2700$, $x = \dfrac{2700}{12} = 225$ hence B(225, 0) is a point on the line. We plot the points A and B and the line AB is denoted by $12x + 5y = 2700$.

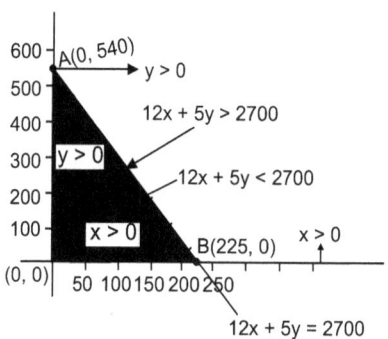

Fig. 8.3

The line divides the plane in two parts on one side of the origin (0, 0) lies. We substitute $x = 0$, $y = 0$ in the equation and evaluate.

$$(12 \times 0) + (5 \times 0) = 0 < 2700$$

Thus, the side containing origin is denoted by $12x + 5y < 2700$.

Clearly the side $12x + 5y > 2700$ corresponds to non-origin side.

Note : If the line passes through origin then any other point can be used to determine which part satisfies the inequality.

Example 8.4 : *Solve the following L.P.P. graphically :*

$$\text{Maximize} \quad z = 10x + 15y$$
$$\text{Subject to } 12x + 5y \leq 2700$$
$$5x + 10y \leq 2000$$
$$x \geq 0, \ y \geq 0$$

Solution : We need to plot the lines given by the inequalities in the constraints.

The line $12x + 5y = 2700$ passes through (0, 540) and (225, 0).

To plot $5x + 10y = 2000$, let us take $x = 0$ then we get $y = 200$ and for $y = 0$, $x = 400$. Therefore, the line joining the points (0, 200) and (400, 0) give the required line.

Substituting the (0, 0) in first equation $12x + 5y$ we get $(12 \times 0) + (5 \times 0) = 0 < 2700$, hence the required region is origin side region (See Fig. 8.4 (a)).

Substituting the origin in second line we get $(5 \times 0) + (10 \times 0) = 0 < 2000$. Hence the region containing origin gives $5x + 10y < 2000$ (See Fig. 8.4 (b)).

Plotting both the region we get a common region, where both the constraints are satisfied. Non-negativity restrictions $x \geq 0$, $y \geq 0$ confine the region to the first quadrant. (See Fig. 8.4 (c)).

Thus we get

Line	Points on the line
$12x + 5y = 2700$	(0, 540), (225, 0)
$5x + 10y = 2000$	(0, 200), (400, 0)

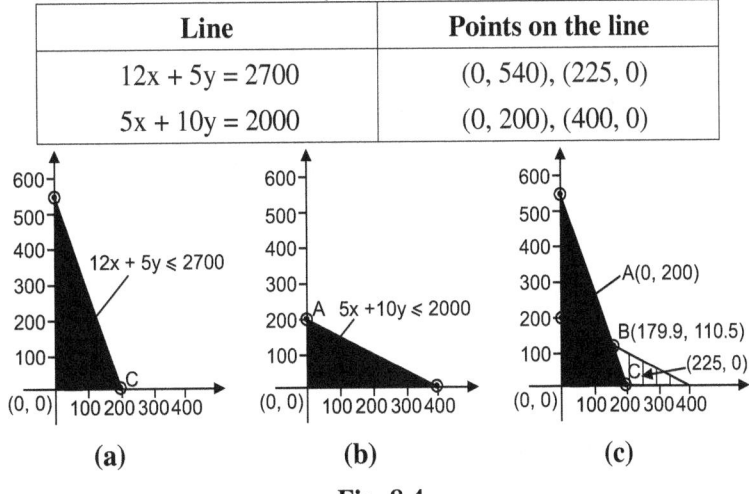

Fig. 8.4

The feasible region or solution space is given by a polygon OABC. We evaluate the objective function at every vertex.

Vertex	$z = 10x + 15y$
O (0, 0)	0
A (0, 200)	3000.0
B (178.9, 110.5)	3446.5 Maximum
D (225, 0)	2250.0

Thus the solution of L.P.P. is $x = 178.9$, $y = 110.5$ and $z = ₹\ 3446.5$ by rounding-off we get $x \approx 179$, $y \approx 111$, $z = ₹\ 3455$.

Solutions of L.P.P. : There are two types of L.P.P. : (i) minimisation, (ii) maximisation.

L.P.P. has following types of solutions :

(a) **Unique optimal solution.**

(b) **Multiple optimal solutions or alternate optimal solution :** This situation arises when the line given by objective function is parallel to any of the boundary of the feasible region. The two vertices by such constraint will give the optimal solutions with the same value of z. In fact every point joining these two points will be a solution to L.P.P. Thus, there will be multiple or infinitely many solutions.

(c) **Unbounded solution :** The feasible region may be unbounded with unbounded value of z.

(d) **No solution or infeasible solution :** If there is no point in the feasible region which satisfies all the constraints then L.P.P. has no optimal solution.

(e) **Degenerate solution :** If any of the decision variable is 0 in the optimal solution then the solution is degenerate. If the vertex at which optimal solution exists is on any of the axis then degenerate solution is possible. This situation will arise if (i) there is only one constraint (ii) the objective function has only one variable in it, (iii) the cost coefficients c_1 and c_2 differ too much relatively etc.

Example 8.5 : Solve the following L.P.P. (Formulated in example 3)

Minimize $\quad z = 4x + 3y$

Subject to $\quad 4x + 12y \geq 18$

$\qquad\qquad 16x + 4y \geq 24$

$\qquad\qquad 8x + 6y \geq 24$

$\qquad\qquad x, y \geq 0$

Is the optimal solution unique ? If not then find the alternate solution.

Solution : To plot the lines we find two points on line

The line corresponding to the constraint	The points on the line
$4x + 12y = 18$ ... (1)	(0, 1.5), (4.5, 0)
$16x + 4y = 24$ ... (2)	(0, 6), (1.5, 0)
$8x + 6y = 24$ ... (3)	(0, 4), (3, 0)

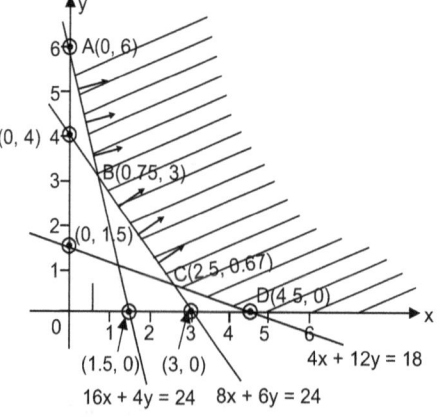

Fig. 8.5

Note that the line $4x + 12y = 18$ divides the x-y plane in two regions. Since origin (0, 0) gives $(4 \times 0) + (12 \times 0) = 0 < 18$, the region containing (0, 0) is $4x + 12y < 18$. The complementary part is $4x + 12y \geq 18$. Similarly, the regions given by $16x + 4y \geq 24$ and $8x + 6y \geq 24$ are also the regions in which (0, 0) is not included. The non-negativity restrictions give the region as the first quadrant. Thus, the shaded region with vertices A(0, 6), B(0.75, 3), C(2.5, 0.67), D(4.5, 0) is a feasible region. We search optimal solution at the vertices.

Vertex	The value of objective function $z = 4x + 3y$
A(0, 6)	$z = (4 \times 0) + (3 \times 6) = 18$
B(0.75, 3)	$z = (4 \times 0.75) + (3 \times 3) = 12$ Minimum
C(2.5, 0.67)	$z = (4 \times 2.5) + (3 \times 0.67) = 12$ Minimum
D(4.5, 0)	$z = (4 \times 4.5) + (3 \times 0) = 18$

The optimising function has minima at B and C. Thus, there are two solutions of L.P.P.

Solution 1 : At B (0.75, 3), $z = ₹ 12$

∴ $x = 0.75$ kg, $y = 3$ kg, $z = ₹12$

Solution 2 : At C (2.5, 0.67)

$x = 2.5$ kg, $y = 0.67$ kg, $z = ₹ 12$

Thus, the optimum solution is not unique the alternate solution is at C.

Note : 1. The objective function $z = 4x + 3y$ is parallel the constraint $4x + 3y = 24$, hence there are multiple solutions. Infact every point on the line joining B and C is a optimal solution to L.P.P. with common value of z as ₹ 12.

2. If (x_1, y_1) and (x_2, y_2) are the two solutions then $(ax_1 + (1 - a) x_2, ay_1 + (1 - a) y_2)$ is also a solution for $0 < a < 1$. Choosing any value of a between 0 and 1 we get a solution. Hence there are infinitely many optimum solutions to L.P.P.

Example 8.6 : *Solve the following L.P.P. using graphical method*

Maximise $\quad z = x_1 + x_2$

Subject to $\quad x_1 + x_2 \leq 1$

$\quad\quad\quad\quad\quad 2x_1 + 3x_2 \geq 6$

$\quad\quad\quad\quad\quad x_1 \geq 0, \ x_2 \geq 0$

Solution : $x_1 + x_2 = 1$ passes through (1, 0), (0, 1), $2x_1 + 3x_2 = 6$ passes through (3, 0) and (0, 2). The region $x_1 + x_2 \leq 1$ is the origin side region and the region $2x_1 + 3x_2 \geq 6$ is the non-origin side region.

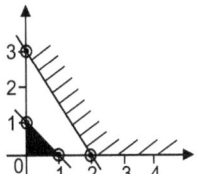

Fig. 8.6

From the figure we get there is no region which satisfies both the constraints. Hence there is no solution to L.P.P.

Example 8.7 : *Show that the following L.P.P. has unbounded solution*

Maximize $z = 2x + y$
Subject to $x - y \leq 10$
$2x - y \leq 40$
$x, y \geq 0$

Solution :

The line corresponding to the constraint	The points on the line
$x - y = 10$	$(0, -10)$, $(10, 0)$
$2x - y = 40$	$(0, -40)$, $(20, 0)$

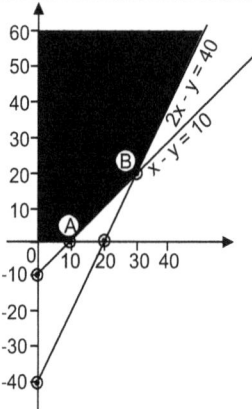

Fig. 8.7

Note that feasible region is unbounded hence solution is unbounded.

Example 8.8 : *The vertices of feasible region of a L.P.P. are given by A(0, 1), B(0, 4), C(4, 6), D(7, 5), E(10, 2). Solve the L.P.P. for the objective functions and state the nature of solutions.*

(a) Maximize $z_1 = x + y$
(b) Minimize $z_2 = x - y$
(c) Maximize $z_3 = 2x + y$

Solution :

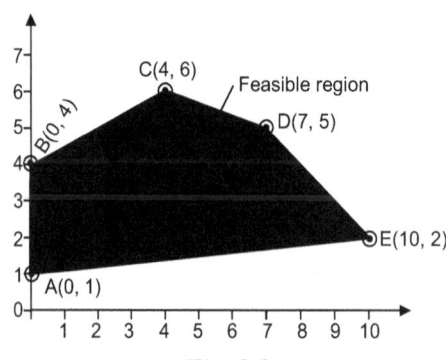

Fig. 8.8

Vertex	Max. $z_1 = x + y$	Min. $z_2 = x - y$	Max. $z_3 = 2x + y$
A (0, 1)	1	– 1	1
B (0, 4)	4	– 4*	4
C (4, 6)	10	– 2	14
D (7, 5)	12*	2	19
E (10, 2)	12*	8	22*

Nature of solutions :

(a) $z_1 = x + y$ has two solutions

Solution (1) : $x = 7, y = 5, z = 12$

Solution (2) : $x = 10, y = 2, z = 12$

Hence there are infinite solutions

General solution $\quad x = 7a + 10(1 - a) = - 3a + 10$

$\quad\quad\quad\quad\quad\quad\quad\quad y = 5a + 2(1 - a) = 3a + 2$

$\quad\quad\quad\quad\quad\quad\quad\quad z = 12$

We get solution for every a, $(0 < a < 1)$

(b) $z_2 = x - y$ has unique solution at $(x = 0, y = 4)$ and $z = - 4$.

It is a degenerate solution since only one variable is non-zero.

(c) $z_3 = 2x + y$ has unique solution at $(x = 10, y = 2)$ and $z = 22$.

Exercise 8.1

Theory Questions :

1. Explain the term 'Linear Programming'.
2. Explain the following terms used in L.P.P. Decision variable, constraint, objective function, feasible solution, optimal solution, alternate solution, convex set.

Exercise 8.2

Numerical Problems :

1. A manufacturing company produces two types of batteries low volt and medium volt. A low volt battery requires 1 hour processing time on machine and 2 hours of labour time. A medium volt battery requires 2 hours of processing times on machine and 1.5 hours of labour time. In a week, processing machine is available for 70 hours and labour time available is 60 hours. The profit due to each of the low volt battery is ₹ 60 where as due to medium volt battery it is ₹ 75.

Formulate the problem as L.P.P. with a view to maximise the total profit and solve it graphically.

2. A and B are two types of fertilizers available at ₹ 30 per kg and ₹ 50 per kg respectively. Fertilizer A contains 20 units of potash, 10 units of nitrogen and 40 units of phosphorus. Fertilizer B contains 15 units of potash, 20 units of nitrogen and 10 units of phosphorus. The requirement of potash, nitrogen and phosphorus is atleast 1800, 1700, 1600 units.

   Formulate the problems as L.P.P. in order to minimize the total purchasing cost. Also obtain the solution using graphical method.

3. A farmer has 100 hectares of land for cultivation. He grows potatoes and tomatoes. He is expected to get profit of ₹ 5000 per hectare for potatoes and ₹ 6000 per hectare for tomatoes. He needs 100 kg fertilizer per hectare for potatoes and 300 kg fertilizer per hectare for tomatoes. The cost of fertilizer is Re. 1 per kg and he can spent maximum ₹ 15,000 on fertilizer. The labour required for sowing, cultivation and harvesting for potatoes and tomatoes is 3 man days and 1 man day respectively. Total man days of labour available is 150.

   Formulate and solve the problem as L.P.P. to maximise the profit.

4. A cold drink company has two plants one at each place Mumbai and Pune. It produces three brands of cold drinks A, B and C. The number of bottles produced per day are as follows :

Brand	A	B	C
At Mumbai	900	1800	1200
At Pune	900	600	3000

   A market survey reveals that in the month of April the demand for the types of cold drinks A, B, C is respectively 12,000, 24,000, 26,400 bottles. The operating cost per day for plants at Mumbai and at Pune are 500 and 380 monetary units. Formulate and solve the problem as L.P.P. so as minimise the total operating cost if the plant at Mumbai is run for x days and at Pune is run for y days in the month of April in order to meet the demand.

5. Suppose there are two types of food items First type of food contains 3 units of vitamin A and 4 units of vitamin B per kg. The second type of food item contains 1 unit of vitamin A and 3 units of vitamin B per kg. The minimum requirement of vitamin A is 12 units and that of vitamin B is 24 units. The costs per gram of food of type 1 and type 2 are respectively ₹ 50 per kg and ₹ 60 per kg. The minimum quantity to be ordered for each type of food is 1 kg. Formulate and solve the L.P.P. to find the quantity to be purchased of each type of food so as minimise to total cost.

6. Solve the following L.P.P. graphically
   Maximize $z = 20x_1 + 17x_2$
   Subject to $2x_1 + 2x_2 \leq 22$
   $12x_1 + 10x_2 \leq 120$
   $x_1, x_2 \geq 0$

7. Solve the following L.P.P. graphically
   Minimise $z = 2x_1 + 4x_2$
   Subject to $6x_1 + x_2 \geq 18$
   $x_1 + 4x_2 \geq 12$
   $2x_1 + x_2 \geq 10$
   $x_1, x_2 \geq 0$

8. Solve the following L.P.P. using graphical method
   Maximize $z = x + 2y$
   Subject to $x + y \leq 100$
   $0 \leq x \leq 75$
   $0 \leq y \leq 60$

9. Solve the following L.P.P. using graphical method
   Maximize $z = x + 3y$
   Subject to $2x_1 + 3y \leq 20$
   $x + y \geq 12$
   $x, y \geq 0$

10. Solve the following L.P.P. using graphical method
    Maximize $z = 4x + 3y$
    Subject to $2x + 3y \leq 6$
    $2x + 2y \geq 20$
    $x \geq 0, y \geq 0$
    Show that there is no solution to L.P.P.

11. Solve the following L.P.P. using graphical method
    Minimize $z = x + 5y$
    Subject to $x + 3y \geq 12$
    $x + y \geq 9$
    $4x + 2y \geq 20$
    $x \geq 0, y \geq 0$
    Show that the solution is degenerate.

12. Solve the following L.P.P. using graphical method

    Minimize $\quad z = x + y$

    Subject to $\quad x + 3y \geq 12$

    $\qquad\qquad x + y \geq 8$

    $\qquad\qquad 4x + 2y \geq 20$

    $\qquad\qquad x \geq 0,\ y \geq 0$

    Show that there is a alternate solution. Hence find the general solution.

13. Solve the following L.P.P. graphically

    Maximise $\quad z = 3x + 5y$

    Subject to $\quad x + y \leq 30$

    $\qquad\qquad x \geq y \geq 0$

    $\qquad\qquad 0 \leq y \leq 10$

14. A manufacturer makes two types of lamps shades A and B which require treatment by a cutter and a finisher. Lamp shade A requires 2 hours of cutter's time and 1 hour of finisher's time. Lamp shade B requires 1 hour of cutter's and 2 hours of finishing time. The cutter has 104 hours and finisher has 70 hours of available time each month. Profit on one lamp shade A is ₹ 6 and on one lamp shade of B is ₹ 11. How many of each type of lamps shades should be manufactured to obtain the best returns. Formulate and solve L.P.P. graphically.

15. A small manufacturing firm produces two types of Gadgets A and B. They have to undergo two processes. First in foundry and then in machine shop.

    The following table gives the men hours of labour required for each of the processes and for each type of Gadgets.

Gadget	Foundry	Machine shop
A	10	5
B	6	4
Capacity	1000	600

    The profit on the sale of A is ₹ 30 per unit and on that of B it is ₹ 20 per unit. How many units of A and B should be produced in order to maximise the profit ?

16. A company makes two kinds of leather belts. Belt A is of high quality and B is of lower quantity. The respective profits are 4 ₹ and 3 ₹ per belt. Each belt of type A requires twice as much time as a belt of type B. If all the belts were of type B the company could make 1000 belts per day. The supply of leather is sufficient for only 800 belts per day (Both A and B combined). Belt A requires a fancy buckle and only 400 such buckles are available per day. There are only 700 buckles a day available for type B. Determine the number of belts to be produced for each type so as to make maximum profit.

17. A manufacture produces bicycles and tricycles each which must be processed through two machines 'A' and 'B'. Machine 'A' has maximum of 120 hours available and machine 'B' has a maximum of 180 hours available per week. Manufacturing of a tricycle requires 6 hours on machine 'A' and 3 hours on machine 'B'. While a bicycle requires 4 hours on machine 'A' and 10 hours on machine 'B'. The profits are ₹ 45 for a tricycle and ₹ 65 for a bicycle. Formulate L.P.P. to have a maximum profit.

Answers 8.2

1. Maximize $z = 60x + 75y$
   Subject to $x + 2y \leq 70$
   $2x + 1.5y \leq 60$
   $x \geq 0 \quad y \geq 0$
   x = No. of low volt batteries,
   y = No. of medium volt batteries.
   $x = 6, \ y = 32, \ z = ₹ \ 2760$.

   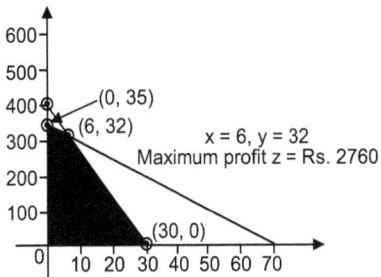
   Fig. 8.9

2. Minimize $z = 30x + 50y$
   Subject to $20x + 15y \geq 1800$
   $10x + 20y \geq 1700$
   $40x + 10y \geq 1600$
   $x, y > 0$
   x = Amount of fertilizer of type A
   y = Amount of fertilizer of type B.
   $x = 42$ kg, $y = 64$ kg, $z = ₹ \ 4460$.

   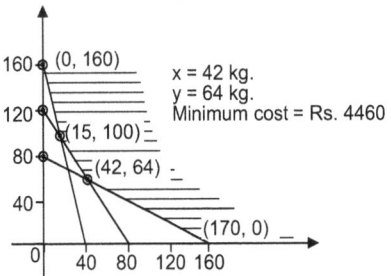
   Fig. 8.10

3. Maximize $z = 5000x + 6000y$
   Subject to $x + y \leq 100$
   $100x + 300y \leq 15000$
   $3x + y \leq 150$
   $x \geq 0 \quad y \geq 0$
   x = No. of hectares for potato.
   y = No. of hectares for tomato.
   $x = y = 37.5$ hectares, $z = ₹ \ 4,12,500$.

   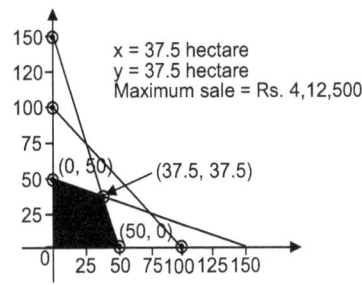
   Fig. 8.11

4. Minimize $z = 500x + 380y$
   Subject to $900x + 900y \geq 12000$
   $1800x + 600y \geq 24000$
   $1200x + 3000y \geq 26400$
   $0 \leq x \leq 30$
   $0 \leq y \leq 30$
   x = No. of days to run the Mumbai plant.
   y = No. of days to run the Pune plant.
   $x = 12$ days, $y = 4$ days, $z = ₹ \ 7520$.

   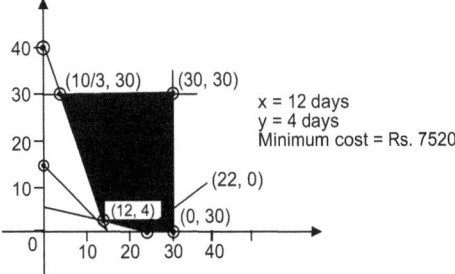
   Fig. 8.12

5. Minimize $z = 50x + 60y$
    Subject to $3x + y \geq 12$
    $4x + 3y \geq 24$
    $x \geq 1 \quad y \geq 1$
    x = Food of type 1 in kg.
    y = Food of types 2 in kg.
    $x = 5.25$ kg, $y = 1$ kg, $z = ₹ 322.5$.

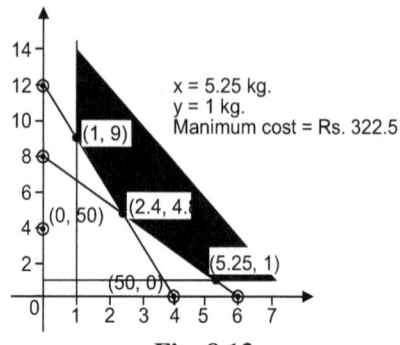

Fig. 8.13

6. $x_1 = 5$, $x_2 = 6$, $z = 202$
7. $x_1 = 4$, $x_2 = 2$, $z = 16$
8. $x = 40$, $y = 60$, $z = 160$
9. No solution
11. $x = 12$, $y = 0$, $z = 12$, solution is degenerate since, $y = 0$.
12. There are two solutions :
    (a) $x = 2$, $y = 6$, $z = 8$ (b) $x = 6$, $y = 2$, $z = 8$
    General solution $x = 2a + 6(1 - a)$, $y = 6a + 2(1 - a)$, $z = 8 \quad 0 < a < 1$.
13. $x = 20$, $y = 10$, $z = 110$
14. x : No. of lamp shades of type A.
    y : No. of lamp shades of type B.
    Max. : $z = 6x + 11y$
    Subject to $2x + y \leq 104$
    $x + 2y \leq 70$
    $x \geq 0, \quad y \geq 0$
    Solution : $x = 44$, $y = 16$, $z = ₹ 440$.
15. x : No. of gadgets of type A, y = No. of gadgets of type B
    Max. : $z = 30x + 20y$,
    Subject to $10x + 6y \leq 1000$
    $5x + 4y \leq 100$
    $x, y \geq 0$
    Solution : $x = 40$, $y = 100$, $z = ₹ 1000$
16. x = No. of belts of type A
    y = No. of belts of type B
    Max. $z = 4x + 3y$
    Subject to $2x + y \leq 1000$
    $x + y \leq 800$
    $0 \leq x \leq 400$
    $0 \leq y \leq 700$
    Solution : $x = 200$, $y = 600$, $z = ₹ 2600$.

OCTOBER 2014

F.Y.B.B.A. : BUSINESS STATISTICS

(Semester – II) (2013 Pattern) (New Syllabus)

Time : 3 Hours　　　　　　　　　　　　　　　　　　　　　　　Maximum Marks : 80

Notes :
1. All questions are compulsory.
2. Figures to right indicate full marks.
3. Logarithmic tables and statistical tables will be supplied on request.
4. Use of private non-scientific electronic calculator is allowed.
5. Carrying/using Mobile is strictly prohibited.

1. **Attempt any FOUR of the following :**　　　　　　　　　　　　　　(16)

   (a) Define the following terms :
   　　(i) Statistics.
   　　(ii) Sample.

   (b) Find mean, median and mode from the following data :
   　　Height in inches ; 61, 62, 63, 62, 63, 62, 64, 64, 60, 65.

   (c) State requisites of an ideal measure of dispersion.

   (d) Calculate Pearson's coefficient of correlation from the information given below :
   　　$n = 7$, $\sum X = 21$, $\sum Y = 20$, $\sum X^2 = 91$, $\sum XY = 74$, $\sum Y^2 = 84$.

   (e) Explain simple Random sampling in detail.

   (f) State limitations of Index numbers.

2. **Attempt any FOUR of the following :**　　　　　　　　　　　　　　(16)

   (a) Write a note on "Scope of Statistics in Management Science" in detail.

   (b) Find the missing frequency from the following data when mean is 15.38.

Size	10	12	14	16	18	20
Frequency	3	7	?	20	8	5

   (c) Calculate quartile deviation for the following data :

Age	10	11	12	13	14
No. of Girls	2	4	7	4	3

   (d) Write a note on 'Correlation" in detail.

(e) Draw a multiple bar diagram for the following data :

State	Birth Rate	Death Rate
Telangana	35,000	15,000
jammu and Kashmir	28,000	8,000
Kerala	14,000	6,000

(f) State properties of regression coefficients.

3. **Attempt any FOUR of the following :** (16)

(a) Draw a pie diagram to represent the following data giving the sales of different salesman of a company.

Salesman	Sales (in ₹)
A	1000
B	1240
C	1560
D	800
E	1400
Total	6000

(b) The average marks secured by a group of 45 students were 41. Later on it was discovered that a score of 92 was misread as 29. Find the correct average marks secured by them.

(c) Calculate standard deviation for the following data :

Class	0-5	5-10	10-15	15-20	20-25	25-30	30-35
F	3	7	12	18	13	10	7

(d) Calculate Karl Pearson's coefficient of correlation from the following data relating to the attendance of Rohan and the marks obtained by him in 10 sets of examinations.

Rohan Attendance	30	32	35	40	48	50	52	55	57	61
Marks	1	0	2	5	2	4	6	5	7	8

(e) State problems in construction of index numbers.

(f) Fit a straight line trend for the following data using method of semi averages :

Year	2003	2004	2005	2006	2007	2008
Production ('000 units)	22	26	24	30	28	32

4. Attempt any FOUR of the following : (16)
   (a) Draw histogram for the following frequency distribution :

Classes	10-20	20-30	30-40	40-50	50-60	60-70
Frequency	6	22	47	36	27	15

   (b) In a certain college there were 12 professors, 15 clerks and 20 peons and their average salaries were ₹ 38,000, ₹ 21,000 and ₹ 14,000 respectively. What was the average salary of all employees ?

   (c) Given below are daily wages paid to the workers in two factories A and B.

Daily wages	No. of Workers	
	Factory A	Factory B
12-13	15	25
13.14	30	40
14-15	44	60
15-16	60	35
16-17	30	12
17-18	14	15
18-19	7	5

   Which factory pays higher average wage ?

   (b) The regression equations are $8X - 10Y = -66$ and $40X - 18Y = 214$. Find the correlation coefficient between X and Y.

   (c) Define the following terms :
      (i) Secure trend.
      (iii) Seasonal variations.

   (f) Obtain correlation coefficient if $b_{yx} = +0.929$ and $b_{xy} = +0.979$.

5. Attempt any TWO of the following : (16)
   (a) Obtain both lines of regression from the following :

X	4	5	6	8	11
Y	12	10	8	7	5

   (b) Calculate seasonal indices from the following data using link-relatives method.

Year	1st Quarter	2nd Quarter	3rd Quarter	4th Quarter
2004	20	40	60	80
2005	30	30	40	90
2006	40	60	30	120
2007	50	50	70	150

(c) Construct Index Numbers of price from the following data by using :
   (i) Marshall-Edgeworth Method.
   (ii) Dorbish-Bowley's Method.

Commodity	2005 Price	2005 Quantity	2006 Price	2006 Quantity
A	2	8	4	6
B	5	10	6	5
C	4	14	5	10
D	2	19	2	15

www.ingramcontent.com/pod-product-compliance
Lightning Source LLC
Chambersburg PA
CBHW062133160426
43191CB00013B/2291